Hunger 1994
Transforming the Politics of Hunger

Fourth Annual Report on the State of World Hunger

Bread for the World
INSTITUTE

1100 Wayne Avenue, Suite 1000
Silver Spring, MD 20910
(301) 608-2400

Cover and text
printed on recycled paper

Bread for the World Institute

©1993 by Bread for the World Institute, 1100 Wayne Avenue, Suite 1000, Silver Spring, MD 20910, USA
Telephone: (301) 608-2400   FAX: (301) 608-2401

Printer: The John D. Lucas Printing Company

Cover photo: NASA

Manufactured in the United States of America

First edition published October 1993

ISBN 0-9628058-9-0

Table of Contents

Introduction

by David Beckmann

I am doing a new thing; now it springs forth, do you not perceive it?
– Isaiah 43:19, *Revised Standard Version*

People in the United States are concerned about hunger. More than half contribute to hunger relief. Ninety-three percent of U.S. voters say that hunger in the United States is a serious problem.

Ninety-three percent of U.S. voters say that hunger in the United States is a serious problem.

People in the United States contribute over $2 billion a year to more than four hundred private organizations that provide relief and development assistance internationally. At home, during the 1980s, food pantries and soup kitchens sprang up all over the country. There were few soup kitchens or food pantries in 1980, but more than 150,000 private organizations now pass out food to hungry people. They distribute $3 billion to $4 billion worth of food annually. They rely heavily on volunteers and donations from the general public.

Hunger 1994 argues that private charity needs to be complemented by stronger government efforts. Government cannot end hunger by itself, but government must do its part. Widespread hunger persists in the world, even in a country as wealthy as the United States, mainly for lack of political will.

The many individuals and organizations now working to help hungry people have it within their power to create the necessary will. But they need to direct some of the time and money now devoted to charity into transforming the politics of hunger.

The rapid growth of the private feeding movement is a wonderful demonstration that people in the United States do not want to let others go hungry. Yet the number of hungry people in the United States has grown even faster than the feeding movement. At any given time, twenty million to thirty million people in the United States face hunger. Between the late 1960s and the mid-1970s the United States reduced hunger, and the nation has the means to virtually eliminate hunger within its borders. Yet hunger is more widespread in the United States now than it was ten or fifteen years ago.

In the United States, every fifth child lives below the poverty line and faces hunger. As a result, many of these children suffer permanent learning and health losses. Many grow up in neighborhoods wracked by violence and criminality. The nation has economic and security reasons, as well as reasons of conscience, for reversing the cancerous growth of hunger and poverty in its midst.

Worldwide, 1.3 billion people are too poor to afford enough food to keep them fully productive. Television brings the U.S. public face to face with their misery. Massive hunger around the world also affects the United States through the violence, forced migrations, and environmental destruction it spawns.

At the international level, too, we know from experience that progress against hunger is possible. Between 1950 and 1980, the developing countries made rapid economic and social progress. Even during the 1980s, the number of children in the world who died from hunger-related deaths dropped from forty thousand to thirty-five thousand a day. But general economic and social progress was reversed in many countries over the past ten or fifteen years. As the regional overviews in this book document, hunger is on the increase in many places, notably in Africa, parts of the Middle East and Latin America, and in countries where communism has collapsed.

Why isn't the substantial effort that Americans are making to reduce hunger succeeding? Could people who are actively concerned about hunger be more effective than they are?

Why Politics?

Many charitable people believe that government programs are ineffective, or that they reduce incentives for poor people to change behaviors that contribute to their problems. Other charitable people are just preoccupied with the urgent needs of people right around them. They may not be well-informed about issues of government policy, and doubt the influence they could have on policy decisions.

Government policies often affect hungry people on a scale that dwarfs the impact of private assistance, however. U.S. government policies are partly to blame for the growth of hunger in the United States during the 1980s. For example, the government cut taxes and social spending. It tolerated high levels of unemployment. A "thousand points of light" could not make up for what these economic policies took away.

To cite a positive example, federal food programs currently provide $39 billion annually to low-income people in the United States, far exceeding the $4 billion that the private feeding movement gives away. Private feeding agencies are weak or nonexistent in some places where need is especially great. Federal food programs include food stamps, the Special Supplemental Food Program for Women, Infants, and Children (WIC), and school feeding. The majority of those served by these programs are low-income children.

U.S. government policies also powerfully affect hungry people around the world. The U.S. foreign aid budget is about $15 billion a year – only 1 percent of all federal spending, but still more than seven times what private sources contribute to U.S. private voluntary organizations that work overseas.

Some U.S. "aid" has supported dictators and in other ways contributed to the problems of poor people. The United States gave almost $1 billion to Somalia in the 1980s, most of it military aid. This money propped up a dictator, Mohammed Siad Barre. In exchange, he allowed the United States access to military facilities along the Red Sea, just across from Saudi oil fields. The U.S. government eventually stopped aid because of human rights abuses, and lost interest in Somalia when the Persian Gulf War established U.S. military facilities inside Saudi Arabia. Barre had encouraged clan rivalries and killed many political leaders to secure his own power. So when his government fell, Somalia collapsed into political chaos and, as a result, mass hunger.

In 1991, Bread for the World (BFW), a Christian citizens' movement against hunger, launched a campaign to change U.S. government policies in Somalia and neighboring countries. Concerned citizens sent nearly 100,000 letters to Congress that year, mostly during the Gulf War and long before Somalia became front-page news. BFW's Horn of Africa bill passed Congress, and President Bush signed it into law in April 1992.

This grassroots citizen effort helped shift U.S. policies from Cold War patterns toward support for peace, democracy, and development. For example, in early 1992, U.S. diplomats facilitated a peace agreement in Ethiopia that may have saved half a million lives that would have otherwise been lost to war and hunger. The most effective form of relief for hungry families in Ethiopia is peace, and private agencies

Government policies often affect hungry people on a scale that dwarfs the impact of private assistance.

could not have matched the U.S. government's efforts to bring relative peace to Ethiopia.

BFW and other citizen efforts that tackle political causes of hunger are often overwhelmed by more powerful political forces. So Bread for the World Institute has been exploring possible actions to build stronger political will to reduce hunger in this country and worldwide. Millions of people in the United States work through tens of thousands of organizations to help hungry people. Could this massive movement be transformed into a dynamic social and political movement with enough clout to end U.S. hunger and reduce world hunger?

Hunger 1994 analyzes networks of institutions that seem especially promising to transform the politics of hunger: agencies that directly assist hungry people, religious communities, low-income people's organizations, the mass media, and advocacy groups. BFW Institute convened a series of consultations to test our findings with leaders in these networks, including sponsors and cosponsors of *Hunger 1994*.

We also carried out original research on the scope of these networks.

Based on our analysis and consultations, we recommend that people and organizations focus on seven key areas for action. (See box, this page.) These are high-impact, strategic activities for transforming the politics of hunger.

Complementing Assistance With Advocacy

Our first recommendation is that individuals and agencies who assist hungry people expand what they do to influence government policies. Many leaders of charitable agencies have already been convinced by their experiences to speak out on public policy issues.

Some of those who set up "emergency" feeding programs in the early 1980s are frustrated that these have become permanent institutions – always scrambling to cope half-adequately with massive need. Second Harvest, the main network of food banks, is now urging government actions

---

Transforming the Politics of Hunger

Some of the effort devoted to helping hungry people should be directed toward transforming the politics of hunger. *Hunger 1994* **recommends seven priority areas for action:**

1. Individuals and agencies assisting hungry people can expand what they do to influence government policies.

2. Religious communities can teach how social concern flows from a relationship with God and help motivate involvement in effective political action.

3. Low-income people's organizations can be strengthened, especially in their capacity to influence government policies that affect them.

4. Organizations which help low-income people can more fully engage people of color, especially in decision making.

5. The media can move beyond stories of pity and charity to explain the causes of hunger, and people and organizations concerned about hunger can make a bigger effort to influence the media.

6. People can expand and strengthen anti-hunger advocacy organizations.

7. People and organizations working against poverty and hunger can become more aware of themselves as parts of a large, potentially dynamic movement.

to reduce hunger. To inform public opinion and public policy, Second Harvest is surveying thousands of food banks, food pantries, and soup kitchens to draw information from their hands-on experience.

Catholic Charities, which provides almost $2 billion annually in assistance to people in need, has also become involved in lobbying. Joe Heiney-Gonzales of Catholic Charities says, "We are managing a huge network of services, but feel that God is calling us to help make a society where such massive charity would not be needed." Catholic Charities, too, is grounding its policy work in a survey of its local staff, which is in a good position to know the public policy changes most needed.

Private voluntary organizations that provide relief and development assistance in developing countries have been through a similar experience. The international debt crisis and other problems in the global economy provoked economic trauma in nearly all developing countries in the 1980s. Many countries have yet to recover. Private agencies found their efforts in low-income communities swamped by the effects of economic malfunction at the national and international levels. Many of the local people who work with U.S. private agencies abroad urged their U.S. friends to help sway U.S. government policies regarding international debt, aid, and trade.

Some U.S. private agencies have responded. Oxfam America, for example, has expanded its education and advocacy efforts. World Vision has established an office for advocacy and education with an annual budget of $500,000. Catholic Relief Services spends an identical amount on development education. These agencies base their advocacy work on their on-the-

ground experience overseas. The International Development Conference is urging its member organizations to devote 5 percent of their budgets to public education and another 5 percent to advocacy.

Organizations that help low-income people are always hard-pressed to meet immediate needs – another evicted family or, for international agencies, another disaster or development project. These organizations are usually struggling to raise funds for pressing needs. But the *combined* budgets of all private organizations assisting poor and hungry people total tens of billions of dollars. By contrast, the combined budgets of the anti-hunger advocacy organizations total a little over $13 million. As assistance agencies make even modest shifts in the use of their resources, the impact will be far-reaching.

Other Priority Areas For Action

Hunger 1994's second recommendation addresses religious communities. Sharing with the poor is important in all religions. The Bible certainly stresses that God requires justice and mercy toward the poor. Faith in God provides spiritual resources to help people wrestle with the individualistic materialism that dominates U.S. culture. Religious inspiration and leadership have been important to many of the movements of social concern that have reformed the United States in the past.

Several surveys suggest that over half the 350,000 local religious communities across the country now give significant attention to the problem of hunger. They feature hunger in worship, youth activities, food pantries, hunger walks, and letter writing to Congress. Many denominations use some of their funding and influence for hungry people. Some theologically

Religious inspiration and leadership have been important to many of the movements of social concern that have reformed the United States in the past.

The people in low-income communities nationwide who lead community organizations, church-related agencies, unions for low-income workers, and other groups of low-income people are heroes of the anti-hunger movement.

conservative churches that are now growing rapidly are also taking an increased interest in hunger and its causes.

But the religious communities' response to hunger is, for the most part, limited to charity. While 40 percent of all Americans go to religious services every week, political candidates know that few voters want the government to do more about world hunger or even hunger in this country. Churchgoers, like others, usually vote their own pocketbooks.

There will not be a transformation of the politics of hunger without a powerful stirring of the spirit. The movement needs more people who are actively and persistently committed to justice for God's sake. Religious communities also need to help those members who are concerned connect effectively to specific political decisions. This is what Bread for the World does.

A third priority area for action is strengthening organizations of low-income people, especially in their capacity to influence government policies. Low-income people can speak for themselves with unique insight, passion, and persistence.

The people in low-income communities nationwide who lead community organizations, church-related agencies, unions for low-income workers, and other groups of low-income people are heroes of the anti-hunger movement. Some community groups have become forces to be reckoned with on local issues, and they provide valuable experience and training for their members.

BFW Institute and Interfaith Impact for Justice and Peace together convened a consultation with representatives of low-income people's organizations. Participants made it clear that major changes are needed at the national level, but that their organizations tend to be weak and preoc-

cupied with local issues of immediate concern. They asked for two kinds of outside help – financial support for their organizations and assistance in connecting to national policy debates.

Low-income people's organizations in developing countries tend to be even weaker than in the United States. They need the same kinds of assistance. But they are affected by decisions in Washington, Bonn, and Tokyo, as well as in their national capitals. People in the United States can help low-income groups from other countries be heard on U.S. government decisions that affect them.

Within the United States and worldwide, a disproportionate share of hungry people are people of color, so racial politics are intertwined with the politics of hunger. It is impossible to imagine a successful anti-poverty movement in U.S. politics without prominent African-American, Native American, and Latino leadership and participation. Internationally, movements against hunger and injustice are mainly movements of people of color. Additionally, a disproportionate share of women suffer poverty, so the leadership and participation of women are also important.

Thus, organizations dedicated to helping low-income people should include people of color and women in every aspect of organizational life, especially decision making. Oppressed people often gain strength by meeting and working together. Therefore, organizations focusing on the needs of women and disadvantaged racial and ethnic groups are also important to the politics of hunger.

Mass media, including television, newspapers, magazines, and radio, do not devote much attention to hunger, and when they do, it is usually in terms of pity and charity. Who doesn't remember stories in the media of poor families receiving Thanksgiving baskets or emaciated Africans receiving food aid? The structural causes of hunger are frequently ignored; poor and hungry people are portrayed as dependent and helpless, and coverage is disproportionately focused on crises.

Chapter 4 notes that there are about 150,000 public relations people in the United States, pitching stories to 130,000 journalists. But seventy of the largest organizations that work against hunger and poverty together employ only about one hundred media staff. Just ten of them work to get media coverage of the underlying causes or public policy issues related to hunger. The other ninety focus on institutional self-promotion. People and organizations concerned about hunger have a big opportunity to change media coverage. It is quite feasible for them to double or triple their current effort to influence the media.

A relatively small network of anti-hunger advocacy organizations concentrates on influencing government policies. These include Bread for the World, the Food Research and Action Center, RESULTS, World Hunger Year, and state and local anti-hunger coalitions. By connecting with these organizations, people who are busy with their own lives *can* make a difference on national and international issues. Members of advocacy organizations also find that political action need not be cold and abstract, but can, in its own way, offer comraderie and fellowship.

While anti-hunger advocacy organizations have won important victories over the past three decades, they have lost more battles than they have won. To strengthen these organizations, more people must get involved. The history in

chapter 5 shows that various advocacy groups have been destroyed or crippled by financial crises, so strong and diverse funding is also key to strengthening anti-hunger advocacy.

Becoming a Movement

The last of seven recommendations in *Hunger 1994* is that individuals and organizations working against hunger and poverty become more aware of themselves as part of a large, potentially dynamic movement.

Our own thinking about the anti-hunger movement is on three levels – economic, political, and religious. At one level, this report addresses the question of how to get more results from the billions of dollars and millions of volunteers already working to help the hungry. This is an economic question. In some cases, an organization will achieve more with its resources by assisting an allied group than by doggedly expanding its own program. In other cases, an organization will have the most impact with its individual distinctive work, knowing that allied organizations are covering other areas.

This report also has a political vision for the anti-hunger movement. U.S. politics and culture have been repeatedly rocked by social movements – the civil rights and peace movements of the 1960s, the women's and environmental movements of the 1970s, and conservative movements of the 1980s. During the 1990s, we just might witness the emergence of a major social movement to overcome poverty and hunger – a transformation of the politics of hunger. The movement could inspire increased efforts to assist people in need, religious ferment, lifestyle changes, and community activism, as well as political change at the national level. It would

Members of advocacy organizations also find that political action need not be cold and abstract, but can, in its own way, offer comraderie and fellowship.

There cannot be progress against poverty unless our institutions of government help make it happen, and we as a nation have not supported some of the most obvious and uncontroversial steps our government could take.

focus on U.S. need but encompass concern about hunger worldwide. One precondition for a social movement against poverty and hunger is that a few committed people and organizations begin planning and praying to make it happen.

Finally, BFW Institute is inspired by a religious vision of God's movement in history. People of faith believe that God hears the cries of the hungry and brings justice to bear. They thank God for the many efforts made to reduce hunger, and ask how their own efforts can best fit into God's movement to rescue hungry people. In the passage of scripture from Isaiah cited at the outset of this introduction, the prophet claims that God is coming to the rescue through events that appear entirely secular.

An Agenda for Policy Change

Many people stay out of the politics of hunger because of controversies and doubts about the role of government. But there is a remarkably broad and long-standing consensus about government policies that would reduce hunger. The Presidential Commission on World Hunger articulated this consensus in 1980. More recently, a wide array of experts and leaders have endorsed the Medford and Bellagio Declarations, which spell out programs of action that could virtually end hunger in the United States within a few years and reduce world hunger by half within a decade. Chapter 6 is our restatement of these long-overdue policy changes.

The Medford Declaration stresses that expanding the federal food programs would quickly eliminate the widespread hunger we have come to take for granted in the United States. Some other anti-poverty programs have also proven their

effectiveness, but are underfunded. Ending poverty would require deeper changes, and government action would solve only part of the problem. But the expansion of existing federal programs could virtually eliminate hunger *per se* and reduce poverty more generally.

Similarly, some foreign aid programs, especially those that work with community groups, are effective in reducing hunger abroad. Child health programs have dramatically reduced child mortality, for example. Credit programs have helped millions of poor people establish and expand small-scale businesses. Yet less than a third of U.S. foreign aid goes to programs that focus on reducing poverty, protecting the environment, or providing emergency assistance.

U.S. policies toward international trade, banking, and security have an even bigger impact on world hunger than aid programs. Policies in these areas are often formulated with little consideration of their impact on hungry people in other countries.

There cannot be progress against poverty unless our institutions of government help make it happen, and we as a nation have not supported some of the most obvious and uncontroversial steps our government could take.

Outside Our Focus

While this report concentrates on networks of institutions that we judge to be especially promising, other institutions are also important to the politics of hunger. Electoral politics are enormously important, but *Hunger 1994* does not include a study of political parties or elected politicians.

We have given only passing attention to other important networks of institutions. Hungry people are usually victims of injustice and violence, so various justice and peace organizations are relevant. Children's advocacy organizations are closely allied with anti-hunger organizations, because poverty is at the root of many children's problems and also at the root of hunger.

The environmental movement is powerful and could become allied with poor people. Desperately poor people are encroaching on rain forests and other fragile ecosystems in developing countries. Moneyed interests are also encroaching, but it is impossible to save these threatened ecosystems without helping the poor people involved to improve their livelihoods in sustainable ways. Environmental and justice issues also overlap in the United States. Dirty industries, toxic waste dumps, and other environmental hazards are often placed in low-income regions of the country and in low-income, African-American, Native American, and Latino neighborhoods.

The environmental movement finally "arrived" when business leaders began to weave environmental concerns into advertising and corporate practices. Some corporate leaders are already providing leadership on hunger and poverty issues. For example, a few business leaders have testified before Congress in favor of funding for WIC and food stamps. Most important to poor people are good jobs, and business leaders need to be involved in measures to improve the job market for low-skill workers.

Another sign of success for U.S. social movements is support from popular culture – popular music, movies, and entertainment television. The Live Aid Concert and the "We Are the World" recording engaged tens of millions of people in responding to the Ethiopian famine of 1984. Popular culture has a powerful influence on values, especially among young people. *Hunger 1994* only touches on popular culture in its discussion of media.

The educational system, from kindergarten through college, could make a powerful contribution by teaching more about hunger and poverty. Social movements have often drawn support from universities, and many of today's students are keenly interested in justice and environmental issues.

Our Next Steps

The discussions and consultations that led up to *Hunger 1994* have already influenced the thinking and planning of a number of organizations and networks, notably Second Harvest, Catholic Charities, World Vision, InterAction, and the Food Research and Action Center. We hope that the publication of *Hunger 1994* will help other organizations and individuals as well.

For our part, Bread for the World Institute will follow up with a series of hunger leadership conferences in cities across the country. We will plan these conferences together with other interested organizations. The conferences would give state and local anti-hunger leaders an opportunity to find new ways to collaborate and sharpen their leadership skills and knowledge.

To help people see that overcoming hunger calls for more than charity or even government assistance programs, we are planning to make *Hunger 1995* an educational resource on the basic causes of hunger.

Bread for the World, the public interest lobby with which BFW Institute is affiliated, is also planning to follow up on *Hunger 1994*. In keeping with chapters 1 and 3, Bread for the World plans to expand its cooperative advocacy work with some service agencies, low-income people's

The educational system, from kindergarten through college, could make a powerful contribution by teaching more about hunger and poverty.

organizations, and organizations of people of color. Chapter 2 on religious communities confirmed the practical importance of BFW's grounding in Christian faith. Chapter 4 reaffirmed Bread for the World's media work, since so little media work on the causes of hunger is being done.

Finally, *Hunger 1994* has led Bread for the World to a renewed commitment to developing its distinctive strength – its nationwide network of forty-four thousand religiously inspired citizen advocates. Bread for the World intends to give high priority to strengthening the local leadership structure of this grassroots movement, involving more people of color and low-income people, and increasing the number of people involved.

Acknowledgements

We are deeply grateful to the sponsors and cosponsors of this report. Many contributed valuable insights, and we could not have financed this report or the consultations that shaped it without their help. The collaboration in producing this report is itself an indication that many anti-poverty agencies are becoming more keenly aware of themselves as part of a broader movement, and that assistance agencies are increasingly involved in education about basic causes and public policy advocacy.

We are grateful for the involvement of several European cosponsors this year. This is a sign of growing international cooperation on global justice issues.

We began planning this initiative with a grant from Lilly Endowment.

We also appreciate the comments we received on all or part of this report from the following people, many of whom participated in our consultations:

Robert Berg, International Development Conference; Lynn Brantley, Capital Area Community Food Bank; Pamela Butt, San Antonio Food Bank; Jo Luck Cargile and Jim DeVries, Heifer Project International; Rob Fersh, Jud Dolphin, Ann Kittlaus, Michele Tingling-Clemmons, and Lynn Parker, Food Research and Action Center; Anthony Gambino and Karen Donovan, InterAction; Dick Goebel, St. Paul Food Bank; John Hammock, Janet Green, and Michael Briggs, Oxfam America; Sr. Georgia Greene, So Others Might Eat; Sam Harris, RESULTS; Joe Heiney-Gonzalez, Catholic Charities USA; Ken Horne, Society of St. Andrew; Maria Elena Hurtado, World Development Movement; David Korten, People-Centered Development Forum; Boyd Lowry, CODEL; Paul McCleary, Christian Children's Fund; Mark Winne, Hartford Food System; Col. James Osborne and Commissioner Kenneth Hood, Salvation Army; Brian Sellers-Petersen and Jerry Levin, World Vision; John Swenson and Nancy Martin, Catholic Relief Services; Angela Van Rynbach and Lee Mullane, Save the Children (U.S.); George Alagiah, BBC; Msgr. Robert Coll, Interfaith Hunger Appeal; John Coonrod, The Hunger Project; Christie Goodman, General Board of Church and Society, United Methodist Church; Yussuf Hassan, Voice of America; Peter Mann, World Hunger Year; Jerry Michaud, The End Hunger Network; Michael McManus; Julia Muggia, U.S. Committee for UNICEF; Mark Mooney, Tribune Broadcasting; Suzy Shure, Shure Communications; John and Eleanor Smith; Chuck Woolery, Alliance for Child Survival; Angela Roffle, ROWEL; Ann Lennon, Project Uplift; Antonio Diaz, Southwest Network for Envrionmental and Economic Justice; Bill Troy, Tennessee Industrial Renewal Network; Carlos Marentes, Sin Fronteras; Catherine Moore, SMILE; Ana Elsa Avilés, Dora Genovés, and Mary Ann Hoehenstein, Service Employees International Union; elmira Nazombe, Jim Bell, and Robert Greenwood, Interfaith Impact for Justice and Peace; Flora Punch and Jean Dever, National Welfare Rights Union; Garnett Day, Christian Church (Disciples of Christ); Gaye Evans, Committee on Religion in Appalachia; Guillermo Chavez, National Hispanic Council on Aging; Janece Boyd, Women's Economic Agenda Project; Jean Stone, Tennessee Hunger Coalition; Jenni Wierwille, United Church of Christ; Juan José Gloria, California Catholic Conference; Lisa Henderson and Betty Coates, Washington Office of the Episcopal Church; Lora Rinker, Arlington Street People's Assistance Network; Louis Head and Maria Chavez, Southwest Organizing Project; Margie Ellison, Federation for Rural Empowerment; Marian Nickelson, Lutheran Office on Government Affairs; Nancy Atkins, Toledo Metropolitan Mission; Rachel Jones and William Dunbar, St. Peter's Community Outreach Center; Ralph Paige, Federation of Southern Cooperatives; S. Tootie Welker, Montana Alliance for Progressive Policy; John Carr and Martin McLaughlin, U.S. Catholic Conference; John DeHaan, World Relief Commission, Christian Reformed Church; Rev. Dr. Lorenzo DuPree, Church of God in Christ; Ken Flemmer, Adventist Development and Relief Agency International; Herbert G. Hassold, Brot für die Welt; Lani J. Havens and Carol Capps, Church World Service; Rev. Leonard Jackson, First AME Church, Los Angeles; Hershey Leaman, Mennonite Central Committee; Sr. Peggy Loftus, U.S. Catholic Conference Mission Association; Sr. Patricia McCann, Mercy Institute; Bryon Peachey, Nazarene Compassionate Ministries; Al Senske, Lutheran Church - Missouri Synod World Relief; Robin Shell, Food for the Hungry International; Rev. Bucky Sydnor, American Baptist Church; Prof. Delane Welsch, University of Minnesota; Prof. Daria Donnelly, Boston University; Norman Hicks, The World Bank; Jo Marie Griesgraber, Center of Concern; Larry Brown and John

Cook, Center on Hunger, Poverty, and Nutrition Policy, Tufts University; Prof. Ben Wisner, Hampshire College; Prof. Robert Chen, World Hunger Program, Brown University; Joe Stork, *Middle East Report*; Howarth Bouis, Patrick Webb, and colleagues, International Food Policy Research Institute; Christian Foster, Carol Levin, Dick Brown, Margaret Missiaen, Stacey Rosen, Mike Kurtzig, and colleagues, U.S. Department of Agriculture; Prof. George Ayittey, The American University; Prof. Murray Feshbach, Georgetown University; Barry Davidson, Canadian Association of Foodbanks; Charles Hanrahan and Remy Jurenas, Congressional Research Service; Barbara E. Cohen, The Urban Institute; Thea Lee, Economic Policy Institute; Prof. Luther Tweeten, Ohio State University; Craig Etcheson, Campaign to Oppose the Return of the Khmer Rouge; Berta Romero; Roger Rumpf, Asia Resource Center; Marianne Leach, CARE; Katie Cook, *Seeds Magazine*; Prof. Janet Poppendieck, Hunter College; Jayne Wood, Devres, Inc.; Leon Howell; Steve Hellinger, Development GAP; Christina Martin, Foodchain; Mark Dunlea, HANNYS; Judith Walker, New York City Coalition Against Hunger; Rosemary Spendlove, National Anti-Poverty Organization (Canada); Susan Scruton, Centre for International Statistics on Economic and Social Welfare for Families and Children (Canada); Marge Connor, Caritas; Diana Melrose and colleagues, Oxfam UK Ireland; André Hubert, European Federation of Food Banks; Christine Carroll, European Anti-Poverty Network; Karen Hauser, Lutheran World Relief; Bob Stix, Ruth Mott Foundation; Hiram Ruiz, U.S. Committee for Refugees; and James Mackie, Liaison Committee of Development NGOs to the European Community.

We are grateful to the following for help in preparing the tables and providing other data: Dr. Janos Ay and colleagues at the Food and Agriculture Organization of the United Nations; Dr. Marito Garcia, International Food Policy Research Institute; Tessa Wardlaw, UNICEF; Rae Galloway, The World Bank; Karen Jones, U.S. Census Bureau; Jessie Marcus, U.S. Bureau of Labor Statistics; Sylvia Grave, U.S. Agency for International Development, Office of Food for Peace; Cheryl Tates-Macias and colleagues at the Food and Nutrition Service, U.S. Department of Agriculture; and Caroline Pfeifer, European Foundation for the Improvement of Living and Working Conditions.

The following Bread for the World/BFW Institute staff and board members provided comments and other assistance with this report: Ingrid Acevedo, Nancy Alexander, Teresa Amott, Marie Bledsoe, Mike Calhoun, Susan Clifford, Gary Cook, Alma Faith Crawford, Jennifer Cross, Peter Doyle, Rick Doyle, Newman Fair, David Fouse, Larry Goodwin, John Halvorson, Michael J. Harning, Barbara Howell, Lorraine C. Kennedy, Lynn Heichel Kneedler, Chris Matthews, Steve Nunn-Miller, Maria Otero, Susan Park, Kathy Pomroy, Kathleen Selvaggio, Arthur Simon, Katherine Smith, Joel Underwood, Sr. Christine Vladimiroff, William Whitaker, Fr. Clarence Williams, Donald D. Williams, and Carole Zimmerman. ■

David Beckmann is president of Bread for the World Institute.

Feeding People –
Half of Overcoming Hunger

Photo: World Vision, Jay Hubbard

The past decade has seen a quiet explosion of emergency efforts to feed hungry people in the United States. This spontaneous, grassroots effort is likened to a sleeping giant, unaware of its size and potential.

PART ONE:
The U.S. Feeding Movement – Fertile Ground For An Anti-Hunger Movement

by Richard A. Hoehn

Every single day across the country, tens of thousands of adults and teenagers squeeze anti-hunger activities into their busy schedules. Some rise before dawn to pick up day-old doughnuts and deliver them to soup kitchens. Others spread peanut butter on day-old bread and fire up soup pots, or make the rounds of hotels to pick up leftover steak dinners.

The past decade has seen a quiet explosion of emergency efforts to feed hungry people in the United States. This spontaneous, grassroots effort is likened to a sleeping giant, unaware of its size and potential. This chapter describes this feeding movement and some of its cautious steps toward becoming an anti-hunger movement that addresses root causes of hunger.

Emergency Efforts Multiply

In the 1980s, religious organizations and service agencies were newly confronted first with hundreds, then thousands, of people coming off the streets for emergency food assistance. In response, neighborhoods and towns across the nation established food pantries to provide several days worth of groceries. The food pantries banded together through local food banks – community-based warehouses that receive, store, and distribute emergency food to other agencies – and, at the national level, Second Harvest. In fourteen years, the Second Harvest national office has become the third largest recipient of private charitable gifts (mostly food) in the United States – ahead of the American Red Cross, the American Cancer Society, and Harvard University.

Feeding organizations have grown at a phenomenal rate. For example, in 1981, thirty soup kitchens and food pantries in New York City served meals mostly to single men with substance abuse or mental problems. By 1992, 750 emergency food providers served an estimated 2.5 million to 3 million meals a month.[1]

Thousands of new groups have sprung up across the country to respond to specific needs. For example, Project Open Hand began in San Francisco, in 1985, when Ruth Brinker noticed that a friend with AIDS often was unable to fix meals for himself. Within its eight-year history, the project has grown to include a $7 million budget, a kitchen, and food bank that provide assistance to people with HIV symptoms. A staff of 75 and 210 volunteers serve more than two thousand meals daily.

Nationally, the number of food services and free-food distribution organizations increased 29 percent between 1987 and 1989; housing and shelter organizations 35 percent.[2] Meanwhile, as a nation, we are further from a solution to hunger than we were fifteen years ago.

Concern and Compassion In Action

A 1992 poll indicates that 93 percent of U.S. voters think that hunger in the United States is either "very serious" or "serious." (See graph 1.)

Seventy-nine percent of the respondents to the same poll indicated they had personally contributed food or participated in some volunteer anti-hunger activity. That translates into more than seventy million

voters. If non-voters and youth under age eighteen were added to this figure, it is likely that more than half the people in the United States contributed to hunger relief.

It is possible to get a sense of the scope of the movement by surveying some of the limited data that exist. The Second Harvest network received food valued at more than $1 billion in 1992. And, there are food banks which are not part of the Second Harvest network.

If food banks, pantries, and soup kitchens were added together, BFW Institute estimates $3 billion to $4 billion in emergency food is being distributed each year in the United States. Tens of thousands of religious congregations have small food pantries for members and the neighborhood. BFW Institute research suggests that there may easily be 150,000 food pantries in the United States – one for every two thousand persons.

The feeding movement is ample testimony that people want to do something. But they prefer it to be concrete, local, personal, and visibly effective, or at least connected with a local, familiar organization, such as a church. "Voluntary giving tends to go to places where the impact of the contributions is seen by the giver," says Craig Dykstra of Lilly Endowment.[3]

Part of BFW Institute's vision of creating the political will to end hunger includes the development of strong national networks among feeding groups. As these networks develop, they might begin to ask why hunger persists in spite of their extraordinary efforts. Such prodding can spark public

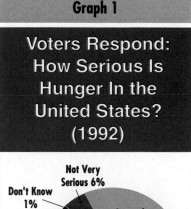

Graph 1

Voters Respond: How Serious Is Hunger In the United States? (1992)

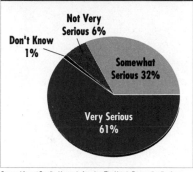

Don't Know 1%
Not Very Serious 6%
Somewhat Serious 32%
Very Serious 61%

Source: Vincent Breglio. Hunger in America: The Voter's Perspective (Lanham, Maryland: Research/Strategy Management)

Feeding the Hungry in Waco
by Rick Huber

Early in 1993, the town of Waco, Texas was thrust into the headlines as the site of a tragic fifty-one-day standoff between federal agents and the Branch Davidians. But behind the headlines is another Waco, one which serves as a prime example of how communities across the country have organized to combat increasing hunger.

Waco is a relatively poor city near the geographical center of Texas. In 1990, Waco's poverty rate (28.5 percent) was more than twice the national average of 13.5 percent. Unemployment is not exceptionally high; however, wages are extremely low. Hunger grips many in this town of 104,000. Churches and concerned citizens have banded together and are working in various ways to ease the pains of hunger.

Baylor University students and local youth plant the gardens of infirm senior citizens. Members of congregations collect canned goods, operate Meals on Wheels programs, and contribute money to anti-poverty efforts. On opening day of the annual Heart of Texas Fair and Rodeo, admission is a dollar plus four cans of food for Waco's needy.

Caritas is the largest provider of emergency food in Waco. Begun in 1967 by Catholic Charities of the Diocese of Austin, Caritas now distributes 1.4 million pounds of privately donated and government surplus food annually. More than three hundred volunteers a month (forty-five-thousand volunteer hours a year) help operate a food bank, pantry, and four thrift stores, as well as provide emergency grants for rent, medicine, and other necessities.

Two-thirds of those who come for help are referred from elsewhere, often government agencies whose eligibility requirements are too stringent or complex for people to meet. Caritas' program, Food for People, distributes surplus food to both families and other agencies. Each month, the pantry distributes $45,000 to $85,000 worth of groceries to about one thousand families. Families are normally limited to one food package per month. As the regional distributor for surplus government commodities, Caritas is able to help an additional four thousand to five thousand households monthly. As a food bank, Caritas also distributes food to thirty-one agencies in McLennan County.

A large portion of the food is received through the Can Do food drive, held from September to December each year. Can Do

discussion about the role of politics and public policy in creating and solving hunger.

Givers, Gleaners, Servers, And Advocates

Givers, or donors, contribute money or food because of religious conviction and human compassion. People who have less tend to give proportionately more of all they have – the biblical widow's mite.

The variety of ideas that people have used to raise money for emergency hunger relief is a testimonial to human imagination – bake sales and poverty banquets, golf tournaments and celebrity balls, hunger hikes and youth group "lock ins."

- In 1992, 322,000 people participated in Church World Service CROP walks to raise money for anti-hunger efforts.

- That same year, Share Our Strength raised $3.5 million, mostly through Taste of the Nation events in which chefs in one hundred cities served culinary delicacies to crowds of donors.

- In St. Louis, 350 volunteers at Feed My People distribute $1 million worth of food to fifty thousand people a year and provide other services to fifty thousand more.

- Grocery stores in the Washington, D.C., area post $2 and $5 coupons at checkout stands for shoppers to tear off and have them added to their grocery bill. The proceeds are donated to the Capital Area Community Food Bank, which in the first three weeks of this program received $80,000.

Gleaners, or gatherers, scavenge for food, raw or packaged, to distribute to people in need. They see the irony of surplus food juxtaposed with abject hunger and reason that the solution to hunger lies in getting food from places where it is being wasted to people who need it.

Rural gleaners track through fields after mechanical devices have gathered the bulk of the harvest. The Potato Project of Virginia, for example, has distributed 150 million pounds of produce in its ten-year history. Sometimes, gleaners ship tons of unsalable (due to low market prices) produce to community food banks which store and then distribute the food.

HandsNet, a California-based computer network, was first used to link a food bank with a surplus of tomatoes to a food bank with excess milk. Being able to instantly communicate with each other, food banks can trade items and arrange proper storage for food that might otherwise spoil.

Urban gleaners take day-old food from grocery stores and bakeries to shelters and soup kitchens. Or, they arrange to pick up cans and boxes of food from homes, religious congregations, or other convenient locations. In many urban areas, mail carriers pick up canned foods while delivering the mail. In 1991, the Boy Scouts collected 57,316,892 cans of food with an estimated value of $57 million to $86 million.

The newest and fastest growing segment of the urban gleaners consists of food rescuers, people who collect excess, unsold food from restaurants, hotels, catering companies, and other food service establishments and then distribute it to nonprofit agencies serving meals to people in need. For example, a hotel might plan dinner for five hundred guests, but only 450 show up. The food is frozen and later picked up by staff or volunteers associated with Prepared and Perishable Food Rescue Programs, one hundred of which recently banded together to form a national association called Foodchain. The United Parcel Service Foundation is supporting

'92 brought in a record 280,000 pounds of food. The centerpiece of Can Do is Food for Families, a one-day food drive spanning seven counties. Sponsored by KWTX-TV, the Waco Board of Realtors, and H.E.B. food stores, the drive is held on the Friday before Thanksgiving. For the preceding two-weeks, KWTX airs announcements during the news urging viewers to donate non-perishable food. Features on people who receive assistance also air. Virgil Teeter of KWTX describes the interviewees as "working people, often two-parent families, who don't have enough and lack the coping skills to manage the rough times." H.E.B. puts grocery bags in their newspaper ads, urging customers to fill them with food for the needy.

All Food for Families food collected in McLennan County goes to Caritas. The 1992 event brought in over 100,000 pounds of food for Waco, and 240,000 pounds for the seven-county area. Caritas also reaps the benefit of community charity through events like church and school food drives, hunger walks, and the annual Feast of Caring where, says Executive Director Eugene Jud, "You pay what you would normally pay at a nice restaurant. Only you get soup and bread. And you go away a little hungry."

H.E.B., a San Antonio-based grocery chain, is a major contributor to Caritas and to Texas food banks. The six stores in Waco each donate 2,000 to 3,000 pounds of perishables per month, while another three semi-truckloads (100,000 to 150,000 pounds) of food come from H.E.B.'s San Antonio warehouse.

Caritas operates five trucks, including a donated refrigerated truck, which pick up food. Food service employees at both area medical centers freeze prepared food that never reached the cafeteria line, and Caritas picks it up weekly. Albertson's Grocery Store donates dairy products. Pop's Deli & Bakery provides bread and sandwiches daily, and about twenty other local stores and food manufacturers make regular donations.

Nevertheless, Caritas is not the only provider of emergency food in Waco. In addition to efforts mentioned earlier, many churches, such as Robinson United Methodist and First Baptist, run their own small pantries. Salvation Army workers serve 150-200 meals a day, including sack lunches and dinners to street people, residents of a halfway house, and formerly homeless residential volunteers. In 1991, fifteen hundred people donated time to help with the Salvation Army's various programs. A gleaning program, Harvesters for the Hungry, has been organized to gather Waco's portion of the 137 million tons of crops wasted each year in U.S. fields and distribute it to the needy.

Feeding People – Half of Overcoming Hunger

Though the bulk of its anti-hunger activity is in emergency food distribution, Waco is also home to initiatives to create hunger awareness and address global poverty. The Seventh and James Baptist Church next to Baylor University has become the headquarters of *Seeds*, a quarterly Christian magazine on hunger issues. *Seeds*, started by a Baptist congregation in Atlanta, was rescued from financial difficulties in 1990 by a group of people in Waco who were committed to its mission and its survival. World Hunger Relief, Inc., begun in Waco in 1976, operates a farm where missionaries and others are trained in agricultural techniques to take to people of developing countries.

The achievements of the citizens in Waco demonstrate the tremendous outpouring of support and the variety of resources mobilized to meet a growing need. Efforts like these, multiplied thousands of times every day in communities across the country, are testimony to the depth and breadth of the anti-hunger movement.

Rick Huber is a research assistant at Bread for the World Institute.

the expansion of this food rescuers network through a $4 million grant.

Emergency feeding organizations tend to become more established over time, though they often begin when someone is starkly confronted with a specific instance of poverty or hunger. What starts out as a short-term effort to meet an immediate need typically becomes an established community institution.

Will people grow weary of the hunger issue when the problem does not go away? Will they doggedly slog on, drop out, or seek alternative solutions? Some participants in the feeding movement see a need to unite the thousand points of light into a grid that will empower a politics of hunger and rewire public policies to end widespread hunger in the United States.

In addition to donors and gleaners, another group of anti-hunger activists are the servers who have to find the money and the means to prepare and deliver food to places where people reside.

The best known deliver-and-serve program is Meals on Wheels. The program began in Philadelphia in 1954 as a private effort to bring meals to homebound seniors. Today fifteen thousand nutrition sites and four thousand private nonprofit groups participate in meals on wheels. More than half the programs have no paid staff, often depending on elderly volunteers. In the early 1970s, the federal Older Americans Act began to pour money into meals on wheels and congregate (on-site) feeding. In fiscal year 1993, the federal nutrition program for the elderly spent $475 million on 245 million meals to feed approximately one million people. The history of meals on wheels provides a clue to the direction some volunteer programs are likely to take. Though largely dependent on volunteers, meals on wheels could not now operate without government funds. Similarly, in 1992, New York City emergency food programs not only received private charitable donations but more than $12.8 million in federal, state, and local government emergency assistance.

Site-servers usually prepare and serve the meals at places where people gather or live. In 1991, churches and neighborhood centers served 137 million meals to 2.6 million senior citizens at fifteen hundred sites where people gathered at a cost of $243 million to the federal government and unknown millions of dollars in private contributions. Nearly 350,000 people volunteer daily with various senior nutrition programs. Most of the twelve thousand emergency homeless shelters offer food programs as do many drug and alcohol rehabilitation centers and centers for abused women and children.

Hospitals, prisons, and residential facilities (e.g., senior citizen) probably provide more nutritious meals than many residents would receive at home or on the streets. Schools and summer recreation programs provide government-funded breakfast and lunch to children. Most of these efforts are heavily supported by public funds.

One of the challenges of the 1990s will be to determine the right balance between public and private efforts to solve major social problems. Private charitable agencies that serve poor people have the flexibility to initiate innovative programs which sometimes become models for larger government programs. Such programs often help people who otherwise become bogged down in large bureaucracies.

At the National Hunger Forum sponsored by the U.S. Department of Agriculture in June 1993, representatives of charitable agencies remarked repeatedly, "We can't do it all. The problems are too big." At this same meeting, which was the largest federally-sponsored hunger symposium since 1969, the largest corporate funder of anti-hunger activities echoed, "Corporate America can't do it all. The public sector has to take the initiative to end hunger."

BFW Institute believes that lasting solutions require transforming public efforts. Bad policies can wipe out the benefits of voluntary efforts and good policies can go a long way toward providing education, jobs, and income. We need a politics that affirms people, a politics that sustains and renews creation and community, a politics which can help transform the spirit and the substance of our era.

Charities Link With Justice

Politics is the most comprehensive activity of human communities. . . . Politics is the mobilization of a people's power for the preservation and ordering of its common life.[4]

Political advocacy groups typically plead, argue for, and support public policies that can alleviate both the symptoms and root causes of hunger and impoverishment. Advocacy that truly speaks in behalf of the genuine interests of poor people gives voice to those who otherwise are not heard in public forums.

A complete map of the agencies working to eliminate hunger would also have to include community organizations and groups that work against racism, that seek to eliminate gender discrimination, that support low-income labor organizing, and that work on housing, community development, and health-care issues. All these are related.

Bread for the World and other advocacy organizations engage people in writing letters, getting media coverage, making phone calls, and visiting members of Congress about specific legislation that affects poor and hungry people. Chapter 5 describes a wide range of advocacy organizations that respond to hunger.

Some charitable agencies are just beginning to engage in advocacy. Such agencies work daily with clients who are impoverished and can speak with particular authenticity about the depth and complexity of their situation.

Food banks and other direct service agencies can draw on a wealth of resources to turn toward advocacy. They have powerful community leaders on their boards, mailing lists of concerned people, and relatively large budgets. Even 5 percent of those budgets devoted to education and 5 percent to advocacy would make a major difference. Charitable organizations have, by and large, earned the respect of the public. That respect forms a reservoir of good will that can be gently tapped to draw more people from service

Bad policies can wipe out the benefits of voluntary efforts and good policies can go a long way toward providing education, jobs, and income.

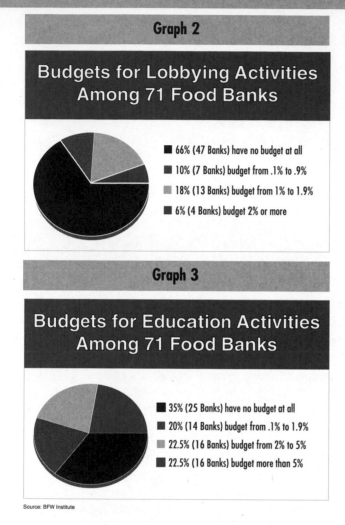

Graph 2

Budgets for Lobbying Activities Among 71 Food Banks

- ■ 66% (47 Banks) have no budget at all
- ■ 10% (7 Banks) budget from .1% to .9%
- ■ 18% (13 Banks) budget from 1% to 1.9%
- ■ 6% (4 Banks) budget 2% or more

Graph 3

Budgets for Education Activities Among 71 Food Banks

- ■ 35% (25 Banks) have no budget at all
- ■ 20% (14 Banks) budget from .1% to 1.9%
- ■ 22.5% (16 Banks) budget from 2% to 5%
- ■ 22.5% (16 Banks) budget more than 5%

Source: BFW Institute

to citizenship.

A BFW Institute survey of seventy-one food banks indicates that thirty-eight have at least one staff member who does lobbying work occasionally. An even greater number of food bank directors indicated that they would like to include advocacy as a program activity. However, many do not have boards that currently support this type of activity. Overall, very little of food banks' budgets go toward lobbying. (See graphs 2 and 3.)

Our survey elicited the following response to the question: "If you have taken a position on legislation, what has been its focus?"

Food banks are more likely to lobby for issues that directly affect their services and government food programs than for broader policies that affect hungry people. (See graph 4.) When asked whether or not the food pantries and other community service agencies that use food banks' services are involved in political issues, 85 percent of the respondents indicated that few or none of these agencies are politically active. BFW Institute's survey shows that many food banks distribute information about hunger and poverty in various community settings.

Half of the responding food banks include information about legislation and urge readers to take action. But political material is generally less than 10 percent of any food bank's newsletter space. Whether a food bank or pantry is ready to advocate political solutions to hunger, they play a very important role in sensitizing the general public about human need and are in an excellent position to interpret advocacy and policy needs.

In Toronto, Canada, leaders of the Daily Bread Food Bank say, "Food banks are becoming permanent beyond repair" even though many view them as temporary fixtures desiring to put themselves out of business by seeing that everybody is fed. Now, Daily Bread views itself as an "activist charity" which not only distributes food but also engages in advocacy directed toward reducing hunger.

"Food bank operators no longer ask whether they should shut down, but what role they can play in the elimination of hunger in Canada," says Gerard Kennedy, executive director of Daily Bread. He suggests that food banks have a "window of responsibility" to feed *and* work for systemic change.

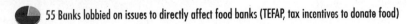

Graph 4

Advocacy Issues Among 71 Food Banks

55 Banks lobbied on issues to directly affect food banks (TEFAP, tax incentives to donate food)

40 Banks lobbied on government nutrition programs (WIC, food stamps)

13 Banks lobbied on other governmental programs (Head Start, Welfare)

17 Banks lobbied on government policies that affect poor people (tax policy, military vs. social spending)

5 Banks lobbied on issues that involved all four of the above

7 Banks lobbied on issues that affect hungry people outside of the United States

Source: BFW Institute

Is a Powerful Hunger Movement Possible?

Social movements rise when people are discontented with the course of events in a society and believe that a possibility for change exists. Public consciousness has to reach a critical mass. And, organizations that are dealing with the problem have to maximize their common efforts.

The environmental movement is a fairly successful social movement. The Sierra Club, founded in 1892, had 5,000 members in 1950 and today has 650,000. The National Wildlife Federation has 6.2 million contributors and members. Widespread public concern about the environment is recent, based on twenty-five years of activism and interpretation.

Robert Cameron Mitchell of Clark University credits the success of the environmental movement in mobilizing public support to four factors:

- The first-generation issues had a direct and powerful appeal to a sympathetic public and to activists. The vivid and picturesque nature of these issues makes them easy to sell.

- Second, the potential threat to health and life posed by many of the pollution issues allows the groups to motivate contributors by portraying the potential losses if these conditions are allowed to persist. The fact that the threat is not confined to a particular group but potentially affects everyone gives these issues a broad appeal.

- Third, the multiplicity of environmental issues allows the groups to appeal to numerous segments of the population. People concerned about toxic wastes might not necessarily be motivated by wildlife appeals, and vice versa.

- Fourth, the continued emergence of new environmental issues such as toxic waste dumps keeps the environmental cause in the news, particularly when dramatic events occur, such as the contamination of Love Canal and the accident at Three Mile Island.[5]

Hunger has a direct and powerful appeal, and allows many points of entry for involvement. But hunger does not as obviously pose a serious threat to most potential contributors, and only sporadically hits the evening news. The disease and joblessness caused by malnutrition are easier to

Feeding People – Half of Overcoming Hunger

The solution to hunger does walk on two legs. But the legs need to be more equal in size, attached to the same body, and walking in the same direction.

ignore than oil spills or pollution in the air.

The feeding movement is a first-generation expression of American discomfort with domestic hunger. Hunger can be the "door" through which people enter an introduction to larger problems of poverty, powerlessness, and distorted public values. Charities can help educate people from their entry point to a sophisticated understanding of the causes of hunger and its international and national dimensions.

An anti-hunger movement is likely to lack a vocal self-interest constituency like the civil rights, feminist, and environmental movements. On the other hand:

> *Many movements in the recent period, such as animal rights and prolife, have been staffed and funded exclusively by conscience constituents.[6]*

The anti-hunger movement may not become as large as the environmental movement, but smaller movements have also had dramatic effects on social problems. The anti-drunk-driving movement has been relatively successful in garnering media attention, changing social attitudes, and influencing legislation.[7]

Most people who collect cans and donate money and time are not even aware they are part of a large social movement. But everyone, from household recyclers to Sierra Club lobbyists, has a sense of being part of a large environmental movement that is making a difference in changing society.

The environmental movement first captured public attention through the national media. The feeding movement has built from the ground up, food pantry by food pantry. While local media may advertise local food drives, the national media have not paid much attention to the feeding movement. To do so could trigger a more self-aware and effective movement against hunger in this country.

Arthur Simon, founder and president emeritus of Bread for the World, says that the solution to hunger walks on two legs – charity and political justice. Both are necessary. People who are hungry cannot wait for our society to sort out its larger social, economic, and political problems. They need daily food. But unless long-term food security solutions are found, the tide of hungry people will continue to rise.

The solution to hunger does walk on two legs. But the legs need to be more equal in size, attached to the same body, and walking in the same direction. The difference between a feeding movement and an anti-hunger movement depends not only on self-awareness and increased activity, but a willingness to attack basic causes, to transform the politics of hunger and the policies that can eliminate hunger. ∎

Dr. Richard A. Hoehn is director of Bread for the World Institute.

Rick Huber, BFW Institute research assistant, collected and analyzed data for this chapter.

Intern Paige Hennessey gathered additional data.

Photo: World Vision, S. Watkins

Croatian girl receives emergency aid.

PART TWO:
From Relief Toward Development and Empowerment

by Doug Siglin

During the second half of 1992, U.S. nongovernmental relief organizations repeatedly pressed the federal government to provide security for feeding operations in Somalia. As controversial as the deployment of troops to Somalia was, the decision to use U.S. forces in a humanitarian role helped save Somali lives. Relief agencies played an essential role in creating the "critical mass" that led to the decision. Achieving an end to hunger – even in the short term – is often as much a matter of political will as of food supplies and logistics.

NGOs and the Politics Of Hunger

Alleviating hunger, whether in high-visibility crises such as Somalia, or in low-visibility but chronic manifestations, quickly crosses into the realm of political decision making. Whether the issue is security for relief operations or access to land, jobs, and credit, public policy has an undisputed effect on hunger.

Since World War I, nongovernmental organizations (NGOs) have implemented relief programs in cooperation with the federal government, often seeking to

NGOs and Europolitics: An Overview
by Rick Huber

While individual European Community (EC) countries have generally maintained autonomy over their foreign policy goals and programs, a large portion of the foreign aid they give to developing countries is now distributed through centralized EC institutions. Thus, NGOs wishing to influence European aid, trade, and development policy toward the Southern Hemisphere turn increasingly to EC headquarters in Brussels to make themselves heard. Mick Wilkinson of the University of Hull, U.K., has done a thorough study of the advocacy of European NGOs at the EC level.

The EC consists of Belgium, Denmark, France, Germany, Great Britain, Greece, Ireland, Italy, Luxembourg, the Netherlands, Portugal, and Spain. The community distributes a large share of its foreign aid through NGOs. From 1976 to 1990, the EC funded four thousand projects through 450 different relief and development agencies. The EC has also funded NGO educational efforts aimed at EC residents. Over the same time period, the EC helped fund 773 development education projects through NGOs. The 1993 EC budget for funding development projects through NGOs is 135 million European Currency Units (ECUs), approximately U.S. $154 million.

The relationship between NGOs and the EC has been institutionalized within the EC system. In 1976, an NGO-EC Liaison Committee was established, largely to help coordinate the awarding of these contracts and projects to various NGOs. In recent years, however, the committee has begun to advocate specific development and trade policies that would benefit poor countries. In fact, the advocacy component of the Liaison Committee has progressed to the point where only one-fifth of the NGOs surveyed still see its central purpose as procuring contracts.

The staff of the various European institutions welcome NGO input. Wilkinson cites statements by each of the EC bodies praising NGOs and affirming their valuable role. It is easier to lobby the EC institutions directly than to mobilize grassroots campaigns or hold popular rallies, due to the multinational nature of the EC's constituency. NGOs also lobby their national governments and parliaments to influence the stands they take in these EC bodies.

European NGOs recognize the strengths they bring to lobbying – knowledge of and connection to Southern grassroots change policy in ways that facilitated their efforts. Today, most U.S. NGOs involved in international development activities seek to eliminate the long-term causes of hunger and poverty. Their emphasis, however, usually remains on providing services to hungry or poor people. Their policy advocacy in crisis situations has seldom been matched by sustained advocacy of policies to eliminate chronic hunger and poverty. In the past few years, however, some international development NGOs have taken steps toward greater emphasis on public education and advocacy to address such structural issues.

The NGO community is quite diverse, comprised of hundreds of organizations, each with its own mission and operating style. A few agencies, such as the Unitarian Universalist Service Committee and Oxfam America, have chosen policy advocacy and its necessary correlate, constituent education, as principal organizational missions.

Others, such as CARE, which played a leading role in the Somalia debate, devote substantial resources to advocacy. Church World Service and Lutheran World Relief are important players through their joint international development policy advocacy office in Washington, D.C. Church World Service is also a leader in the field of "development education." World Vision recently decided to allocate $500,000 annually to advocacy and education. Catholic Relief Services has a development education budget of $480,000 annually. Its staff frequently testify before Congress, and the agency's parent organization, the U.S. Catholic Conference, is heavily involved in advocacy.

At the other end of the continuum, several NGOs adamantly eschew activity related to policy change. For example, Interchurch Medical Assistance procures and distributes medical supplies for overseas health-care ministries of Protestant churches and agencies. According to Executive Director Paul Derstine, "[A]s per our ByLaws, I.M.A. does not engage in any form of advocacy work."[1]

In 1992, Bread for the World Institute and the American Council for Voluntary International Action (InterAction), an association of U.S. international development NGOs, conducted a survey of Inter-Action members. About half of the twenty-five respondents were not interested in advocacy, or were only willing to play a passive role in support of others. The other half wanted to play an active role in changing policies and legislation, but primarily through educational efforts.

The reluctance of many NGOs to devote significant resources to education and advocacy contrasts sharply with the activities of many similar groups in Canada and Europe. Aggressive NGO advocacy could help foster a stronger U.S. government commitment to combatting global hunger and promoting sustainable development. NGOs' years of on-the-ground experience in the developing world means that they have much to contribute to debates about U.S. foreign assistance.

Overview of U.S. International Development NGOs

The community of U.S. international development NGOs comprises several hundred separate organizations whose annual budgets range from more than $1 billion (the American Red Cross, including its domestic operations) to just a few thousand dollars (Surgical Aid to Children of the World spent $137,000 in fiscal

organizations and people, a broad-based Northern constituency, and the moral authority of altruistic motives.

The NGOs have had some successes in lobbying the EC. They have pushed for and gotten language about human rights, racism, sexism, and other concerns into EC positions on overseas development. In 1992-1993, the NGO-EC Liaison Committee was invited for the first time to participate in the EC Council's internal working groups, specifically the Development Cooperation and Food Aid Working Groups. The NGOs have helped the EC to maintain a focus on Africa in recent years despite the preoccupation with Eastern Europe, and have attained some debt reduction on behalf of the developing world. They have also provided indigenous NGOs and others from the countries in which they operate with insights into the EC process, to help them become effective advocates for themselves.

On trade and agricultural issues, however, NGOs face a formidable challenge. Debt and trade are the two most important developing country issues, according to NGOs answering Wilkinson's survey. Yet they are the most complicated. Compared to the NGO lobby, the farming and business lobbies are well-funded and powerful – so powerful that three fourths of NGOs surveyed indicated that it is virtually impossible to compete with them. In addition, responsibility for trade and debt matters falls across several EC departments, while NGOs generally focus on those institutions concerned with development assistance.

Challenges to the NGO lobby in Europe are many. One is its relatively small size. Twice as many NGOs indicate that the NGO-EC Liaison Committee is underfunded as think it is sufficiently funded. Over three-fourths of the NGOs surveyed believe that NGOs should do more lobbying, especially in Brussels. Indeed, the majority believe that the role of northern NGOs should increasingly be that of fund-raiser and advocate for southern NGOs and people, leaving project design and administration in the hands of local populations. This vision is still distant, however, and NGOs remain reluctant to commit resources to any endeavor, such as coalition building or lobbying, which is outside their traditional overseas development work. Almost two-thirds of European NGOs indicate that there should be a permanent NGO lobby in Brussels, but only 12 percent are willing to contribute additional funds for its maintenance.

Another challenge to building a cohesive NGO lobby is the

diversity of perspectives and opinions among organizations. The NGO-EC Liaison Committee tries to set priorities for a coalition of twelve national platforms representing seven hundred agencies. All of these agencies pride themselves on their independence and autonomy, and many compete with one another for EC funding.

In addition to the NGO-EC Liaison Committee, smaller, independent (not EC-funded) trans-European NGO coalitions have formed, most in the past few years. The most significant include APRODEV (Protestant), EURO-CIDSE and Caritas Europa (Catholic), and EUROSTEP (secular). Each attempts to influence EC policy. An association of twenty-four NGOs called EuronAid cooperates with the EC in the programming and procuring of food aid. Smaller, specialized networks emphasize a specific field of development (debt, the environment, South Africa, and trade).

In sum, European NGOs recognize the need for advocacy and are slowly but surely reflecting this insight in their program emphases. Only 10 percent of NGOs responding to the survey opposed lobbying, and the vast majority are in fact moving toward greater involvement in advocacy. Support for development education for EC citizens is even stronger. And NGOs are solidly in agreement that resources available for lobbying and development education are insufficient.

The consequences of trade, debt, and development policies of the world's largest trading block are enormous for the future of developing countries. If European NGOs take the steps needed to increase their influence in Brussels and their educational efforts at home, they could significantly increase their overall impact.

Rick Huber is a research assistant at Bread for the World Institute.

percent of the member agencies, as a matter of policy, accept no government assistance.[2]

The largest U.S. international development NGO outside of InterAction is Catholic Relief Services. In 1991, it raised $260 million, with $54 million (21 percent) coming from private U.S. sources and the rest from governments (mainly the U.S. government) and international organizations.[3]

Altogether, U.S. NGOs provided $2.7 billion in overseas development aid in 1991.[4]

Many of the largest and best known NGOs have existed since the first half of this century, when they were established to provide emergency relief. The American Red Cross, by far the oldest and largest of the international NGOs still active, was established in 1881. Since the turn of the twentieth century, it has operated under a congressional charter, carrying out several U.S. international treaty obligations.

World War I spawned other relief agencies. Some continue to operate today, including the American Jewish Joint Distribution Committee (created in 1914), the Near East Foundation (1915), the American Friends Service Committee (1917), and the Organization for Rehabilitation through Training (1922).

A subgroup of NGOs was formed during the period between the world wars to assist overseas orphans through child sponsorship: Save the Children Federation (1932), Childreach (formerly Foster Parents Plan, 1937), and Christian Children's Fund (1938). In the past two decades, these agencies and several smaller ones have generally moved away from working with orphans to assisting with the development of low-income communities where sponsored children live.

1991). Its members are known variously as "international service organizations," "international charities," "NGOs," and "private voluntary organizations." All have a nonprofit character, an altruistic or humanitarian overseas mission, and a special tax status.

Many of these organizations belong to InterAction. Member organizations (152 in May 1993) currently receive $1.5 billion annually in private contributions and $600 million from the U.S. government (half in the form of commodities). Thirty-five

World War II gave impetus to new relief organizations: the Unitarian Universalist Service Committee (1939), Catholic Relief Services (1943), World Relief Corporation (1944), Lutheran World Relief (1945), CARE (1945), Church World Service (1946), Meals for Millions (1946), and Direct Relief International (1948). A significant number of additional agencies, many tied to churches and focused on medical needs, were established during the subsequent decade.

Dozens of additional NGOs, principally secular and oriented toward technical assistance and training, were formed during the 1960s and 1970s in response to growing recognition of the long-term nature of the problems of hunger and underdevelopment. Some were founded by returning Peace Corps volunteers. Many of these agencies were well-positioned to take advantage of the U.S. foreign assistance program's shift in 1973 to emphasis on meeting "basic human needs." For many of them, the U.S. Agency for International Development (AID) remains a prime source of funding. Groups in this category include Africare, America's Development Foundation, Appropriate Technology International, and the Center for Development and Population Activities.

A final significant subgroup of the NGO community is composed of agencies established to carry out activities within the United States which have subsequently created international divisions. Because of their particular expertise, some became involved in overseas activities at AID's request. They include Goodwill Industries, the Salvation Army, the Young Men's Christian Association (YMCA), the Young Women's Christian Association (YWCA), and cooperatives, such as the National Cooperative Business Association, the National Rural Electric Cooperative Association, and the Credit Union National Association.

Development theorist David Korten points to an evolution in NGO development program strategies over time – from relief and welfare to an emphasis on small-scale, self-reliant, local development. NGOs in developing countries have often undergone a similar evolution. For example, the Bangladesh Rural Advancement Committee, which provides credit and training to rural poor people, began as a disaster relief group. Korten sees the emergence of "third generation strategies," in which NGOs facilitate changes in policies and institutions at the national and regional levels to permit long-term development locally. Partnerships between developed and developing country NGOs – with Northern groups increasingly seeking to serve as catalysts to empower people and organizations in the South – along with education and advocacy, are essential elements of this strategy. Korten stresses that a given NGO may pursue all three strategies through a variety of programs.[5]

Symbolic of the kinds of changes Korten describes is the change which Meals for Millions has undergone. In changing its name to the Freedom from Hunger Foundation, it has also changed its mission from relief to "empowerment," with an emphasis on providing credit and non-formal education to poor women. Many other NGOs have similarly evolved during the 1970s and 1980s.

Korten's thinking has had considerable influence in the U.S. NGO community. Recently, he has encouraged NGOs with a vision of equitable, sustainable, and participatory development to "become facilitators of a global people's development movement" – the fourth generation

Today, most U.S. NGOs involved in international development activities seek to eliminate the long-term causes of hunger and poverty.

Oxfam United Kingdom and Ireland

by Diana Melrose

Oxfam United Kingdom and Ireland (Oxfam UKI) is best known as a relief and development agency. Yet it has engaged in advocacy since its founding. Upon establishing the Oxford Committee for Famine Relief in 1942, its founders pressed the British government to exempt relief supplies for needy civilians from the allied blockade.

Oxfam UKI's main emphasis, however, was initially on providing humanitarian relief. In the 1960s and 1970s, when other Oxfams, including Oxfam America, were set up, the focus switched to working with developing country counterparts on community development. Only during the 1980s did Oxfam UKI return to outspoken advocacy. It worked on unethical infant formula and pharmaceutical marketing and the suffering caused by the international isolation of Cambodia, apartheid in South Africa, and conflict in Central America. Campaigns on such issues generated controversy because of legal restrictions on British charities' political activities.

Oxfam UKI staff and trustees nevertheless became increasingly convinced of the value of advocacy in tackling the structural causes of poverty, particularly those rooted in North-South injustice. They saw lobbying and campaigning as "adding value" to relief and development work.

Today, Oxfam UKI views advocacy as part of a "single" program approach to poverty and preventable suffering. By lobbying successfully to increase the quantity or quality of foreign aid, reduce debt burdens, or improve terms of trade for poor producers, Oxfam UKI can help bring about positive change for millions of the world's poor people far in excess of the impact of its 1992 overseas grants of $92 million.

Oxfam UKI's trustees have decided to increase lobbying expenditures over the next five years from approximately $1.5 million to $4.5 million. Currently another $9 million is allocated annually to campaigning, public education, development education, and mass communication.

Oxfam UKI's advocacy once targeted primarily the British and Irish governments and multilateral organizations such as the United Nations (UN), European Community (EC), and World Bank. Now, it is becoming increasingly international. Oxfam UKI is anxious to work with Southern counterparts and colleagues to

strategy. As he notes:

Social movements have a special quality. They are driven not by budgets or organizational structures, but rather by ideas, by a vision of a better world.[6]

Barriers to NGO Advocacy

Despite these changing perspectives, NGOs face many obstacles when they seek to get involved in policy advocacy. These include organizational inertia and structures, the nature and interests of the NGO constituency, NGOs' relationship to the U.S. government, and funding and operational issues.

Organizational Inertia And Structures

A key factor is inertia. The very idea that direct service agencies should serve as advocates is rather new. Many U.S. NGOs were established during an epoch when the U.S. government was not very involved in international humanitarian affairs. Contemporary foreign aid as we know it dates only from the Truman administration. Conceived, established, and managed for years as agencies to provide relief, technical, or other direct services to persons overseas, it is natural that U.S. NGOs should have some difficulty modifying their missions to include education and advocacy.

Several U.S. NGOs have taken pride in being "apolitical." Some even have longstanding charters or bylaws prohibiting political action. Some NGO leaders mistakenly view lobbying Congress as incompatible with nonprofit tax status.

Certain mundane organizational considerations also have a practical effect on organizational evolution. NGO board members are usually selected to emulate sitting members. Many boards are made up of prominent citizens or business people who have little interest in engaging in political action which may be perceived as threatening the status quo. Board chairs have often served for many years, rising under the tutelage of a past generation of leaders. Chief executives are likewise often hired in the mold of their predecessors. Most managerial and program staff are chosen for their overseas program experience, not on the basis of political or advocacy skills. Knowledge of how to plan effective policy advocacy and its value often is not present in the agency.

Nature and Interests Of the NGO Constituency

As organizations whose boards and financial supporters are drawn from the U.S. public, NGOs' programs are necessarily related to public attitudes. The U.S. public tends to know little about countries outside of the United States unless there is a specific ethnic tie or a dramatic crisis. This is particularly the case for developing nations. The U.S. educational system has done little to foster an understanding of, or interest in, international development issues, despite growing global interdependence. Also, many U.S. citizens doubt that foreign aid is effective in reducing poverty and hunger, although there is strong public support for helping poor and hungry people overseas.[7]

Moreover, the public is motivated to donate generously to relief efforts by images of starvation. The public is significantly less interested in supporting work on long-term, often political, solutions to the deeper problems. Convincing the public to support longer-term efforts, particularly in the realm of advocacy, requires NGOs to educate their donors.

develop their abilities to undertake advocacy work in their own countries, as well as at regional and international levels. This new priority is in response to demands of partners in the seventy countries where Oxfam UKI works.

Southern NGOs are increasingly calling on Northern NGOs not only to do more advocacy work, but also to facilitate Southern access to Northern decision makers. For example, with another British agency, Christian Aid, Oxfam UKI arranged for representatives of small-scale banana producers from the Caribbean to talk to senior EC officials. The banana producers' livelihoods depend on preferential access to the European Single Market. Similarly, Oxfam UKI has joined with Brazilian partners to lobby the World Bank.

To be effective, Oxfam UKI believes that its advocacy needs to be driven by its overseas experience in response to needs identified by partners and beneficiaries. Lobbyists must then analyze the decision-making process in the target institution, identify the key lobbying opportunities, and formulate specific proposals to put to policy makers. For example, last year Haitian counterparts asked Oxfam UKI to help address the problems they faced as a result of political repression and the embargo on official development assistance. Together, the Haitian groups and Oxfam UKI lobbied successfully for a new EC budget line for Haitian NGOs.

Networking is critically important to Oxfam UKI's advocacy. The organization is actively involved in issue-specific coalitions and other networks of like-minded agencies within the UK and Ireland, in Europe, and internationally. Together with other European agencies, Oxfam UKI works closely with government officials in the member state holding the six-month EC presidency to identify ways of moving forward the shared advocacy agenda, as well as reacting and contributing to relevant policy debates.

European NGOs are actively seeking trans-Atlantic advocacy partnerships. New coalitions are emerging among NGOs from the South, North America, and Europe, representing not just development agencies but environmental organizations and those working on human rights. Such networks are needed, for decisions made in the United States are of critical importance to poor people throughout the developing world. Poorer developing country governments have lost what little autonomy they had over their economic policies to Washington-based international financial institutions such as the World Bank and International Monetary Fund. The New York headquarters of the United Nations has assumed new political significance with the end of the Cold War, and the United States is today the sole superpower.

Oxfam UKI's experience shows the need to couple policy advocacy with proactive media strategies. Key international meetings offer pegs for lobbying and generating media interest. On a number of occasions, Oxfam UKI has placed full-page ads in national newspapers to try to influence public debate. For example, in 1992, it was widely rumored that the British government planned to cut foreign aid. Oxfam UKI succeeded in getting the media to focus on the threatened cuts and their implications for the world's poorest citizens by placing provocative newspaper ads to remind Prime Minister John Major of the fine words spoken at the Rio Earth Summit.

Direct advocacy and indirect lobbying through the media are not enough. Successful advocacy usually requires broader public pressure. In the case of the threatened aid cuts in 1992, Oxfam UKI mobilized supporters to write to their members of parliament and government ministers. In the end, the aid budget increased.

Today, NGOs have unprecedented opportunities to participate in policy dialogue with governments and multilateral agencies. Reflecting this growing appreciation of the role of NGOs in generating pressure for policy change, the U.N. Development Program's 1993 *Human Development Report* describes advocacy as "NGOs' greatest strength." It is a strength on which NGOs need to capitalize in pursuing collaborative strategies to tackle poverty and injustice.

Diana Melrose is public policy director at Oxfam UKI.

NGOs' Relationship to the U.S. Government

Tax Status. Virtually all international development NGOs (and most domestic direct service agencies) are classified as 501(c)(3) organizations (the term refers to the relevant section of the tax code). This status permits contributors to deduct the full amount of the donation from their federal taxes, and relieves the organizations from having to pay federal taxes.

The law prohibits 501(c)(3) organizations from actively taking sides in elections. It also limits the right of these organizations to "lobby." Until the law was rewritten in 1976 and the accompanying

regulations were finally clarified by the Internal Revenue Service (IRS) in 1990, widespread confusion existed about how much lobbying was allowed and about the penalty for doing too much.

This led most NGO leaders to eschew policy advocacy altogether, or at least to approach it with extreme caution. Although the new law and regulations are now clear and permissive, most NGO leaders are not familiar with them and remain unduly cautious.

In general, a 501(c)(3) organization can spend only an "insubstantial" amount (generally interpreted to mean 6 percent) of its annual budget on a set of narrowly defined "lobbying activities." Few non-profits come close even to that limit. Organizations which choose to provide IRS with more detailed accounting can spend a larger share of their revenues (no more than 20 percent of the first $500,000, 15 percent of the next $500,000, 10 percent of the next $500,000, and 5 percent of the remainder) on lobbying, up to a maximum of $1 million.

The definition of lobbying focuses on efforts to influence specific congressional legislation. No more than 25 percent of lobbying expenditures can go to "grass-roots lobbying," i.e., attempting to enlist people around the country (as opposed to advocacy efforts by officers and employees of the organization) in legislative initiatives. The more than one hundred pages of IRS regulations are complex and difficult for a non-lawyer to understand, but the basic principles are simple enough.[8]

A great number of education and "advocacy" activities fall outside of the narrow IRS definition of lobbying, e.g., providing policy makers with research findings, presenting testimony, offering general suggestions for policy change, encouraging executive branch officials to take particular actions, and tracking the voting records of members of Congress. These are not counted against the total spending limitation.

Funding Relationships. Many NGOs draw on U.S. government resources. Several have become dependent on such resources. This is particularly the case for many of the small, technically-oriented NGOs, which may receive 50 to 80 percent of their funds from the federal government. For example, Planning Assistance, which provides technical assistance for organizational management in developing countries, received 76 percent of its revenue from the federal government in fiscal 1991. Such dependence is not limited to small, technical NGOs; huge agencies such as Catholic Relief Services and CARE devote a major part of their program to the distribution of U.S. government food aid.

The close relationship between the U.S. NGO community and the government dates back to World War II, when NGOs wishing to provide relief, even if privately funded, were required to register with the U.S. government and receive permission to operate. After the war, regulations were relaxed. But today NGOs are required to meet certain conditions and gain formal recognition to receive and distribute U.S. government funds or commodities. AID's shift to an emphasis on meeting basic human needs in the mid-1970s significantly strengthened the financial relationship between the agency and NGOs. The new program directions and pressures to reduce full-time government staff led AID to use NGOs to implement rural development programs. In 1981, Congress declared that at least 13.5 percent of U.S.

development assistance should be channelled though NGOs. The United States provides by far the most dollars of development assistance (about $1 billion in fiscal 1992, including food aid) through NGOs of any donor nation.[9]

This close financial relationship has clear advantages for the budgets of NGOs, and often assists poor and hungry people in a more effective manner than AID could otherwise manage, but it is a two-edged sword. Reliance on government funds makes some groups hesitant to criticize government policies. But fear of losing government funding does not always prevail. CARE received 81 percent of its fiscal 1992 revenue from the U.S. government. Yet CARE has often sharply criticized U.S. government policies regarding poor coordination of food aid and child survival programs, the negative impact of AID and multilateral development bank loan conditions on poor people, and other issues.

Funding and Operational Challenges

A very practical problem for NGOs considering more active involvement in advocacy is the relative unavailability of funds for such activities. By law, U.S. government funds cannot be used to advocate changes in U.S. government policies. Foundations face their own legal restrictions against funding lobbying, and most are reluctant to fund advocacy work permitted by law.

Individuals provide most unrestricted funds for NGOs, but they usually respond generously to images of hungry people, and prefer to have their contributions go directly to a recipient. They want to feel that their contributions will do something concrete for someone in need. Convincing

Many NGOs draw on U.S. government resources. Several have become dependent on such resources.

NGOs in developing countries have increasingly called on U.S. NGOs to do advocacy and education in the United States.

people that their contributions are just as well – or better – used to fund policy advocacy is often difficult. Organizational fund-raisers, who must be cautious, often fear that asking people to support advocacy will alienate donors who do not believe that the organization should be "political." Related to this, organizations which rate the effectiveness of charities usually view advocacy and education as "overhead" rather than a part of the organizational mission.

Finally, there are clearly funding trade-offs at stake as NGOs choose to move toward more aggressive advocacy. To the extent that budgets are stable, funding the capacity to analyze public policies and develop advocacy strategies may well mean a cutback in direct services.

Factors Encouraging More NGO Advocacy

Although the obstacles to more NGO advocacy are significant, there are several sources of outside encouragement. Perhaps most importantly, NGOs in developing countries have increasingly called on U.S. NGOs to do advocacy and education in the United States. Many developing country NGOs have now developed the capacity for effective technical assistance and training for their country people (and policy advocacy in their own countries), and no longer need expatriate help. They still need financial assistance, but they also need help in making U.S. government policies on international trade, debt, security, and aid more favorable toward their countries.

Second, there is some evidence that the public may be gradually becoming more knowledgeable and understanding of long-term hunger and poverty issues. The

nearly 140,000 former Peace Corps volunteers now living throughout the United States have contributed to increased understanding of development issues. The inclusion of global education materials in many school curricula is also welcome, but much more effort is needed in this area, and NGOs can help.

When famine in Ethiopia became front-page news in 1984, most Americans thought it was mainly due to drought and that Ethiopians needed food aid. When famine in Somalia became front-page news in 1993, however, most Americans thought it was mainly due to political factors and were willing to support both private assistance and action by the U.S. government and the United Nations.

Finally, NGO umbrella groups are pressing for increased education and advocacy efforts. InterAction has long encouraged members to move in this direction. It sponsors advocacy skills-building workshops at its annual conferences, and has challenged each member agency to spend a minimum of 5 percent of its budget on advocacy. The group's Public Policy Steering Committee is seeking additional resources for its members to establish programs in these areas.

The International Development Conference, a biennial gathering to discuss critical international development issues, has also recently challenged NGOs to spend at least 5 percent of their annual budget on development education and 5 percent on advocacy supporting poverty alleviation and sustainable development. The conference's ongoing Public Policy and Development Education Committees are seeking to facilitate NGO activities to meet this challenge.

Conclusion

Many U.S. NGOs presently choose not to be particularly active in advocating changes in U.S. policy which could assist in reducing or eliminating international hunger and poverty. There are several understandable reasons for their reluctance. On the other side of the ledger, there are several important encouragements for NGOs to become more active in advocacy. Many, including some of the largest agencies, seem willing to try.

The need for NGOs to share their experience in developing countries with U.S. policy makers is compelling. Increased NGO advocacy could significantly reduce hunger and promote equitable, sustainable, and participatory development among the communities worldwide that U.S. NGOs assist. ■

Doug Siglin is director of Congressional Relations at the World Wildlife Fund and chairman of the National Peace Corps Association.

A. Cecilia Snyder, a BFW Institute research assistant, collected and analyzed data for this chapter.

The need for NGOs to share their experience in developing countries with U.S. policy makers is compelling.

Religious Communities Respond To Hunger

Photo: Joseph Crachiola

Religious communities have taken the lead in responding to hunger.

by Richard A. Hoehn

Give Us This Day Our Daily Bread

Hunger has stalked humanity from the earliest days. Nomads sought divine help for a successful hunt. Farmers prayed for a bountiful harvest as they tilled the soil. "Give us this day our daily bread" is probably the most oft-repeated human prayer.

In the Bible, God tells Adam and Eve: "All green plants I give for food." Following the flood, God says to Noah: "Every creature that lives and moves shall be food for you." In Exodus, soon after the Israelites leave Egypt, they run out of food and water. They complain, "If only we had died at God's hand in Egypt, where we . . . had plenty of bread to eat! But you have brought us out in this wilderness to let this whole assembly starve to death." God shows Moses how to make the bitter water drinkable and sends quail and manna for food. "Each had just enough to eat." No one had a lot; no one went without.

The compassionate feeding of the multitudes is the only miracle story which appears in all four Gospels (twice in Matthew and Mark). The gospel writers emphasized the feeding miracle because it prefigured the Last Supper and Jesus as the bread of life.

The Christian eucharistic meal has both divine and human dimensions. There, no race, class, gender, age, ability, or nationality distinctions exist. Everyone belongs. The table of the Lord is the table of the world. The eucharist anticipates the reign of God when "They shall never again feel hunger or thirst."

Food produced, prepared, shared, and consumed has a spiritual dimension and has thus always been a central part of

Table 1

Anti-hunger Activities of Congregations (by %)				
	Syracuse	**Evansville**	**Spokane**	**Average**
Donate food or time	86	76	70	77
Worship	61	63	60	61
Hunger walk, e.g. CROP	71	50	39	53
Youth activities	52	49	54	52
Help food pantry	82	66	63	70
Have food pantry	63	35	46	48
Adult education	36	23	41	33
Soup kitchen	20	16	12	16
Letter writing	21	10	11	14
% responding	25	19	29	25
# responding	56	80	103	239

Source: BFW Institute

religious observance. The filled stomach and the shared table dwell close to the heart and hearth of religious imagery, liturgy, and practice. Religious communities, therefore, have taken the lead in responding to hunger.

Congregations Confront Community Hunger

About 36 percent of adults in the United States attend worship on an average weekend, up to 75 percent attend at least sometime during the year, and 70 percent claim membership in a religious denomination. Sixty-four percent identify as Protestant, 28 percent Roman Catholic, 2 percent Jewish, 1 percent Orthodox Christians, 1 percent Mormon, and 4 percent other (including Muslim and Buddhist).[1]

The *Yearbook of American & Canadian Churches* indicates that of the $17.9 billion given by congregations, approximately 18 percent went to benevolent causes.[2]

In 1991 almost as many congregations offered programs in human services, such as housing programs for the homeless, food kitchens, and family counseling, as offered religious education.[3]

A 1993 BFW Institute survey of religious congregations of all types (from National Baptist to Nazarene and Buddhist) in three communities – Syracuse, New York; the Evansville, Indiana area; and Spokane, Washington – found high involvement in anti-hunger activities.[4] (See table 1.) It also showed a relatively consistent pattern of activities in congregations. Most congregations donate food or time. Just under two-thirds have hunger-focused worship. Half have programs that introduce youth to anti-hunger concerns and over one-

third have adult education opportunities that deal with anti-hunger concerns. Twelve to 20 percent have soup kitchens and an average of 14 percent engage in letter writing to influence public policies on hunger.

More than three-fourths of responding congregations say they contribute food or time to alleviate hunger. Caution has to be exercised in projecting from this sample to the United States as a whole because congregations that are actively involved are more likely to return a survey questionnaire than those which are not active. But, if the percentage of congregations which contribute food or time were multiplied by the total number congregations in the United States, more than 250,000 congregations donate to emergency hunger relief. Forty-eight percent of congregations have food pantries. That would come to 150,000 congregational-based food pantries in the United States.

A recent study of six mainline Protestant denominations found that 85 percent of these churches are either active or place "some emphasis" on anti-hunger concerns.[5] A United Church of Christ survey found that 93 percent of their congregations think hunger is a "very important" or "important" issue.

In addition to these activities, religious people sew quilts, contribute clothing, work in night shelters, and engage in hundreds of other projects that help alleviate the poverty that leads to hunger. Habitat for Humanity's program of home building for low-income people has attracted widespread support among Christian people. Religious people make up the bulk of volunteers at food banks, community centers, soup kitchens, and in feeding programs both inside and outside formal religious auspices. They contribute much of the money that goes toward the alleviation of hunger through interreligious and secular organizations as well as through their denominations.

Mainline Denominations

Most mainline denominations teach that faith leads to acts of charity and justice. Many denominations, such as the Episcopalians, have a hunger fund which raises and disburses funds for anti-hunger activities. Even though overall funding to the Evangelical Lutheran Church in America (ELCA) national office has been dropping, the Hunger Appeal continues to bring in more money each year – from $10.8 million in 1989 to $12.3 million in 1992.

Catholic Charities does domestic relief and development work and Catholic Relief Services does international work in behalf of the nation's fifty-six million Roman Catholics. Catholics also support poverty reduction through their social teachings, the activities of religious groups such as the Society of St. Vincent de Paul and the Campaign for Human Development (CHD), which raises about $12.5 million to fund local empowerment projects and community organizations.

CHD funds projects that have low-income people as at least half of the decision-making board, work to change the conditions that create poverty, and aim at self-sufficiency. Following the 1992 riots, CHD awarded $100,000 to help fund the Source for Empowerment and Eco-

nomic Development (SEED) in Los Angeles. The archdiocese is matching this grant with another $100,000 to develop this program of loans to small businesses, especially those owned by minority and low-income entrepreneurs.

The Department of Social Development and World Peace of the United States Catholic Conference helps U.S. bishops to share the social teachings of the Catholic church, apply their teachings to social issues, advocate for justice and peace, and build the church's capacity to be active in social matters. Recent statements by the bishops on peace and economic issues have received wide attention, and the Catholic Conference has developed an effective advocacy arm in Washington, D.C.

The Methodist Board of Church and Society promotes social justice, both in the United States and internationally. The United Methodist Committee on Relief (UMCOR) works on relief and development in the United States as well as abroad. UMCOR has also been effective in promoting advocacy on hunger issues within the Methodist church.

The $10 million raised by the Presbyterian Church U.S.A. (PCUSA) annually through One Great Hour of Sharing is used for disaster relief, development work, self-help projects, education, and advocacy. Over the years, Presbyterians have developed a system of Hunger Action Enablers (HAEs), currently ninety-nine staff and volunteers, who promote hunger concerns at local and regional levels. The HAEs provide education and sensitization in local congregations, send newsletters about hunger events, and assist with public policy advocacy. Perhaps because of this strong, well-staffed, emphasis on hunger, Presbyterian congregations are more active than many other Protestants when it comes to hunger issues.

A PCUSA survey in spring 1993 indicated:

- 98 percent of congregations participate in food distribution programs;

- 94 percent contribute money through One Great Hour of Sharing;

- 85 percent conduct food distribution at Thanksgiving/Christmas;

- 64 percent participate in a meals on wheels type program;

- 41 percent participate in hunger education programs; and

- 32 percent are involved in public policy advocacy.

PCUSA congregations give large quantities of food, money, and volunteer time to local food distribution programs. Surprisingly, 17 percent of congregations gave $10,000 or more toward hunger programs within their community; 12 percent gave a similar amount to programs outside their community.

The Mennonites are a small Christian denomination noted for commitment to service. Mennonites, rooted in farming communities, have a particular interest in hunger and food production. The Mennonite Central Committee was begun in 1920 to help starving Russian Mennonites in the aftermath of the Russian Revolution. Over time, their relief and development projects have included people of all faiths.

In 1991, Mennonites gave $1,017 per member to their churches, almost three times the national average. In 1992, the Mennonite Central Committee raised $11.8 million for relief and development projects, an impressive sum from a denomination of only 150,000 people in the United States. The committee also ships donated food from farms and churches to needy areas.

Evangelical Churches

Since the 1950s, evangelicals have experienced massive growth.[6] The evangelical movement was initially made up of low-income people who were politically conservative and, at the same time, suspicious of politics.

The rapid growth of independent (not attached to any particular denomination) evangelical-based relief and development organizations, such as World Vision and Food for the Hungry, indicates the widespread support for anti-hunger activity among evangelicals. World Vision's magazine goes to 750,000 subscribers, its television programming reaches millions, and World Vision's funding from U.S. sources is $250 million.

Evangelicals, like their mainline counterparts, differ in goals and strategies around public problems. A relatively small subset of evangelicals, attracted to hard-line fundamentalist beliefs, emerged to promote political activism on a conservative agenda which combined piety, patriotism, and politics.[7] By articulating concerns of some Protestant evangelicals and Roman Catholics, the new religious (fundamentalist) right was able to pull together a funding and activist base for a sophisticated and powerful movement. Recently they have expressed fresh interest in mobilizing their constituency to respond to economic issues alongside of issues such as abortion and pornography.

Traditional (i.e., not part of the new right) evangelicals are also becoming more interested in poverty and hunger. A National Survey of Evangelicals on Christian Relief and Development indicated that evangelicals gave "helping poor in America" a slightly higher mean score than abortion and pornography as "important for Christians to be actively involved in;" and

Evangelicals and Hunger

"During the past year and a half, it has been my privilege to visit some thirty-six denominational and missions headquarters of the member denominations of the National Association of Evangelicals. It is remarkable to me to understand the commitment to holistic ministry that has emerged in the evangelical church in America. Over the past decade, a dramatic expansion of vision has occurred.

"The evangelical denominations see the task of the church as threefold: 1) discipling the membership of their churches; 2) evangelizing those who have not heard the Good News; and 3) doing works of mercy, love, and justice worldwide.

"The emerging commitment to this holistic gospel has caused organizations like World Relief to enjoy the greatest time of cooperation with the churches in the United States that we have ever enjoyed. Not only is this seen with the increase of offerings for poor people, but the training in relief and development that many of the on-the-field missions people now have.

"The trend toward coalition response in times of need is likewise encouraging . . . . Evangelical agencies such as World Vision, World Relief, Mercy Corps, and some seventeen other organizations participated in [the] coalition effort on behalf of hungry and needy people in Somalia.

"The Association of Evangelicals of Liberia, along with World Relief, sponsored the National Day of Prayer and Reconciliation Workshops in June 1993. The ministry of Christians in reconciliation, so that the hungry can be fed in safety and security, is of prime importance today. This coordinated view at seeking spiritual and physical solutions is something that is important in every part of the world today.

"The evangelical church has proved its tremendous capacity in worldwide evangelization over the past two centuries. Now, with the emergence of a holistic view of the task of the church, the mobilization of the church to care for the hungry and needy around the world can be raised to a new level. There is reason for optimism, even in the midst of a world filled with war, greed, and need."

Arthur Evans Gay, Jr. is executive director of World Relief of the National Association of Evangelicals.

ranked "helping poor people around the world" only slightly lower.

> *Over half (54 percent) of evangelical collegians and seminarians claim the pursuit of justice is just as, or almost as, important as evangelism. More typically, evangelism and social justice are combined.*[8]

The Sojourner community is another example of an organization that successfully combines evangelical commitment with as much attention to political activism as to non-consuming lifestyles. *Sojourners* magazine says:

> *Just as food links the body and soul, it also connects us as individuals with the rest of creation – not only with the soil and sunshine and water from which our food is formed, but with the many human beings whose work has brought it to our tables.*[9]

Poverty-Focused Churches

Many evangelical and mainline, especially slum, congregations minister primarily to a lower-class constituency and devote a much higher than average percent of resources to hunger and homelessness. The Salvation Army is an interesting case study because it has the largest organized network of feeding centers and shelters in the nation. Of the ten thousand Salvation Army units in the United States, more than eight thousand (including twelve hundred shelters) have a feeding or grocery distribution component. Nearly 1.3 million workers, mostly volunteers, served sixty-five million meals in 1992. The army, perhaps more than any other denomination, visibly symbolizes the church for the down and out.

The Salvation Army is best known for its Christmas bell ringers, collection pots, uniformed brass bands, and secondhand stores. Unlike such secular agencies as Goodwill (which had church origins) or the Volunteers of America (a Salvation Army spin-off), the Salvation Army is a worshipping community.

The Salvation Army began in England in 1865 as an evangelical crusade among poor people and came to the United States in 1880. The army believes that when people are hungry and homeless it is difficult for them to hear the gospel message. The army responds, both spiritually and physically, to the plight of people in need.[10]

Salvation Army uniforms identify adherents as set apart for mission and evangelism. They live in relative poverty and are committed to a highly-disciplined personal lifestyle. In a recent Washington, D.C., survey, the top executive of the army had the lowest salary of any nonprofit organization leader. Many members have themselves been saved from poverty, homelessness, or addiction.

The army is mostly nonpolitical but did support the establishment of the Select Committee on Hunger of the U.S. House of Representatives in 1984. Some army members would like to see a greater balance between service and advocacy develop over time.

African-American Denominations

Black, or African-American, churches are churches of survival and resistance, of charity combined with justice; faith combined with faithfulness. The African-American church is grounded in the experience of enslavement.

A "black theology," which implicitly or explicitly shapes church life, can be seen

BROT FÜR DIE WELT – Bread for the World (Germany)
by Don Reeves

Bread for the World (U.S.A.) has the same name as BROT FÜR DIE WELT (Germany). Although the two organizations are not otherwise connected, they share similar views on sustainable development. Bread for the World (U.S.A.) is exclusively an advocacy and education group.

BROT FÜR DIE WELT is an association of German Protestant churches which, as an expression of their Christian faith and convictions, seeks to overcome poverty and hunger in developing countries by funding relief and development programs. Founded in 1959, BROT has funded more than fifteen thousand programs in more than one hundred nations in Africa, Latin America, and Asia.

The emphases of the programs funded by BROT have shifted from relief to development to empowerment in its nearly thirty-five-year history. In its early years, BROT made grants to overseas partners for traditional charity or relief work. These often evolved into longer-term development programs emphasizing human rights, democratic participation by poor people, attention to the roles of women, and environmental protection. In recent years, many of BROT's developing country partners have engaged in a variety of social or political change activities, with BROT's open or, in some instances, quiet support.

In India, BROT supports many organizations dealing with the problems of bonded labor, especially among children. These organizations began by assisting with legal advice and protection. Resistance to change and corruption, however, limited the success of such efforts, and led to protest campaigns aimed at raising public awareness through media coverage, with BROT's support.

BROT has also undertaken educational campaigns in Europe. One Indian partner asked BROT to help raise the consciousness of European buyers of Indian carpets. Consumers have persuaded European importers and their Indian export partners to pressure loom owners not to use bonded child labor. Indian and German nongovernmental organizations are now promoting a "child labor-free" label for carpets. This campaign has gained attention at trade fairs, in the popular press, and even on financial pages.

The carpet-labelling program is only one instance of BROT's

outreach in Germany which emphasizes the impact in developing nations of social, economic, and political decisions in industrial countries. Educational work stresses the trade-linked impact of affluent lifestyles on Southern countries. BROT emphasizes both the potential benefits and problems inherent in export-led growth and the power of industrial nations to distort trade to their own advantage.

BROT, with its Southern partners, has conducted a decade-long campaign linking European imports of feed from Southern nations, e.g., cassava from Thailand and soybeans from Brazil, to the surplus of meat and dairy products which Northern nations dump on world markets, thereby harming Southern producers of similar products. BROT has also exposed how export cropping often uses the best lands, driving local food production onto marginal lands, while prices rise for basic foods. BROT highlights policy decisions which distort trade: Northern export subsidies and Southern export promotion.

BROT calls attention to working conditions, e.g., of flower growers in Colombia. Perhaps its most successful campaign to date has been for Fair Trade Coffee, now found in supermarkets in Germany, the Netherlands, and Switzerland. BROT has not sponsored boycotts, noting that trade has the potential for mutual benefits.

Similarly, BROT's concern is rising over the impact of Southern debt, and the conditions international lenders link to new loans. This concern also grows from experience. Southern partners, churches in Africa in particular, are requesting more support from BROT because their governments are cutting back on education and health services as part of their economic adjustment programs. In developing a sense of responsibility in Germany, BROT stresses the heritage of colonialism and the continuing effects of more recent military and economic domination.

BROT's programs of education in Germany are intended to lead to changes in understanding and lifestyle at the personal level, and to policy changes at the national, European Community, and international levels. Such expectations create tension. Historically, BROT has appealed to German Christians for contributions primarily on the basis of charity. Education and appeals based on justice are more challenging to donors and, if not well introduced, may yield less funds for badly-needed work, at least in the short term.

On the other hand, BROT is finding that its contributors are increasingly aware that acts of charity do not solve deep-rooted

as early as slave songs and as recently as a political rally.[11] It rises out of struggles for personal identity, pride, and power; but also the realization that the personal is political – that the battle for freedom not only lies inside oneself and in inter-personal relations, but outside oneself in the larger society. The black church is committed to changing the basic structures that can restore and renew the twin pledges of freedom and equality.

The civil rights movement in the 1960s would not have existed but for the African-American church, sometimes called "a spiritual refuge with a social conscious-ness."[12] Faith in God cannot be separated from faithfulness toward individuals and society. Rev. Eugene Rivers of Azusa Christian Community in Boston claims that when you ask "Who is doing something to help low-income people in our urban areas?" the answer is "The church; especially the black church."

African-American churches have seen their own "evangelical" revival through the growth of neo-Pentecostalism, for example in the African Methodist Episco-pal (A.M.E.) Church. But their brand of evangelicalism takes a somewhat different political turn than in the new religious right. This revival combines Pentecostal piety with A.M.E. progressive politics.

The Church of God in Christ (COGIC) is the fastest growing Pentecostal church in the world and reported to be the fastest growing Protestant church in the United States. COGIC has stood firmly against racism, been active in the fight against drugs, established very active food pantries, and increasingly expresses its concern through political advocacy.

A survey of members of traditionally black churches found that 91 percent approve of their clergy "taking part in protest marches on civil rights issues," and 91.6 percent of clergy think churches should "express their views on day-to-day social and political questions."[13] African-American churches are more heavily committed to political advocacy as a necessary part of the solution to hunger and poverty than are most predominantly white denominations. Insofar as black churches are continuously struggling against racism they are implicitly addressing one of the root causes of hunger alongside their direct charitable and political anti-hunger activities.

Muslims

Though about 20 percent of the slaves brought to the United States were Muslims, the Muslim faith largely died out in the African-American community. There has been a sharp increase in the number of Muslims in the United States in recent years, partly through conversion and partly through immigration. An estimated one million of the six million Muslims in the country are African-American. Approximately twenty thousand are estimated to belong to the Nation of Islam led by Minister Louis Farrakhan, successor to Elijah Muhammad. Most U.S. Muslims profess the Sunni faith as it exists in Africa, Asia, and the Middle East. While exact statistics about the extent of Muslim anti-hunger work are not available, Muslims traditionally show considerable concern for poverty and the environment. The Islamic concept of *zakat* (Arabic for *justice*) is, above all, about the rich sharing with the poor.

Ecumenical Agencies

Hunger concerns are often addressed through ecumenical and interfaith agencies

problems. They also recognize that the earth cannot support affluent lifestyles for everyone.

Church and state are not divorced in Germany in the same way as in the United States. Churches are subsidized by the state in many ways. The state collects a church tax from all members of each state-sanctioned church. This tax is calculated as 8 to 10 percent of each member's income tax. The state subsidizes or reimburses most of the cost of all social work the German churches carry out – day care, hospitals, programs for the handicapped, and education. The German government also gives churches considerable funds for overseas development work.

Such tax support does not preclude criticism of the government or of prevailing policies; church funds are not subject to annual appropriations. Nonetheless, there is a "chilling effect" on the boldness of critique or support for alternative policies, just as some charities in the United States are concerned about the impact that criticism of the government might have on the availability of grants, food aid, or other services on which their programs depend.

BROT has gained some freedom by using only privately contributed funds for its program grants and advocacy. Its annual funding also serves as a barometer of whether contributors support the total program, including the education and advocacy components. BROT's income has grown steadily since its founding.

Education and advocacy seem certain to become an increasing share of the work of BROT FÜR DIE WELT and its cooperating agencies. Witnessing to Christian love through attempts to overcome poverty in poor communities wherever they may be is increasingly seen as a matter of justice. This justice must be addressed not only in acts of charity, but in social, economic, and political change – at the personal, community, national, and international levels.

Don Reeves is economic policy analyst at Bread for the World Institute.

such as the National Council of Churches, councils of congregations at state and city levels, and ministries that cover a sector of a city. The Greater Dallas Community of Churches (GDCC) and local agencies such as North Dallas Shared Ministries are two such organizations that cooperate in the same city.

Table 2

North Dallas Shared Ministries
Yearly Comparative Summary of Assistance

	1985	1987	1989	1991	1992
Families served	2,287	5,589	7,355	9,573	...
Food assistance value of food	$ 74,634	201,824	320,568	435,845	481,400
Financial assistance					
Rent	40,623	110,635	132,449	129,991	147,726
Utilities	10,868	21,706	22,491	41,456	42,409
Gasoline	3,266	3,951	3,084	3,540	3,342
Total*	$ 60,807	141,708	165,272	182,568	302,596
Total aid	$135,442	343,510	485,840	618,413	684,238

* Includes items not listed above

Source: North Dallas Shared Ministries

North Dallas Shared Ministries is a cooperative ministry of fourteen faith traditions, with support from congregations as different from one another as Temple Emanuel (Jewish), Mt. Pisgah Missionary Baptist (African-American), Westminster Presbyterian, Our Redeemer Lutheran, Lover's Lane Methodist, Peace Mennonite Church, St. Rita Catholic, and First Unitarian Universalist. Table 2 shows not only that the need for services increased between 1985 and 1992, but that the organization was able to mobilize more and more resources to respond to those needs.

GDCC, with the Dallas Urban League, the Junior League, the North Texas Low-Income Housing Coalition, and twenty-four other community groups initiated an End Hunger Project. The project surveyed the extent of hunger and poverty in the Dallas area, and targeted six of the neediest neighborhoods. The coalition collected data on the use of public and private food distribution programs. Then they convened a Hunger Action Conference "to begin the development of action plans at the neighborhood level to move our community toward the elimination of hunger."

The list of food pantries in the Dallas area

vividly presents the ecumenicity of hunger concerns – eighty-three agencies, including First Presbyterian, Bartimaeus Baptist Temple, First Methodist, Holy Trinity Greek Orthodox, Jewish Family Service, St. James Catholic, Skillman Avenue Church of Christ, Martin Luther King Community Center, Centro de Amistad, Salvation Army, Soul Patrol, the Dallas Inter-Tribal Center, St. John's Lutheran, and All Faith Chapel. Hunger knows no one church, no one political party, no one ideology. It brings people of many faiths together around concerns that transcend many other religious differences. Hunger speaks straight to the heart.

Interfaith Impact brings together the American Muslim Council and Jewish, Protestant, and Catholic agencies to advocate on justice and peace issues. (See chapter 5.) More than forty religious groups from the Seventh-Day Adventist Church to the Korean Presbyterian Church in America participate in relief and development work through Church World Service, affiliated with the National Council of Churches. NCC and the World Council of Churches also organize religious groups to express their concerns through justice education and advocacy.

Charities Serve, Educate, and Advocate

Denomination-based charities are a primary vehicle through which congregations express their concern for malnutrition, poverty, and homeless. A vast amount of feeding occurs at religious-sponsored hospitals and retirement facilities, children's day-care and senior walk-in centers, homeless and rehabilitation shelters and programs.

Many of the largest charities in the United States are sponsored by religious organizations – partly because of the commitment of religious people to end social ills and partly because these charities have functioned as

Table 3

Top Nonprofits[16] ($ million, 1991)

Largest Private Support		Largest Income (Public + Private + Other)	
United Jewish Appeal (National)	668.1	Catholic Charities	1,842.6
Salvation Army	649.0	Lutheran Social Ministry Organizations	1,651.3
Second Harvest	404.5	YMCA of the USA	1,538.1
American Red Cross	386.1	American Red Cross	1,410.0
Catholic Charities USA	368.3	Salvation Army	1,286.9
American Cancer Society	346.3	U.S. Committee for UNICEF	807.0
American Heart Assn.	235.7	Goodwill Industries of America	712.1
United Jewish Appeal — Fed of Jewish Philanthropies of New York City	235.5	United Jewish Appeal	668.2
YMCA of the USA	214.5	Second Harvest	506.0
Boy Scouts of America	209.6	ARC - Association for Retarded Citizens of The United States	474.6
Harvard University	195.6	Girl Scouts of America	437.1
Shriners Hospitals for Crippled Children	186.8		

Sources: *The Chronicle of Philanthropy* and *The Nonprofit Times*.

good stewards of public (often federal) funds to carry out programs. Many secular charities had their origins in the religious community.

By comparison, in 1989 the 33 percent of "civil rights, social action, and advocacy" groups which filed under federal guidelines altogether spent $300 million.[14]

Public support for many charities has increased in recent years. Between 1988 and 1991, support for Catholic Charities rose 81 percent, for the Salvation Army 72 percent, and for U.S. Committee for UNICEF 20 percent. (See table 3.)

The work of Catholic Charities is typical of the many religious-sponsored charities. In 1992, Catholic Charities provided emergency food services to 8.1 million people.

Both Catholic Charities and Catholic Relief Services contract with federal agencies to deliver government-funded programs. A range of two-thirds to three-fourths of these organizations' funding comes from government sources. Private religious organizations are often well-positioned to carry out charitable relief services. But changes in public policies can still swamp the efforts of even the most generous agencies. In the United States:

> *From fiscal year [FY] 1982 to FY 1992, the inflation-adjusted value of federal spending in. . . [such areas as education, training, employment, social services, international affairs], exclusive of Medicare and Medicaid, declined a cumulative total of $119.1 billion compared to what would have been spent had FY 1980 spending levels been maintained.*[15]

Catholic Charities sees an increased need to affect the public policies that lead to this vast need. In 1991, fifty-five Catholic Charities agencies (36 percent of the total) reported involvement in hunger and nutrition legislative action at the national level; eighty-one (53 percent of the total) reported involvement at the state level, and seventy-four (48 percent) reported local legislative involvement around hunger issues. The same number reported legislative involvement at the national level on international justice and refugee issues, while about half as many indicated involvement at the state and local levels on these issues.

Volunteers and staff in charitable agencies, who work with poverty and hunger efforts on a daily basis, can help congregations develop their education, service, and advocacy programs. Many people in these charitable agencies are increasingly seeing the need to add policy education and advocacy (works of justice) to direct service (works of charity). The churches in Germany recently set a good example when they contributed $6.5 million toward educating the public about issues in developing nations.

Political Advocacy

Though millions of religious people are contributing time and money to charity, the political advocacy record is mixed. Seventy-two percent of the adults and 51

MAZON: A Jewish Response to Hunger

by Mia N. Johnson

Sharing one's abundance and good fortune with friends and family brings a measure of kindness to the days of celebration within the Jewish faith. Woven into this rich tapestry of tradition is also the concept of "inviting the poor to the table." In Jewish communities in eastern Europe, it was the law that a celebration could not begin until the poor of the community graced the table.

In contrast to the small, tightly-knit Jewish communities of the past, it is harder to honor this aspect of Jewish tradition today. *Tzedakah*, which is often translated as *charity* but which actually means *justice,* is difficult to practice on an individual-to-individual basis. Nevertheless, *tzedakah* still epitomizes the Jewish attitude toward poor people – justice requires that the world's riches be shared by all. In modern times, Jews fulfill this obligation most often by giving to established charities.

In his article in the April 1985 issue of *Moment*, Leonard Fein, editor and publisher, began with the words traditionally spoken during the Jewish festival of Passover: "Let all who are hungry enter and eat." He set forth a message of social justice and responsibility, applying to the contemporary world that wonderful part of Jewish tradition which asks all to act justly toward poor people. From this union came the concept for MAZON: A Jewish Response To Hunger, founded by Fein and Irving Cramer in 1986.

MAZON (Hebrew for *food*) asks Jews to contribute 3 percent of the cost of life-cycle celebrations, such as weddings, birthdays, anniversaries, and bar and bat mitzvahs (coming of age ceremonies for thirteen-year-olds) to efforts to fight hunger. During Passover, when Jews are asked to recall when they were "strangers in the land of Egypt," MAZON asks them to respond to the needs of a hungry stranger by contributing the dollars they would have spent to feed one extra guest. On Yom Kippur, a day of fasting and atonement, MAZON asks that Jews give the money they ordinarily would have spent to feed their family. Throughout the year, MAZON receives thousands of contributions marking personal achievements and honoring family members and friends at special times in their lives.

In 1986, 175 synagogues joined MAZON as synagogue partners, which agreed to institutionalize MAZON into congregational life and to encourage members to adopt the 3-percent idea. Today, there are nearly seven hundred synagogue partners, from all the major branches of Judaism, located throughout the United States. This network encompasses over one million people, and total contributions reached nearly $2 million in 1992.

Twice a year, MAZON makes grants to nonprofit organizations, principally in the United States, but also overseas. Recipients provide immediate assistance to hungry people or address the percent of youth in six mainline Protestant denominations said they "never marched, met, or gathered with others to promote social change" and 78 percent of adults "never spent time promoting social justice."[17] Yet, religious congregations have a distinguished history of involvement in political advocacy in the United States.

A century and a half ago, congregations fought for the abolition of slavery. Following the civil war, many congregations turned their attention to prohibition, understood as a way to attack the problem of alcoholism and the disruption it brought to many families.

In the early part of this century, some congregations gave important support to the rise of labor unions. The 1940s saw a surge in religious involvement in domestic social ministries and the establishment of charities to respond to problems abroad. For the most part, however, the dominant religious view was that the best way to influence society was to influence individuals.

A series of papal encyclicals and pastoral statements renewed Roman Catholic social teaching, giving increased emphasis to justice and peace, and urging attention to aid, trade, and other policies which affect developing countries. Simultaneously, the World Council of Churches focused heavily on Third World issues, with increasing attention to liberation theology. U.S. church-based overseas assistance organizations began to complement traditional relief and welfare activities with development and empowerment projects.

In the 1960s and early 1970s, shaped by the civil rights movement, religious organizations shifted from influencing politics through shaping individual consciences to using the authority and money of government to shape the lives of individuals.

Transforming Congregations

The religious community can, by virtue of its size and moral authority, have an important influence on the alleviation of hunger and on public policies that affect hunger. Why has this large force been unable to stop hunger at home and abroad? More important, what can be done about it?

There is little doubt that religion in the United States and worldwide is undergoing an identity crisis. It has been a long time since the Sunday sermon was a chief vehicle of entertainment, information, or cultural identity; since religion was the sacred canopy uniting various pieces of private and public life; since extended families coincided with the geography of worship and work.

Throughout history, religious congregations have lived in varying degrees of tension with their culture – dominating, withdrawing, supporting and/or criticizing. Priest-kings cloaked themselves in divine right to justify the rules they made for the populace. Monastic communities of the third and fourth centuries separated themselves from their era to preserve faith and culture from corrosive social decadence. Through their teaching and service, they sometimes had a profound impact on abutting communities.

Today's religious organizations are chameleons caught on a historical plaid, struggling to determine which parts of the cultural pattern they should reflect and which parts they should reject. What is the proper role of a congregation in this fast-paced, high-tech, consumer-oriented, individualistic culture?

In 1979, the United States Catholic Conference released a document, *Political*

causes of hunger and seek effective long-term solutions. MAZON awarded $20,000 in 1986; grantmaking in 1992 topped $1.5 million, bringing the cumulative total to more than $5 million. MAZON grants have provided help to poor Jews in New York and Chicago (nationally, 16 percent of the Jewish community lives at or near the poverty line[1]); to Central American refugees in Los Angeles; to African-American farmers in the deep South; to homebound victims of AIDS in San Francisco; and to peasant women in Guatemala.

Grants typically range from $4,000 to $15,000. In recent years, several devastating events have prompted MAZON to provide larger sums: a $78,000 grant to purchase one million oral rehydration units for refugees on the Turkey-Iraq border in 1991; $81,500 in emergency funds for fourteen charities in Los Angeles feeding people left hungry and homeless by civil unrest in 1992; and $62,000 that same year to support the therapeutic feeding program of the International Medical Corps in Somalia. In June 1993, MAZON entered into a partnership with the Sarajevo Jewish community by making an initial grant of $50,000 for food and medical supplies, distributed on a nonsectarian basis at their feeding centers in the beleaguered Bosnian capital.

In the area of research and advocacy, MAZON has helped fund state-level surveys of hunger among low-income children sponsored by local groups and the Food Research and Action Center. Grants have also funded local, state, and national efforts to expand access to federal food programs.[2]

MAZON is probably the only U.S. Jewish organization focused exclusively on hunger. Other local and national groups work against hunger as part of larger domestic and international anti-poverty and economic justice concerns. Many work on a nonsectarian basis, but some focus primarily or even exclusively on needy Jews in the United States and overseas. Many synagogues and local Jewish organizations sponsor pantries and soup kitchens, or participate in cooperative interfaith efforts. The Council of Jewish Federations is one of five charities on the board of the U.S. government's Emergency Food and Shelter Program. The American Jewish Joint Distribution Committee, one of several Jewish international relief and development agencies, is a sponsor of the Interfaith Hunger Appeal. In June 1993, the Synagogue Council of America, a coalition of congregational and rabbinical bodies, joined the U.S. Catholic Conference and the National Council of Churches to call for welfare reform which focuses on "attacking poverty, not the poor."

MAZON hopes its funds will serve a dual purpose. As Executive Director Irving Cramer explains:

We do short-term funding for immediate need, immediate intervention. What we favor most of all is funding multi-service organizations, where we'll provide the food portion and they'll provide the shelter, day care, job training, job referrals, medical and psychological care, clothing and so on. In other words, organizations designed to help lift people out of their poverty.

MAZON is not the answer to hunger, but it offers a way to bring food and justice to those who hunger for both – a way for American Jews to do good as they celebrate doing well.

Mia N. Johnson is program associate at MAZON: A Jewish Response to Hunger.

Responsibility for the 1990s, which says the church's role in the political order includes the following:

- Education regarding the teachings of the church and the responsibilities of the faithful;

- Analysis of issues for their social and moral dimensions;

- Measuring public policy against gospel values;

- Participating with other concerned parties in debate over public policy; and

- Speaking out with courage, skill, and concern on public issues involving human rights, social justice, and the life of the church in society.

This list could be a guide to all religious communities as they seek to integrate faith and faithfulness.

Congregations can explicate the scriptural, theological, and spiritual implications of faith for faithfulness. For Christians that means showing how faith in the risen Christ leads to acts of charity and justice.

"Because God loves and forgives us, we are freed to dedicate our lives to helping people in need," says David Beckmann, president of BFW Institute. He continues, "Commitment to Jesus leads to acts of justice."

The central conclusion of the Search Institute study of the Evangelical Lutheran Church in America, Christian Church (Disciples of Christ), Presbyterian Church

(U.S.A.), Southern Baptist Convention, United Church of Christ, and United Methodist Church, is that "effective Christian education is the most powerful single influence congregations have on maturity of faith." By "maturity of faith," they mean "exhibit a vibrant, life-transforming faith marked by both a deep, personal relationship to a loving God and a consistent devotion to serving others."[18]

The study showed that anti-hunger activists are more likely to engage in prayer and Bible reading than non-activists, contrary to some popular notions. (See graph, p. 44.)

Another study has shown that people who attend religious services regularly are likely to give more generously of their time and money, not only to their congregation but to other charities as well, than people who attend infrequently, or who do not attend at all.[19] The 36 percent who attend weekly or nearly weekly give an average of $1,220 per household and volunteer 3.2 hours of their time per week compared with $227 and 1.4 hours for those who do not attend at all. Sixty-two percent of people who volunteer learned about the volunteer activity through religious institutions.

This is not to suggest that most churchgoers are anti-hunger activists. Most are not. Seventy-three percent of adults in that study say that their congregation is warm, 74 percent say it is friendly, and the following percent say they are "interested" or "very interested" in "studying, learning about, or being involved in:"

- 77 percent – The Bible;

- 75 percent – Developing a personal relationship with Jesus;

- 74 percent – Improving my skills at showing love and concern;

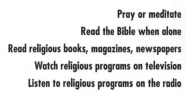

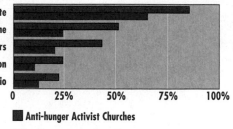

Graph 1

Religious Activities of Anti-Hunger Activists

Anti-hunger activists are more likely to be involved in most religious activities than non-activists. Here are some of the differences, comparing those who do each activity at least two or three times in a month.

Pray or meditate
Read the Bible when alone
Read religious books, magazines, newspapers
Watch religious programs on television
Listen to religious programs on the radio

0   25%   50%   75%   100%

■ Anti-hunger Activist Churches
■ Non-Activist Churches

Source: Eugene C. Roehlkelpartain, "Hunger Activists: Their Beliefs and Behaviors" in *Seeds Magazine*, May, 1992, 19.

- 74 percent – How to be a good spouse or parent;

- 73 percent – Applying my faith to daily living;

- 69 percent – Making more friends at church;

- 41 percent – Christian perspectives on social and political issues;

- 36 percent – Examining my lifestyle in light of the world's poor;

- 36 percent – Community service projects;

- 33 percent – International issues;

- 31 percent – People of other racial and ethnic groups; and,

- 20 percent – Peacemaking and social justice activities.

Private ranks high, public ranks low. Social justice activity ranks last. Fifty-eight percent of adults and 67 percent of youth indicated that they do not want churches to get involved in political issues. But, more than a third of the adults surveyed are interested in developing Christian perspectives on social and political issues, examining their lifestyle in the light of the poor, and in community service projects. Even though only one in five is interested in peacemaking and social justice activities, one in five is still almost thirty million people. And, the survey suggests that if these churches were to root their social concerns in scriptures and spirituality, more people would likely become involved.

Congregations that are active in anti-hunger concerns do not engage in anti-hunger activities at the expense of other activities. Indeed, they are more likely to provide members with love and support, to provide excellent Christian education for children, to teach the Bible, and to encourage personal commitment to Jesus than non-activist churches.

Some congregations are combining hunger with other related social justice issues. Members may be particularly concerned about the environment or poverty while others are motivated by women's concerns or racial discrimination. These issues or causes are all related to hunger. Women and children, especially people of color, are those most likely to suffer from hunger. The wasting of the environment ruins water supplies and strips nutrients from the soil, depriving peasant farmers of the basic means of their livelihood.

Environmentalists and social justice activists each tend to place priority on one part of the creation while neglecting the other. The two movements must join hands. Some efforts along these lines are already under way. For example, the World Council of Churches has combined its traditional social concerns with environmental concerns under the theme of Justice, Peace, and the Integrity of Creation.

Presbyterians and others often bring environmental and hunger concerns together around lifestyle and issues of wasteful

Anti-hunger activists are more likely to engage in prayer and Bible reading than non-activists.

Religious congregations can buck the individualism and consumerism of U.S. culture.

consumerism. The shopping mall symbolizes the good life for many people. People's social identity is established by where they can afford to shop. The mall is a place where people can go to be among, but not truly encounter or take responsibility for, other people.

Religious congregations can buck the individualism and consumerism of U.S. culture. They can show alternatives to the mindless cultural slow dance to mall muzak. Charitable involvement builds compassion. Political involvement is a way of affirming the value of human communities, and thus is an antidote to cultural individualism.

Religious congregations can unite with those communities of low-income people who are seeking relief from poverty, racism, exploitation, and violence. They can also join community organizations and political advocacy organizations that work for policies that empower individuals and contribute to a just society.

Congregations can set an example of simple lifestyles, rejection of consumer values, and transformative politics. They can continuously apply a biblical criterion when the question "What should we do?" arises. That criterion measures possible responses in the light of how they affect the well-being of the poorest and most vulnerable of poor people.

Conclusion

The vision of a just and sustainable society, only achievable through a combination of personal and political means, is close to the heart of the religious vision.

Justice is the form which love takes when dealing with groups. The history of religious involvement in politics (abolition and civil rights) shows the great impact congregations – especially when led by a committed minority can have when they are serious about a problem.

Religious people bring deep spiritual values, profound commitment, and centuries of experience in responding to human need. They bring a sense of the holiness and wholeness of nature and human social life.

Poverty and hunger cannot be solved by individual efforts, no matter how heroic their proportions. By the same token, public programs cannot reach deep enough into human lives to provide sensitive and individualized solutions. Solutions must be found by combining the best compassionate efforts of religious congregations on an individual basis with those efforts required to transform the politics and the policies which affect hunger. Nothing could ennoble or make politics more meaningful than if citizens and legislators decided that ending hunger was a first priority. Religious congregations have the values, the faithfulness, the compassion, the wisdom, and the vision that can make that happen. ■

Dr. Richard A. Hoehn is director of Bread for the World Institute.

Rick Huber, BFW Institute research assistant, carried out the survey research used in this chapter.

WHAT I CAN DO!

	Awareness	Involvement	Leadership
Personal/Family	• Study causes of hunger • Initiate dialogue with hungry/poor person(s) • Study connections between consumption, lifestyle, hunger	• Contribute to, join hunger organizations • Participate in poor peoples' organization • Reduce consumption to share with people in need	• Organize hunger study group • Help organize poor people's group • Form education and advocacy support group
Congregation	• Study scriptures on hunger/poverty • Include hunger concerns in prayer • Contribute to international relief, development work • Learn about denomination's hunger/poverty programs • Bring food to pantry • Study theology of poverty, advocacy, stewardship of human resources	• Teach class about hunger/poverty • Include hunger/poverty in congregational worship • Volunteer overseas • Partner with poor church in U.S., developing world • Volunteer at soup kitchen, pantry, night shelter • Adopt servant-advocate lifestyle	• Conduct "poverty banquet" • Conduct Hunger Sunday, Offering of Letters • Lead effort for overseas education, aid • Take hunger concerns to regional, national church • Find job at hunger/poverty organization • Reorient church programs to servant-advocate model
Workplace	• Talk with people about hunger issues	• Orient part of job toward needs of hungry/poor people	• Enhance workplace's relationship to hungry/poor people
Public Policy	• Study hunger policy • Follow current hunger bills • Study legislator's voting record	• Write letter, editorial to newspaper • Call, write legislators about hunger issues • Contribute, participate in political campaign	• Arrange group visit to editor, news director • Take delegation to legislators • Run for office

For more information, write Bread for the World Institute, 1100 Wayne Avenue, Suite 1000, Silver Spring, MD 20910 phone: (301) 608-2400 FAX: (301) 608-2401.

Speaking For Ourselves

Up And Out Of Poverty Now! offers an example of collaboration between grassroots low-income people's organizations and national advocacy groups.

PART ONE:
Organizing U.S. Low-Income People To End Hunger

by Rick Tingling-Clemmons

Those who are not poor and hungry usually are insulated from the ravages and urgency of social and economic problems. Anti-hunger advocates can be effective insofar as they encourage, accept, and support leadership from those who have their roots and links with the victims on the front lines. Ending hunger requires the full participation of poor and hungry people in the planning and execution of programs to meet their needs, and in providing organizations of low-income people with adequate resources. Anti-hunger organizations must bring these partnerships with hungry people into their own boardrooms and mission.

In an effort to explore the potential for collaboration between national anti-hunger groups and grassroots organizations of low-income people, Bread for the World Institute and Interfaith Impact for Justice and Peace jointly convened a consultation in May 1993. Participants included representatives of U.S. community-based organizations that are composed of or work closely with poor people; funders of anti-hunger and anti-poverty efforts; and staff of national anti-hunger advocacy organizations.

The Consultation

The discussion at this consultation emphasized the need for dialogue and coalition building. Participants also addressed a number of public policy issues:

- In the short run, the need for improvements in federal anti-hunger and anti-poverty programs, due to such problems as low benefit levels, restrictions on participation, and the stigmas attached to participation;

- In the long run, the need for adequate and sustainable incomes that allow families and individuals to obtain an adequate diet and other necessities;

- The importance of strengthening community- and workplace-based organizations seeking justice for poor people; and

- The disproportionate numbers of women and people of color who experience poverty and hunger.

Participants said that organizations of low-income people in the United States are not demanding more soup kitchens or homeless shelters as the solution to hunger, though these are often vital for coping with hunger. Rather, such organizations are seeking jobs, housing, access to health care, and comprehensive reform of the social services system. Eliminating hunger ultimately requires changing the social and economic structures that cause the poverty of which hunger is a symptom.

Attendees defined hunger as:

A physical, mental, and spiritual condition that results from a lack of dignified access to sufficient and secure family, financial, institutional, or community resources to obtain a culturally-appropriate diet for a safe and healthful life.

They also offered a vision of how a broad-based, anti-hunger movement would operate:

A movement to end hunger must respect the dignity of each human being, must redistribute its own resources to those most affected, and must provide institutional channels to power for those working at the grassroots level.

While the focus was primarily on hunger and poverty in the United States, participants looked at a number of international questions. These included U.S. immigration policies and the likely impact of the North American Free Trade Agreement on jobs and communities in both the United States and Mexico.

Models of Collaboration

Too often, well-intentioned organizations working for peace and social justice fail to listen to low-income people. For example, while working as a Third World organizer for the Committee Against Registration and the Draft (CARD), organizing a conference on racism and the draft, this writer found that CARD's slogan, "Just say no to the Draft," failed to address the problems of poverty and unemployment among racial minorities. The reality is that the armed forces offer poor people employment and training. During the Vietnam War era, the draft injected an element of equity, since African Americans, disproportionately in poverty, also made up a disproportionate share of the troops. Although white, middle-class, young men benefitted most from conscientious objector status and other draft deferments, conscription drew more of them into military service.

A more successful example of collaboration comes from the experience of Up and Out of Poverty Now! (UOPN), composed of the National Welfare Rights Union, the National Union of the

Ending hunger requires the full participation of poor and hungry people in the planning and execution of programs to meet their needs.

Hunger and Poverty in the Hispanic Community

by Deirdre Martinez

In the absence of comprehensive data on nutritional status in the United States, hunger trends can be understood in the context of poverty trends. These trends reveal that Hispanics, one of the nation's most diverse and fastest-growing populations, are disproportionately poor and are therefore likely to suffer from malnutrition. (The U.S. Census Bureau uses the term "Hispanic" to identify persons of Mexican-American, Puerto Rican, Cuban, Central and South American, and other Hispanic descent. Here, it is used interchangeably with "Latino").

The 1990 census counted 22.4 million Hispanics, an increase of 53 percent over 1980. Immigration and natural increase are expected to make Latinos the largest ethnic minority in the United States early in the next century.

More than one in every four Hispanic families in the United States – including almost two in five Hispanic children – are poor. Poverty among Hispanic families is rising for a variety of reasons – undereducation, concentration in low-paying jobs, early childbearing, and the impact of recession. Data from the 1990 Census show that:

- Hispanic families are more likely to be poor than non-Hispanic families. One-quarter of Hispanic families were poor, compared to 9.5 percent of non-Hispanic families.

- Married-couple Hispanic families have a higher poverty rate than their white or black counterparts. Almost one in four Hispanic married-couple families was poor (23.5 percent), compared to 12.4 percent of black and 7.7 percent of white married-couple families.

- Hispanic female-headed families face a high risk of being poor. Almost half (48.3 percent) of Hispanic families in poverty were maintained by females without a husband present, compared to 31.7 percent of non-Hispanic poor families.

- While the poverty rate for all children remains high, Hispanic children are especially likely to be poor. Almost two-fifths (38.4 percent) of Hispanic children were living in poverty, compared to less than one in five non-Hispanic children (18.3 percent).

Homeless, and the National Anti-Hunger Coalition. Its founding conference received financial and institutional support from the United Church of Christ.

The National Welfare Rights Union, made up of welfare recipients, stresses that recipients must speak on their own behalf, rather than through representatives or advocates. The union also seeks increased benefit levels, so that anti-poverty programs actually lift people out of poverty.

The National Union of the Homeless, which employs and organizes homeless people, has recruited support from labor unions, religious groups, city officials, technicians, and media specialists to acquire housing projects and other initiatives to provide homeless people with both shelter and respectful treatment. The union has created model facilities and pressured local governments to free up funds and housing for homeless people to operate, renovate, and maintain.

The Food Research and Action Center (FRAC), a Washington-based research and advocacy group, helped establish the National Anti-Hunger Coalition in 1979. The coalition is a grassroots organization of low-income people and their advocates. For many years, FRAC contributed staff time and other resources to the coalition, and it continues to support UOPN with staff and information.

Recently, the National Organization for Women (NOW) has begun working with and providing support to UOPN and its constituent organizations. This has resulted from NOW's desire for its own agenda to better reflect the interests of poor and working-class women as well as women of color. NOW has committed financial and in-kind contributions to UOPN.

Dilemmas of Building Mutual Trust

Gary Cook, of the Presbyterian Hunger Program, has noted that suspicions often accompany efforts to link grassroots and national advocacy organizations:

Suspicions . . . go on with the community-based folks thinking the advocacy folks are just playing with poverty and the advocacy folks look at community-based groups as having unrealistic expectations of the political process.[1]

Building coalitions and true collaboration generally require a conscious values change – away from the business-as-usual method of top-down directing and organizing, to a commitment to self-determination within and without. Many organizations that are committed to such an approach have been known to slip away from their insights, goals, and commitments to the self-determination of low-income people. Such slips often accompany other changes in staff, directors and/or boards, and shifting priorities of funders. A strategy for building coalitions requires open confrontation and evaluation of chauvinisms and assuring the greatest level of democracy possible – with all the fears and risks this entails.

There are numerous effective guides to organizing, adaptable to local political and economic realities.[2] Alliances and coalitions against hunger and poverty pair people and/or organizations who need services with those who can provide resources and services. Resources include "connections," cash, people, time, and in-kind services. Great pains must be taken to make sure that leadership is encouraged, supported, and heeded from among poor and hungry people themselves.

Poverty levels vary among Hispanic subgroups. (See table 1, p.55.) Other factors suggest the presence of hunger in the Hispanic community. With a median age of 26.2 years, Hispanics are 7.6 years younger than non-Hispanics. Of the Hispanic population in poverty, 47.7 percent are less than eighteen years old, compared to 38.3 percent of the low-income, non-Hispanic population. At a time in their lives when nutritional demands are greatest, many Hispanic children who are unable to obtain a nutritionally-balanced diet are at risk of being malnourished.

Latinas have a high rate of teenage pregnancy. Recent National Council of La Raza (NCLR) research found that Latina teens aged fifteen to nineteen are twice as likely to become parents as white teens. In 1989, about one Latina teen in ten gave birth, compared with fewer than one in twenty white adolescent females. Teenage mothers often are poorly informed about the importance of health and nutrition habits during pregnancy. One in three Hispanics lacks health insurance, compared to about one of every seven people in the general population. As a result, pregnant adolescents are vulnerable to a variety of complications, including miscarriages, babies born with birth defects, and in some Hispanic subgroups, low birthweight babies. In addition, because these mothers are teenagers, they lack adequate education and employment opportunities; they also lack parenting and other skills, which contribute to poor socioeconomic status.

Hispanics are highly urbanized. Fifty-two percent live in central cities, compared to 22.4 percent of white non-Hispanics and 56.9 percent of black non-Hispanics. Many urban food shoppers do not have access to reasonably-priced supermarkets. Higher prices, limited choices, poor quality, and a larger proportion of highly-processed foods in small neighborhood stores increase the likelihood of poor or unbalanced diets. Neither poor urban consumers nor taxpayers get the greatest value from food stamps used in these circumstances.[1]

Hispanic migrant and seasonal farmworkers – tens of thousands of workers and their families – have limited access to health care. Health-care providers say that many have never had formal health care, have suffered years of neglect, and do not have a proper understanding of the role of medicine in acute, chronic, and preventive care. Similarly, as for other new immigrants, language barriers, reliance on traditional medicine, and fear of government and other officials contribute to lack of preventive care and poor understanding of nutritional needs.

Hispanics are the most undereducated major racial/ethnic group in the United States. This can contribute to poor understanding of proper nutrition and probably reduces knowledge about services and programs. The Food Research and Action Center (FRAC) notes, however, that poor people lack stoves and refrigerators more often than nutritional knowledge.

In 1991, 1.3 million, or 14.1 percent, of all households receiving food stamps were headed by Hispanics. Similarly, 1.3 million Hispanics participated in the Special Supplemental Food Program for Women, Infants, and Children (WIC), accounting for 23.7 percent of the total population served. The U.S. Department of Agriculture (USDA) and the Congressional Budget Office estimate that only 66 percent of individuals and 60 percent of households eligible for food stamps participate.[2] USDA estimates that WIC will serve only about 60 percent of those eligible in 1993.

In 1990, the California Rural Legal Assistance Foundation conducted a survey in six communities in California's Central Valley, as part of the nationwide Community Childhood Hunger Identification Project (CCHIP), sponsored by FRAC. More than three fourths (76 percent) of the families surveyed were Hispanic. The results show that:

- More than one-third of the families faced severe hunger; 36 percent reported serious problems getting enough food; 98 percent of hungry families ran out of money for food for an average of seven days per month;

- Nearly sixty-six thousand school-age children in the four-county area were hungry;

- Two-thirds of the families faced food shortages and 68 percent reported at least one instance in the previous year when they did not have enough food to eat or money to buy it;

- The average household spent 44 percent of its income on shelter; one-third of the hungry households spent more than half their total income on shelter;

- The average household size was 5.4 persons, while the average household income was $12,500 per year; and

- The participation rates in federal food programs were: food stamps – 48 percent; WIC – 19 percent; School Lunch (free/reduced price) – 92 percent; School Breakfast (free/reduced price) – 57 percent; Commodities – 31 percent; Emergency Food – 36 percent.

Successful coalitions usually grow out of broad agreement on values, vision, and mission, though members may often differ on tactical and policy questions. Accepting that survival is contingent on meeting people's basic needs with dignity as a matter of right is a value that must underlie an anti-hunger movement.

Coalitions of Collective Self-Interest

Across the United States, there are organizations with demonstrated successes in coalition building of this sort:

- The Association of Community Organizations for Reform Now (ACORN) has campaigned to get banks to reinvest in local communities. ACORN has also taken over abandoned housing in an effort to press government at all levels to deal with the affordable housing crisis. In Chicago, for example, ACORN has seventeen groups and over five thousand members in low-income, African-American neighborhoods. In addition to pressing for banks to reinvest in "credit-starved" neighborhoods, Chicago ACORN has worked on housing, utilities, sexual assault, toxic chemicals, and public education.

- The Justice for Janitors campaign is built on collaboration between ACORN and the Service Employees' International Union, an affiliate of the AFL-CIO that organizes low-wage workers. Many unorganized janitors are immigrants who are often subject to exploitation because of their lack of legal status.

- Citizen Action is another national organization with local and regional chapters that organize low-income people around issues which concern them. In western New York, Citizen Action's emphasis is primarily on access to health care. In Buffalo, the organization has sought to organize a multiracial association to improve the quantity and quality of affordable housing.

- The Rural Coalition is composed of a diverse range of organizations concerned about rural America, including small and minority farmers, Native Americans, farmworkers, rural housing activists, and national advocacy groups. The coalition has a long history of recruiting an ethnically-diverse board of rural activists and building programs and initiatives responsive to their needs and vision.

- The Tennessee Hunger Coalition has a board that is controlled by low-income people. The coalition has mounted successful grassroots legislative campaigns to make school breakfast more widely available to children in the state.

- African-American welfare mothers in the Orlando, Florida, area established Single Mothers in a Learning Environment (SMILE) in 1983. It seeks to empower low-income women to make them independent of the welfare system. Projects include developing employment-related skills, voter registration, and short-term efforts to improve public assistance programs.

- Black Workers for Justice, based in North Carolina, seeks to organize working poor people in the southeastern United States to "challenge injustices such as poverty, hunger, [and] exploitation, and to bring about a better quality of life."

- On the Pine Ridge Indian Reservation, the Lakota Fund's Circle Banking Project provides small groups of poor people credit for microenterprises. The project, modelled on the Grameen Bank in

As NCLR and other research have shown, Hispanics are likely to be under-represented in federal programs, including preschool programs such as Head Start, as well as in the Job Training Partnership Act program. Although no separate estimate of the eligible Hispanic population served by WIC and food stamps has been made, these findings suggest that Hispanics are likely to be a considerable part of the unserved eligible population. Factors contributing to low Hispanic participation in these programs include:

- *Lack of community-based services.* Often, Hispanics cannot obtain services or apply for assistance within or near their own neighborhoods. Lack of transportation, lack of evening hours to make services accessible to the working poor, and a fear of seeking services outside their community often discourage eligible Hispanics from obtaining services.

- *Inadequate outreach to the Hispanic population.* Many government programs lack bicultural, bilingual staff. Failure to do active community outreach through the Spanish-language media or visits to community agencies and churches also limits Hispanic community awareness of entitlements, and other available services.

- *Hispanics often rely on other family members for assistance instead of government programs.* This family-centered care does not provide nutrition education and may create a burden on other family members, who may themselves be socioeconomically disadvantaged.

To supplement federal anti-poverty and anti-hunger efforts, Latinos often rely on community-based organizations (CBOs). As trusted and recognized institutions, CBOs are in a position to provide outreach, education, and service. Some are affiliated with NCLR, the nation's largest constituency-based Hispanic organization. Its 150 community affiliates provide services to more than two million people annually in thirty-seven states, the District of Columbia, and Puerto Rico.

For example, El Concilio de Madera, an NCLR affiliate in Madera, California, provides affordable, walk-in medical services to low-income residents. Health education staff have found that the little health education available locally is largely targeted to specific lifestyles, diseases, or conditions. They have also found that inadequate nutrition and ignorance about nutrition and its relationship to health maintenance are major factors in many of the illnesses experienced by Madera Family Health Center patients in nearly all of the life cycles. Staff provide nutritional counselling for children and adolescents and for nutrition- and diet-related diseases such as hypertension, diabetes, and obesity.

Another NCLR affiliate is NAF Multicultural Human Development Corporation (NAF), offering health services to farmworkers in coordination with the Nebraska Department of Health, Nebraska Chapter of the National Hemophiliac Foundation, and United Migrant Opportunity Services, Inc. Programs include health-care access, Hispanic hemophilia outreach, migrant health, HIV/AIDS education and prevention, health promotion, and immunization outreach. NAF facilitates access to WIC, maternal and child health care, and family planning by providing translation, transportation, and information.

CBOs have demonstrated their ability to improve the lives of Hispanic families. This ability should be fostered and strengthened. Failure to do so can have serious consequences for Hispanics and for the school and work force population of which they constitute a significant part.

Deirdre Martinez is a policy analyst for the Poverty Project at the National Council of La Raza (NCLR). She wishes to thank the following NCLR staff for editorial assistance and review: Frank Beadle, director of the Center for Health Promotion; Sonia M. Pérez, senior policy analyst for the Poverty Project; and Emily Gantz McKay, senior vice president for Institutional Development.

Bangladesh, offers loans without collateral and depends on peer pressure to assure pay back.

- Kids 1st was established by low-income Hispanic community organizations in Monrovia, California. It seeks the involvement of parents in public school reorganization and quality education for all children, including poor, minority children.

- The Southwest Organizing Project has challenged national environmental organizations to examine how their programs and hiring practices have contradicted their "lip service" to environmental jus-

tice. This challenge resulted in funding problems for the project, but it has stuck by its principles and survived. The project has also fought for improved worker safety and health in the region's high-technology industries. Maria Chavez, a project activist from Albuquerque, New Mexico, who formerly worked in an electronics plant, says:

You . . . get no safety lessons, no education . . . . [We] want to change the laws so people can get educated. We don't want the companies to move . . . we need the jobs . . . we need to be educated before we go to these companies to work.[3]

Many of these efforts have received funding or technical assistance from national organizations, certain foundations, and the religious community. The Campaign for Human Development, a program of the U.S. Catholic Conference, is a major source of funds for community-based and national anti-poverty projects. Protestant social justice and anti-hunger programs similarly fund such efforts. The Center for Community Change in Washington, D.C., the Midwest Academy in Chicago, the Industrial Areas Foundation (with groups around the country), and the Highlander Center in New Market, Tennessee, among other groups, train community organizers.

In the United States, poverty, and therefore vulnerability to hunger, is often related to race. The majority of poor people are white, but the poverty rate among members of racial minority groups is higher than that of whites. In 1991, the U.S. Census Bureau reported an overall poverty rate of 14.3 percent. For whites, the rate was 11.3 percent; for African Americans, 32.7 percent; and for Hispanics, 28.7 percent. Child poverty rates were 21.1 percent overall; 16.1 percent for whites, 45.6 percent for African Americans, and 39.8 percent for Hispanics. Organizations which promote the rights and well-being of members of racial minority groups often work on hunger and poverty issues.

For example, the oldest, national African-American civil rights organization, the National Association for the Advancement of Colored People (NAACP), established in 1909, is best known for its efforts to oppose racial discrimination in all facets of U.S. life. It has eighteen hundred local chapters and 400,000 members, and is active in litigation and public policy advocacy. In addition, the NAACP assists in the development of low-income housing and offers education and training, job referrals, and child care.

Similarly, the National Urban League, established in 1910, is a civil rights and social service organization which seeks to assist African Americans in achieving social and economic equality. Through 114 affiliates in thirty-four states, it provides assistance and empowers African-American communities in such areas as employment, housing, education, social welfare, AIDS education, and crime prevention. The organization also engages in research and advocacy activities. Its community-based programs around the country involve more than a million people each year.

Along with the efforts of national groups, there are tens of thousands of community-based low-income people's organizations. These include churches (often refuges from a troubled world), parent-teacher associations, and a wide variety of locally-initiated neighborhood improvement efforts.

Low-income people's organizations continue to need considerable support. As welfare rights activist Jean Dever told the May consultation, it is hard to think about contacting your congressional representative when you do not have a phone and you cannot afford the stamp for a letter.

When other organizations provide funds, services, technical assistance, and training, they must not use this to exert control. Partnership is a matter of empowering grassroots groups to articulate their message as they define it.

Conclusion

Locally-determined grassroots efforts should feed into national strategies to end hunger. Only federal policies can achieve the redirection of resources needed to revitalize low-income communities. This coin has two sides: harmful federal policies, as in the 1980s, can overwhelm promising local efforts. Attempts to change federal legislation and policies seldom succeed in fostering lasting change without broad popular support. Thus, Tootie Welker, organizer for the Montana Alliance for Progressive Policy, argues that increased voter participation is the vehicle for obtaining real power.[4] Frances Fox Piven and Richard A. Cloward, academic experts on poor people's movements, add that achieving change often requires acts of protest as well.[5]

A successful movement to end hunger will adopt the strategies, risks, partnerships, and courage necessary to "do the right thing." That means working for the creation of jobs with decent wages for all who can work, secure incomes for all households to meet their needs, and, over the long term, a just society. ■

Rick Tingling-Clemmons is a Vietnam-era veteran and peace activist with twenty-five years' experience as a grassroots organizer. He received his M.A. in Adult Education from the University of the District of Columbia in 1993.

It is hard to think about contacting your congressional representative when you do not have a phone and you cannot afford the stamp for a letter.

Table 1

Poverty Among Hispanic Persons By Place of Origin (1990)

	All Families		Income Below Poverty Line				
	# Families	% of Hispanic Families	# Families	% Families	# Persons	% Persons	% Children
Total U.S. Population	66,322,000	. . .	7,098,000	11%	33,585,000	13%	21%
Total Hispanic Population	4,982,000	100%	1,244,000	25%	6,006,000	28%	38%
Mexican Origin	2,945,000	59%	736,000	25%	3,764,000	28%	36%
Puerto Rican Origin	626,000	13%	235,000	37%	966,000	41%	57%
Cuban Origin	335,000	7%	46,000	14%	178,000	17%	31%
Central and South American Origin	667,000	13%	148,000	22%	748,000	25%	35%
Other Hispanic Origin	408,000	8%	79,000	19%	350,000	21%	36%

Source: U.S. Census Bureau.

PART TWO:
People's Movements: An Alternative Development Vision

by Medea Benjamin

People's Movements Counter Despair

The 1980s have been called the "lost decade" for development, as debt, austerity, deteriorating terms of trade, violent conflict, and environmental degradation reversed some of the progress developing countries made against hunger and poverty in the preceding decades. Yet there were some bright spots, among them the flowering of grassroots organizations. Millions of people have banded together at the community level to press for social and economic justice and a sustainable environment. Sometimes they work in self-help groups to find collective solutions to their problems. Other times they join in "grassroots lobbies" to put pressure on government or international institutions.

The impetus for forming such groups is often sheer economic necessity. In other cases, grassroots groups have emerged with increasing levels of education and, in some countries, income. People in many countries have gravitated toward private organizations to work independently of, and, when possible, oppose dictatorial governments.

The growth of grassroots groups also reflects a desire for alternative approaches to development. Capitalism in the developing world has not delivered the much-heralded consumer paradise. Socialism, once seen by many as an alternative to the inequities and greed characteristic of capi-

Photo: IAF, Wilfredo Garcia

Grassroots people's movements seek to overcome disempowerment in developing countries.

talism, has failed to achieve just, humane societies.

Furthermore, the late twentieth century is a time of challenges to state sovereignty in the Southern Hemisphere. Transnational corporations and global financial institutions are gaining more influence over individual lives than nation-states. Developing country government policies are no longer simply dictated by the particular faction in power, but often are set by multilateral institutions such as the World Bank and the International Monetary Fund (IMF) – institutions with no accountability to local people. Consequently, most citizens feel powerless to determine how society should function. Grassroots groups seek to overcome this disempowerment.

These organizations, known as "people's movements," have cropped up all over the globe:

Millions of people have banded together at the community level to press for social and economic justice and a sustainable environment.

- In Mozambique, where a devastating war has led to massive starvation, hundreds of women formed a cooperative movement called the Green Zones to grow their own food.

- In rural Bangladesh, where commercial banks close their doors on poor people, the Grameen Bank was formed to make small loans (an average of $60) to hundreds of thousands of needy recipients (mainly women), for microenterprises. The repayment rate is over 90 percent, and this model is now being replicated in dozens of other countries, including poor areas of the United States.

- In the Philippines, the debt crisis of the 1980s that plunged standards of living to levels of the 1960s fomented the Freedom From Debt Coalition to fight against what members perceive as usury by foreign lenders.

- In Peru, where constant currency devaluations left women without enough money to feed their children, they came together to form hundreds of collective kitchens, or *comedores comunales*.

Similar grassroots efforts began in Eastern Europe in the late 1970s, and played a major role in the democratic revolutions of the late 1980s. Since then, nongovernmental organizations (NGOs) have proliferated rapidly in Eastern Europe, playing essential roles in such areas as anti-poverty work, human rights protection, education, and ecology.[1]

Southern NGOs and Development: From Welfare To Empowerment[2]

Throughout the developing world, local NGOs have a long history of providing services to poor people. In the 1970s and espe-cially the 1980s, many of these groups shifted their emphasis from top-down welfare to bottom-up empowerment, thereby helping to foster truly participatory people's movements.

In Africa, some churches and ethnic associations sought to meet the needs of poor people from colonial times. More recently, they have supported women's and environmental groups, rural development efforts, and poverty alleviation. NGO involvement in development has spread due in part to governments' weaknesses in delivering services and fostering popular participation in economic and political life. African NGOs seeking to protect human rights and promote political pluralism have frequently faced government hostility and repression.

In South and Southeast Asia, mutual assistance has been important in rural communities for centuries, especially in areas cultivating irrigated rice. In India, voluntary social welfare work and emergency relief was an integral part of the independence struggle. In the 1960s and 1970s, NGOs became involved in appropriate technology, health care, and adult education. Since then, training, consciousness-raising, and building grassroots organizations have become major NGO emphases. In Southeast Asia, local and national democratization have become important objectives, along with environmental sustainability, economic justice, and consumer issues.

Latin American NGOs shifted their focus from welfare to challenging authoritarian governments in the 1960s and 1970s, often under the influence of liberation theology. They came to view local development projects as a way to help communities resist repression. The difficult economic circumstances of the 1980s were a time of explosive growth for grassroots groups.

Since the 1970s, Northern governments and multilateral agencies have channelled significant funds to Southern NGOs, both directly and through Northern NGOs. Some of these groups are part of, or work closely with, people's movements.

Obstacles to People's Movements

Grassroots organizations in the developing world operate in the face of formidable obstacles – obstacles that range from the hostility of local elites, to government repression, to a world economy that is stacked against poor people.

Why hostility? Change is a threat to those in power. For local landowners or business people, community-run businesses could mean new competition, loss of markets, and decreased profits. For the political elite, community efforts to have a say in the political process imply new accountability, sharing in decision making, and fewer special privileges. When NGOs demonstrate that they can deliver services or carry out development efforts more effectively than governments, the authorities may view this as a direct challenge to their legitimacy. Finally, empowering women is often viewed as threatening by men.

The stakes can be high. Demonstrations are broken up, organizations are banned, and holders of economic power resist the redistribution of land and other assets. In the worst of cases, key organizers may be carted off by secret police forces, never to be seen again.

Nevertheless, in the 1990s, people's movements are thriving. Some see them as posing an alternative to the policies promoted by multilateral development institutions. The alternative is neither statist socialism nor elite-controlled capitalism. It is a vision of democratic initiative and community self-management of equity and environmental sustainability.

People's movements have shortcomings. Though they tend to be more democratic and broad-based than government-run institutions, they can succumb to bureaucracy, dependency, and corruption. The initial euphoria of many grassroots groups is slowly sapped by internal rivalries, lack of direction, or financial instability. Too often, indigenous NGOs become dependent on outside funding, whether from official aid or Northern NGOs.

In addition, their chances of success all too often hinge on outside forces beyond their control. International trade and monetary agreements, military conflicts, and national policies that determine access to productive resources are often more critical to feeding people than one community growing its own food.

The most successful people's movements have learned that they must make alliances and form coalitions at the national or even international level. They have often formed umbrella organizations such as FAVDO, a pan-African association of community groups. Ideally, these umbrella organizations serve as representational bodies, drawing from many community sectors to lobby governments and international institutions in the interest of poor people.

Some coalitions have been so strong that they have managed to topple repressive governments. The democracy movement presently sweeping Africa is due in part to the strength of grassroots coalitions pressing for change. Latin American grassroots movements have helped force several authoritarian governments from power. A particularly exciting case is that of Brazil, where the Workers Party – with the backing of popular organizations such as unions, churches, environmental groups, and neighborhood committees – almost captured the presidency in 1989.

International trade and monetary agreements, military conflicts, and national policies that determine access to productive resources are often more critical to feeding people than one community growing its own food.

But there is another key ingredient to the long-term success of people's movements, and that is linking up with similar movements in other countries. This is where Northerners can lend a hand.

How Can Northerners Support People's Movements?[3]

The role of Northerners in the decade of the 1990s goes way beyond the traditional role of furnishing financial support. It requires greater involvement in a wide range of economic and political issues.

One area where supporters play a crucial role is defending grassroots organizers whose lives are threatened. International letter-writing campaigns and public pressure on governments guilty of human rights abuses by such groups as Amnesty International and Survival International have helped save lives and gain the release of hundreds of jailed activists.

In Central America, a movement of internationalists, particularly within the religious community, emerged to accompany local activists in their daily work. Their presence in El Salvador and Guatemala helped reduce the violence governments and armed forces unleashed against grassroots leaders. In Haiti, U.S. activists are playing a similar role in curbing the military's worst excesses.

Northerners can also support people's movements in their efforts to gain access to technical information that can help their organizing work. The Consumers Association of Penang (CAP), Malaysia, a champion of consumers' rights in the developing world, has asked Westerners to furnish information on foreign subsidiaries of multinational corporations, as well as on international covenants protecting the environment and consumers. This type of information helps CAP activists press legal claims against abuses by multinationals.

Another way to support people's movements is through "sister" programs linking cities, churches, schools, and clinics. The 1980s have witnessed the mushrooming of hundreds of such direct ties between Southerners and their Northern counterparts. These partnerships create direct lines of communication and resource exchanges, bypassing government intermediaries and creating lasting bonds of friendship.

For example, Holy Trinity, a Roman Catholic church located in an affluent neighborhood in Washington, D.C., is a sister parish to Maria Madre de los Pobres, a low-income, Christian-based community in San Salvador, El Salvador. Holy Trinity parishioners provide financial support for the sister community's educational efforts and development projects, including a bakery and a carpentry workshop. Of equal importance, many people from Holy Trinity have visited El Salvador, stayed in the homes of sister parish members, and learned firsthand about their endeavors to achieve justice, peace, and dignity.[4]

Southerners have also asked for help in facilitating South-South exchanges, where Third World groups can learn from each other. The international women's group ISIS organizes exchanges of grassroots activists. A Brazilian health-care worker and an Indian social worker might switch posts for a year, taking the lessons of each others' countries back home.

Southern groups have made it clear that another key role for Northerners is to educate their own citizens about global issues, especially complex issues such as world trade and structural adjustment programs. An example of a successful education and action campaign is the Don't Stop the Giving, Stop the Taking campaign organized by Oxfam

UK and Ireland during the height of the African famine in the mid-1980s. It stressed that donating money to help starving Africans was not enough at a time when Northern banks, governments, and firms were extracting resources from the continent. The campaign helped convince the U.K. government to take the lead in proposing global initiatives to forgive African debt.

A critical way to help Southern grassroots organizations is by focusing on larger U.S. trade and foreign policies. The time is ripe to press for restructuring of the U.S. foreign aid program. Even more difficult is the daunting task of challenging the global economic structures that keep poor people poor. In recent years, U.S. groups have joined with their counterparts in other countries to examine how the world trading system affects poor people in developing countries, and to give citizens around the world a voice in normally closed-door trade negotiations. (See chapter 6 for more detail.)

Northern and Southern NGOs have also worked together to challenge the negative consequences World Bank and IMF "structural adjustment" policies often have for poor people and the environment. For several years, a coalition of Northern development, environmental, and human rights groups has joined with Southern partners to lobby the annual joint board meetings of the bank and IMF on these issues. In April 1993, FAVDO and InterAction, the main association of U.S. development NGOs, issued a joint statement on similar concerns to U.S. Rep. Barney Frank (D-Mass.), who chairs the House Banking Subcommittee that oversees U.S. participation in the multilateral institutions. The Bank Information Center, a Washington-based clearinghouse, facilitates the flow of information to try to institutionalize these advocacy relationships. It is at this level of national and international policy where Northerners can wield their greatest power and show the extent of their support for people's movements.

The Challenge of People's Movements

A fundamental change – a "paradigm shift" – may be in the works. The rise of people's movements is *not* just another development trend like the "trickle-down" of the 1960s, the "basic needs" of the 1970s, or the "private enterprise" thrust of the 1980s. Why? Because it was not concocted in the halls of Northern donor institutions.

It is coming to life in the peasant hamlets of Burkina Faso, in the squatter settlements of Mexico City, in the fishing communities of Malaysia. It is being built by women and men tired of watching their children die, young people tired of seeing their future destroyed. It is a product of despair, anger, fear, and hope. It is a slow and steady shift in power.

As we approach the twenty-first century, it is precisely this shift in power that can make it possible to address the grave injustices of our times. Taking on formidable opponents from local landowners to state bureaucracies to international bankers, people's organizations may portend a future in which democracy is defined not simply by elections or legislative structures, but by deeper citizen involvement in public life. ■

Medea Benjamin, a nutritionist and economist, is co-director of Global Exchange in San Francisco, Calif.

Eritrea – A Model for Popular Participation

by Sharon Pauling

After thirty years of war, Eritreans exercised their hard-won right to determine their political status in a referendum held in April 1993. It was no surprise that the final tally revealed an overwhelming 99.9 percent vote in favor of independence from Ethiopia. For most Eritreans, independence was not an option but the culmination of decades of struggle for freedom and the right to overcome poverty and famine. As the spirit of celebration continues, the daunting process of reconstruction and development looms large. A top priority for this multicultural nation is continuing the process of democratic participation that began during the fight for independence as it meets these challenges.

In winning the war, the Eritrean People's Liberation Front (EPLF) scored a military victory. But even more importantly, it had, during the course of the war, unleashed a social revolution that could lay the groundwork for transforming Eritrean society into a unified and egalitarian nation. The liberation struggle was by necessity based on bottom-up mobilization. Early on, the EPLF recognized that lasting change could only be sustained by the involvement of the people themselves.

Beginning in the mid-1970s, the EPLF forged a model for development based on popular participation and organized mass groups of women, workers, peasants, and youth. EPLF members began winning the confidence of the people by dealing with the immediate problems of daily life. They taught health care, nutrition, and simple food production techniques. Later, local committees were established to resolve community and family disputes. The EPLF

supported women, even in their divorce appeals. People began to appreciate the changes and associated further improvements with the front. All over the country, even in the most remote villages, fighters who were engineers, "barefoot doctors," teachers, farmers, and shepherds worked with a broad base of supporters to set up cooperative stores, workshops, field clinics, and schools.

Similarly, staff of the Eritrean Relief Association, which provided relief and rehabilitation aid in the rural areas and towns administered by the EPLF, involved beneficiary populations in helping to shape emergency and reconstruction projects.

This organizing also gave rise to political and social consciousness as people from all walks of life began to challenge traditions that had meant poverty, primitive patterns of land use, and the domination of women by men. Traditionally, peasants and seasonal farmers had been forced to give a share of their crops and labor services to landlords. Transferring social, political, and economic power from landowners and feudal chiefs to women and peasants was a central problem. Basic social services, such as primary health care and education, did not exist in many rural areas. Illiteracy was a major problem. Women lacked legal rights and access to property.

Strategies for land reform, the new roles and rights of women, and the structure of EPLF decision making were developed with wide involvement by the organized population.

Although EPLF training was heavily influenced by Marxism in the early days, the EPLF has since made dramatic policy shifts toward an emphasis on practical issues. Specifically, new realities mean that the EPLF, as it seeks to govern a new nation, has to address the practical issues of how to manage a "mixed" economy, how a multiparty political system might work, how to relate to neighboring countries, and how to foster national unity within Eritrea. The country's new leaders are concerned with how to attract capital and skills back to Eritrea from abroad. Despite the ideological shifts, the local conflict resolution and decision-making structures established by the EPLF in the 1970s should serve the country well as the people grapple with the questions of the 1990s and beyond.

The new government views agricultural rehabilitation, environmental restoration, and basic infrastructure rebuilding as priorities, key to people returning to normal work. "Call committees" were formed to attract Eritreans living abroad to participate in a sort of Eritrean "peace corps." Many invested capital. Others returned to serve as teachers, mechanics, technicians, financial planners, and computer programmers.

During the independence struggle, women made exceptional progress. Askalu Menkorios, head of the National Union of Eritrean Women, says, "Eritrean women will never go back to the way they were before. Women have learned to believe in themselves and many men have changed their ideas about women's traditional roles." One-third of the EPLF's fighters were women. Now, many stay in school up to age fifteen. Women work as truck drivers, mechanics, barefoot doctors, and industrial workers. They now participate actively in political life. Importantly, these changes, along with many others, have occurred at the grassroots level. Askalu, understanding that the struggle is far from over, sums up the importance of broad-based participation when she says, "We

consider what we are doing at the grassroots as the best guarantee of change in the future." ∎

Sharon Pauling is Africa policy analyst at Bread for the World and co-coordinator of the Coalition for Peace in the Horn of Africa. She was a member of a U.S. delegation which observed Eritrea's independence vote.

People's Initiatives for Alternative Agrarian Reform in the Philippines

by Maria Christina M. Liamzon

In 1986, a peaceful popular uprising overthrew Philippine dictator Ferdinand Marcos. The country's NGOs were jubilant and extremely hopeful about the changes that could take place under the new government of President Corazon C. Aquino.

One national NGO network, the Philippine Partnership for the Development of Human Resources in Rural Areas (PhilDhrra), initiated extensive discussion within its membership regarding the implications of the "People Power Revolution" for NGOs involved in development activities and the grassroots groups with which they worked. After considerable dialogue within the network, PhilDhrra issued a call for nationwide consultations on agrarian reform and rural development.

This remains an area of pressing need, since nearly 70 percent of the country's farming households do not own the land they work, and the overwhelming majority of Filipinos rely on agriculture and fishing for their livelihoods. Agrarian reform and rural development programs give farming households secure title to the land and allow them to increase their productivity

CASE STUDIES

The end of the Marcos dictatorship signalled a new climate of openness for political action in the Philippines.

and incomes, thereby enhancing the quality of life for many poor and hungry Filipinos.

In response to PhilDhrra, interested NGOs and peasant associations collaborated to organize consultations at the village, municipal, provincial, sub-regional, and regional levels. These discussions took place over a period of three months and involved more than ten thousand people. Two national meetings were then held to consolidate the results of the consultations. Following these gatherings, the views and demands of the peasant sector were presented to top government officials, including President Aquino. At the second national consultation, a new peasant federation, the National Federation of Peasant Organizations (PAKISAMA) was formed, linking local PhilDhrra-assisted farmer and fisherfolk associations that had not yet joined existing federations.

PAKISAMA was established to seek the political and economic empowerment of its peasant group members. It lobbies for changes in national policy that benefit peasants. It is also involved in development projects aimed at supporting peasant demands at the local level and in creating economic alternatives to tenant farming and low-paid agricultural labor.

The end of the Marcos dictatorship signalled a new climate of openness for political action in the Philippines. Rural development NGOs and peasant associations deliberately moved into a new arena of involvement – agrarian reform and rural development policy advocacy.

In 1987, however, the NGO community saw that its lobbying had only limited influence on the passage of meaningful agrarian reform legislation. Landlords and their allies dominated the Philippine Congress, and peasant groups remained fragmented. The Comprehensive Agrarian Reform Program

(CARP) which the congress approved exempted much of the country's farmland from redistribution, and tied up distribution of the land it did cover ("carpable" land) in massive amounts of red tape.

NGOs recognized the need to bring together the many peasant organizations to present a stronger voice to the government. Various efforts led to the formation of the Congress for a People's Agrarian Reform (CPAR), a significant umbrella group of peasant associations around the country. This coalition was composed of twelve major regional and national farmer, fisherfolk, and rural women's organizations and federations representing a wide range of ideological orientations. It is supported by an equal number of intermediary development NGOs. The process of building this coalition has been slow, and has focused not only on the substance of the coalition's program, but more importantly on establishing trust and cooperation among the coalition leaders. CPAR has drafted a much more substantial agrarian reform law called the People's Agrarian Reform Code, and campaigns actively to replace CARP with this broader legislation.

Since 1989, PhilDhrra has sought to complement this advocacy program with an initiative to carry out agrarian reform on the ground. This program, called the Tripartite Partnership for Agrarian Reform and Rural Development (TRIPaRRD), involves the cooperative efforts of development NGOs, grassroots peasant associations, and the national and local government. Initially, it facilitated the transfer of carpable lands to farmers in three provinces.

Drawing on its early experience and successes, the partnership has expanded to cover other provinces and to involve new NGOs and peasant groups. After taking office in 1992, the new President of the Philippines, Fidel Ramos, appointed a rural development NGO leader as secretary of agrarian reform. This should speed up the process of land redistribution. ■

Maria Christina M. Liamzon, former PhilDhrra national coordinator, is a fellow of the People-Centered Development Forum and a Rome-based international development consultant.

Haiti: Grassroots Development Depends On Democracy

by Juana Rodriguez

International NGOs have worked on development projects in Haiti for many years, often in partnership with grassroots groups, such as farmer associations and cooperatives. Haiti's recent experience shows why countries must address the problems of political stability and representative government before true development can take place at the community level.

One example of the partnerships between foreign development NGOs and grassroots Haitian groups is the Cocoa Project of the Mennonite Economic Development Associates (MEDA). From early 1981 until October 1991, MEDA exported cocoa produced by eleven Haitian cooperatives to the United States. MEDA acted as a "benevolent exporter" to ensure that co-ops paid farmers a dividend on every pound of cocoa they brought in.

The co-ops with which MEDA worked were among hundreds of indigenous groups active in Haiti. These groups seemed to spring up along the country roads travelled by NGOs' jeeps. It is some-

times said that all a NGO needed to perform development work in Haiti was a presence in a local community, a list of needs, and an "animator" (staff person) to "animate" the list right out of the community. The needs for seeds, clean water, and sanitation are tremendous, and rural Haitians are eager to make progress, elect leaders, keep financial records, and organize work brigades.

But drastic changes occurred in October 1991. A military coup dashed the hopes of the vast majority of the population for a new era of democratic government. Community organizations working on development projects became illegal, because the military viewed people working together for economic and social progress as supporting ousted President Jean-Baptiste Aristide. The intense grassroots activity sparked by Aristide's seven-month government quickly fizzled.

The year 1991 had been a special one for Haiti and its people. They had given Aristide, a populist Catholic priest, a landslide victory in the country's first truly democratic balloting after years of dictatorship, including thirty years of autocratic rule by the Duvalier family. The charismatic new president seemed to awaken a people who for years appeared to passively accept their fate. Before 1991, it was common to hear people say, "*Si bondieu voule*" ("If God wants").

At the end of 1990 and during most of 1991, development work became easier because people had a larger stake in the decisions made for both their community and country. At farmers' group meetings, Aristide's phrases were always used to motivate and engage people in activity: *"Pa manje soup demokrasi ak fwochet"* ("You can't eat democracy's soup halfway with a fork, you have to drink it all in");

Haiti's recent experience shows why countries must address the problems of political stability and representative government before true development can take place at the community level.

"Lavalassemen" ("Like an avalanche of mud from overflowing rivers, slow, steady, and strong are the people of Haiti demanding democracy"); *"Tet ansamn"* ("Heads together solving problems"); *"Pral chita sur tab la, pa en ba tab la"* ("We'll sit around the table, no longer under the table"); and *"Men ansamn, chaj pa loud"* ("Hands together, the load is not so heavy"). Development workers often referred to Aristide when encouraging cooperative members to take responsibility for keeping their leaders honest. The president had called for people to take it upon themselves to assure *transparans* (clean books and business affairs).

On January 7, 1991, Haitians had taken such responsibility, flooding the streets of the capital to block the Duvaliers' former secret police chief from staging a coup before Aristide could take office. The demonstrators said, "No one will rob us of the ability to ensure that the person we elected to be our president is sworn in and enters into office, as elected."

Aristide was extremely unpopular with both Haiti's wealthy citizens and the army. They viewed him as a threat to their entrenched privileges. The coup which overthrew him came on September 30, 1991.

The aftermath has been frightening. The military government has suppressed grassroots groups and terrorized its opponents with torture, arbitrary arrests, and random killings. This government has earned money by smuggling and drug dealing, effectively evading the embargo imposed by the Organization of American States to restore democracy. Some aid agencies, desperate to end the political stalemate, have resumed their programs in Haiti. But popular participation in development and efforts to address the root causes of hunger, poverty, and injustice cannot re-

sume until the military regime exits and the legally-elected government is restored.

As this report went to press, there were signs that United Nations mediation efforts would succeed in bringing Aristide back. Perhaps Haiti will again have fertile ground for development. ■

Juana Rodriguez, a former media associate at Bread for the World, worked for Catholic Relief Services and MEDA in Haiti.

Voluntary Agencies In Jordan
by Daniel U.B.P. Chelliah

Over the past few years, Jordan's voluntary agencies have shifted their emphasis from providing welfare to involving poor communities in sustainable development. A major reason for this change has been the need to integrate into society half a million Jordanians and Palestinians who returned from jobs in the Persian Gulf during the 1990-1991 Gulf war.

Many of Jordan's private voluntary agencies have patrons in the country's royal family. Groups, such as Queen Alia's Jordan Social Welfare Fund, the Noor Al Hussein Foundation, the General Federation of Jordanian Women, the local branches of the Young Women's Christian Association, the Jordan Business and Professional Women's Club, the Middle East Council of Churches (Jordan Branch), and the General Union of Voluntary Societies help returnees to resettle. They also provide assistance to development projects in poor communities in rural and urban areas. Other intermediary organizations, such as the Development Employment Fund, Agricultural Credit Corporation, and National Aid Fund, finance income-generating

CASE STUDIES

projects to shield poor people from the impact of sharp reductions in government spending.

Voluntary agency development projects target vulnerable groups, such as women and children, Palestinian refugees, and low-income Bedouin farmers. The projects support day-care and primary health centers, train women in skills that enable them to become wage-earners, and promote income-generating, rural home-based activities, such as gardening, rug weaving, dairy production, animal husbandry, sewing, tapestry making, leather stitching, pottery, embroidery, and food preservation. Women also receive training in family planning, child care, nutrition, and hygiene, so that they can become primary health-care outreach workers.

Agencies offer credit for starting small-scale commercial enterprises, carrying out agricultural activities, and improving rural infrastructure.

Many Jordanian voluntary agencies and churches work in partnership with international nongovernmental development organizations, including Save the Children Federation (U.S.), Catholic Relief Services, Caritas, the Mennonite Central Committee, and the Adventist Development and Relief Agency. The goal is to empower local communities by offering new skills, encouraging the use of appropriate technologies, and stressing sustainability. ■

Daniel U.B.P. Chelliah is coordinator, Refugee Affairs, at BFW Institute.

Over the past few years, Jordan's voluntary agencies have shifted their emphasis from providing welfare to involving poor communities in sustainable development.

Transforming Media Coverage of Hunger

Feeding stories on television vastly outnumber stories on the causes of hunger.

by Kraig Klaudt

Imagine a group of environmental activists planning ways to save the planet. In an effort to publicize their cause and rally public support, they sail out to sea on their ship "Rainbow Servant." En route, they encounter a leaking oil tanker and a few whaling boats. Rather than confront them, the environmentalists quickly navigate around them and head to the location of numerous harpoon-injured whales, seals, and dolphins. With cameras rolling, the crew provides medical assistance to the most desperate-looking of the sea creatures.

As inconceivable as this might seem, these are the very tactics used by the majority of those concerned about hunger.

While the most effective social movements have mobilized the public around the causes of a crisis, anti-hunger organizations have rallied the public around assisting the victims. Certainly, a feeding movement should use these tactics to draw attention to the immediate needs of hungry people. They are at best, however, only partial strategies for mobilizing an anti-hunger movement to eliminate the root causes of hunger.

Most anti-hunger organizations, even those involved in emergency feeding, are usually concerned about addressing the causes of hunger. However, their most widely publicized activities are related to soup kitchens, food shipments, and emergency relief. Anti-hunger activists frequently lament that reporters and the general public show little interest in examining lasting solutions to hunger. Their experience has been that stories about feeding crises get the most media attention. As Bob Geldof, the rock musician most responsible for the biggest media event on hunger, observed, "Long-term aid is less exciting than the Seventh Cavalry arriving with food to bring people back to life. And that's a problem."[1]

While it is easy to fault the media for this coverage, anti-hunger activists share responsibility. Organizations championing hunger issues can be spoiled by the media coverage they receive from journalists who flock to their side during feeding crises. As a result, these organizations have not developed the capacity or commitment to publicize adequately the causes of hunger, especially through television. Nor have they become as savvy or daring as promoters of other social causes.

It is doubtful that a powerful anti-hunger movement can be mobilized without media coverage. It is also unlikely that significant public policy changes to end hunger will be achieved in the absence of the media.

Media Coverage of Hunger in the 1980s

The peak in both media coverage of, and public interest in, hunger during the past decade surrounded the 1984-1985 famine in Ethiopia. For some anti-hunger activists, this frenzy of media coverage surrounding starvation and relief efforts demonstrated television's capacity to draw mass attention to hunger and mobilize a public response. For others, it displayed television's ability to mislead society about important hunger issues.

In either regard, 1984 was the year anti-hunger activists witnessed the enormous power of television. Numerous photos and stories had been printed about the famine in Ethiopia before the first camera crews arrived. In 1983, a photographer for *The Denver Post* returned from Ethiopia with grim photos, which were published in that paper and in a few other dailies.[2] *The Washington Post* had already written five articles, *The New York Times* had printed twelve pieces, and dozens of AP reports had been filed prior to October 1984.[3] The television networks, however, initially delayed covering the famine:

> It is well known that both the European network of broadcasters (Eurovision) and NBC in New York rejected the Ethiopian story. In fact the NBC line-up editor just did not want to know. He suggested that there were far more important domestic stories.[4]

Yet, it was not until camera crews filmed the crisis that the story was able to

"Long-term aid is less exciting than the Seventh Cavalry arriving with food to bring people back to life. And that's a problem."

On July 13, 1985, the LiveAid concert was staged simultaneously in Philadelphia and London, reaching an audience of 1.5 billion people and raising $87 million.

command public attention. On October 23, 1984, footage of massive starvation in Ethiopia, filmed by Mohamed Amin and narrated by Michael Buerk, was transmitted by the British Broadcasting Corporation (BBC). Viewers saw throngs of skeletal bodies. The same day, NBC's London bureau convinced the network to broadcast the footage that evening to a U.S. audience.

After the BBC report alerted the public to Ethiopia's crisis, the entertainment industry popularized the issue and kept it on the national agenda. Within days of the BBC broadcast, Geldof, lead singer of the Boomtown Rats, formed Band Aid and recorded "Do They Know It's Christmas?" In the United States, Harry Belafonte and Ken Kragen organized USA for Africa and recorded the song, "We Are the World." On July 13, 1985, the LiveAid concert was staged simultaneously in Philadelphia and London, reaching an audience of 1.5 billion people and raising $87 million.

While a feeding movement came to life around the famine, far fewer gains were made in mobilizing an anti-hunger movement. Relief workers frequently spoke of the need for long-term development, yet this was reported as a side story to the much larger feeding drama. For example, little if any media attention was given to a legislative campaign on Africa headed by Bread for the World and other anti-hunger advocacy organizations. That campaign ultimately led to an emergency assistance and long-term development bill which provided $800 million to Africa, almost ten times the money raised by LiveAid.

Extensive coverage of hunger within the United States can be traced back to Michael Harrington's book, *The Other America*, and the CBS documentary, "Hunger in America" in the mid-1960s. Both of these exposés

helped mobilize the public to make substantial gains in addressing domestic hunger. Twenty years later, many of those gains had been reversed. Anti-hunger organizations proved to be no match for the budget cuts of the Reagan administration. In 1986, Hands Across America was organized to draw attention to rising hunger and homelessness in the United States. An estimated five million people held hands and formed a human chain at points across the United States to show solidarity with hungry people.

Domestic anti-hunger activists proved more capable than international hunger agencies in forming large coalitions to campaign against hunger. The Coalition on Human Needs and the Coalition for America's Children, for example, focused directly on the root political causes of domestic hunger. Anti-hunger advocacy groups eventually succeeded in winning back some of the funding for federal food programs. However, despite lots of opinion polls, grassroots strategies, and public service announcements, these efforts ultimately failed to provide the drama required to make hunger an urgent political issue during the 1980s.

A Critique of Hunger Coverage

Journalists have prepared many memorable articles and features on hunger. Each year, *WHY* magazine receives hundreds of worthy nominations for its annual awards for excellence in reporting hunger issues. Nevertheless, feeding stories vastly outnumber the occasional anti-hunger story. Anti-hunger activists raise a number of common concerns about coverage of hunger:

The structural causes of hunger are frequently ignored. Journalists often personalize poverty and hunger and approach it exclusively as a human interest story. According to one survey of network news coverage of poverty issues between 1981 and 1986, the networks were twice as likely to tell the personal story of a person living in poverty than to report about poverty as a general social issue.[5] In presenting the details of one person's lack of nutritious food, there is often little mention of the underlying causes or public policies which have caused his or her misfortune. According to Michael Moss, a reporter for *Newsday*:

> *The vast majority of news reporting on hunger that I've found in surveys is merely human interest, and anecdotal, and the political result of such reporting leaves the public focused on the poor themselves. That focus varies in flavor from time to time, from being critical of the poor in blaming them for their plight, to being sympathetic with the poor in feeling sorry for their condition, and perhaps charitable. What seldom is conveyed to media consumers is that there are very real causes to poverty, and to hunger, which can be traced and reported by journalists.*[6]

The media tend to reduce complex stories down to their most basic elements. Radio and television news shows, having limited time to present the day's news, tend to discourage thoughtful explanation and encourage glib sound bites. "It's difficult to explain in thirty seconds why people are starving in Sudan; especially when most people don't know where Sudan is," explained one anti-hunger activist. Hunger is not alone in receiving this kind of coverage. Ernest Hemingway once observed,

> *After I finished high school I went to Kansas City and worked on a paper. It was regular newspaper work: Who shot whom? Who broke into what? Where? When? How? But never Why, not really Why.*[7]

The "whys" of a story do get told when someone has been savvy enough to dramatize their dynamics creatively. In the 1980s, Oxfam UK and Ireland was able to generate extensive media coverage on one of the leading, albeit most complicated, causes of hunger – the international debt crisis. The provocative advertising campaign showed that for every dollar raised from LiveAid events, the Third World was sending $2 back to industrialized nations in debt repayments.

Poor and hungry people are often portrayed as dependent and helpless. Based on the images they see on television, many North Americans believe the people of sub-Saharan Africa are emaciated and unable to feed themselves. Africans are frequently shown as inactive or wandering, passively receiving the aid provided to them by overworked Western relief workers. Similarly, a typical image of a hungry person in the United States is that of an unemployed minority street person. On the contrary, the majority of hungry people in the United States are white, live outside urban areas, and are either children or adults employed at wages below the poverty level.

Anti-hunger agencies are guilty of perpetuating these images by using "point and weep" communications strategies. To draw attention to the severity of the situation, the most explicit photos and footage of destitution and starvation are used to

What seldom is conveyed to media consumers is that there are very real causes to poverty, and to hunger, which can be traced and reported by journalists.

Public Opinions on Hunger and Poverty

Public polls on poverty and hunger challenge the conventional wisdom that people are uninformed or apathetic about the causes and solutions to hunger. Polls show that there is a core audience of perhaps ten million to twenty million people who believe that domestic poverty and homelessness are the most important problems facing this nation. This core constituency is much larger than the constituency for protecting the environment.[8]

Another surprise is the public's lack of confidence in efforts to solve poverty and hunger. One poll showed that only 7 percent of people believe that poverty will be eliminated in the United States in the next ten years. This compares to 42 percent who believe that AIDS will be cured within ten years, and 42 percent who believe we will put an astronaut on Mars.[9]

This pessimism might be attributable to the fact that the public sees a feeding movement and not an anti-hunger movement. According to one poll, 55 percent of the population believes that charitable organizations seldom or never make a difference in solving the problems of poor people. Roughly 60 percent of the population feel the government should spend more to address poverty and childhood hunger.[10]

In polls conducted annually from 1973 through 1989, an average of 74 percent of those polled believed the United States spends too much on foreign aid, and only 5 percent believed the United States spends too little.[11] On the other hand, one of every five adults in the United States purchased the recording, "We are The World," during the Ethiopian famine, indicating a potential willingness to become involved in addressing world hunger.

raise money and attract public attention. George Alagiah, international development correspondent for BBC TV News, calls them "stick baby" photos. These images, while lubricating dollars from the hands of donors, fail to tell the complete story of very ingenious and determined people trying to find a way out of a terrible situation. In reference to Africa, Michael Parenti asks why other stories are not told:

> There are a thousand fascinating stories that could be told about Africa. . . . Africans who have struggled with great courage for independence and revolution; Africans who try to hold their families and cultures together, confront generational and gender conflicts arising from changing social conditions, live in modern African cities and deal with the problems of urbanization, and fall in love and have dreams for themselves and their children; Africans who are underpaid laborers yet organize labor unions, churches, communities, and businesses, fight to get an education, and build mass political organizations under oppressive conditions.[12]

The very language of the hunger debate helps perpetuate images of helplessness and dependence. Foreign *aid* and *welfare*, for example, are terms of a feeding movement. Other terms, such as *food security*, *sustainable development*, and *self-reliance*, might be more useful in articulating that hungry people want the means of feeding themselves.

Hunger and poverty are only reported when there is a crisis. Mohamed Amin, one of the first camera people to film the Ethiopian famine in 1984, explains the realities of the media business:

> In a commercial world where the media have to sell themselves to survive, visual impact is everything. From a ratings point of view, war and suffering are preferable to peace and contentment. Perverse as it may sound, human tragedy now has a certain entertainment value. So if it hasn't got a body count, it's not going to rate.[13]

It also seems to help if the body count is Caucasian rather than African, Latino, or Asian. Somalia had been in the midst of chaos for more than a year before becoming the focus of media attention. As late as July 1992, *The New York Times* was devoting more attention to the fate of African elephants and rhinos than to the situation faced by the Somali people.[14]

The closing or consolidating of foreign news bureaus has contributed to the lack of early reporting on overseas hunger crises. Approximately 150,000 journalists work for U.S. media; only 420 of them are assigned to foreign news bureaus,[15] the vast majority in industrialized countries. As a result, more U.S. reporters cover the New York Yankees than the entire continent of Africa.

Domestic anti-hunger activists face the opposite challenge in presenting their issues to the media. Hunger in the United States does not have a readily visible body count. The peril of hundreds of American children would normally be the week's top news story, as was the case when a search for a group of children missing in a blizzard in Michigan captivated the national media. However, the deaths of more than a hundred children each day from preventable hunger- and poverty-related illnesses is not seen to be newsworthy.

Anti-hunger advocates are seldom television guests. Journalists usually seek the supposedly less-biased opinions of scholars and federal agency spokespeople, rather than the opinions of advocates who are openly biased. In 1989, Fairness & Accuracy in Reporting released a study of 865 episodes of "Nightline" which showed that 80 percent of the guests were professionals, government officials, or corporate representatives, while only 7 percent were from public interest, advocacy, labor, or racial/ethnic organizations.[16] A similar study of the "MacNeil/Lehrer Newshour" guest list found its ratio to be 87 percent to 6 percent.

Hunger issues are rarely framed in moral terms. A study of media coverage of five important social issues in the late 1980s found that journalists framed the issue in terms of its moral implications only 4 percent of the time. Journalists were many times more likely to frame the story in terms of its economic implications, conflict, human impact, or victimization of powerless people. While journalists rarely report on the moral dimensions of social issues, most people become involved in social issues because of deeply-held values. According to the study:

> *Regardless of the medium in which they work, journalists eschew the moral frame which figures prominently in the public's understanding of issues. The public, in contrast, relished and drew out the moral dimension in the human impact of issues, and underscored the moral dimensions of public policies.*[17]

There are some exceptions. Social issues such as abortion, gay and lesbian rights, and pornography are frequently framed in moral terms. Conservative religious leaders such as Jerry Falwell, Pat Robertson, and Bishop John Spong, are often called upon by the media to discuss the ethical consequences of various public policy decisions. It is not uncommon for a *Time, Newsweek,* or *U.S. News* cover story to feature the morality angle of a public policy controversy which involves sexual ethics. Yet the starvation of thousands of people each day in a world of abundant resources is covered almost exclusively as a crisis, human interest or economic story – not a story which concerns personal or public morality.

The very language of the hunger debate helps perpetuate images of helplessness and dependence.

The Public Relations Capacity of Anti-Hunger Organizations

Because of their ownership of media outlets and vast advertising budgets, corporations possess enormous power to shape the words and images consumed by society.

Discussions on improving media coverage of hunger usually end at this point. Anti-hunger activists share their list of frustrations and grievances, and reporters attempt to explain the realities and constraints of their profession. The discussion often fails to consider the potential of news sources, such as anti-hunger organizations, in shaping reports of their issues. Quite often, the discussion also fails to acknowledge the opportunities available to social movements to create their own news coverage.

Very little is known about the public relations capacity of the anti-hunger movement. Little documentation exists on the amount of time, skills, and budget devoted to publicizing hunger. In general, information about hunger comes from political institutions, corporations, and local and national anti-hunger agencies.

Political Institutions

The importance elected officials place on public relations has been well-documented. Presidents, members of Congress, governors, and state legislators are very media-conscious. Federal agencies alone spend more than $2 billion on all public affairs-related activities.[18] Agencies such as the U.S. Department of Agriculture, U.S. Department of Health and Human Services, and the U.S. Agency for International Development (AID) frequently provide the media with information on hunger-related issues. The press secretaries of many congressional offices and committees also provide reporters with valuable information. In addition, various United Nations agencies wage publicity efforts around hunger and development issues.

Corporations

U.S. corporations spend nearly $125 billion each year on advertising,[19] with a growing share devoted to cause-related marketing strategies. Very little of this money, however, is spent on hunger-related issues. Because of their ownership of media outlets and vast advertising budgets, corporations possess enormous power to shape the words and images consumed by society. Various labor unions and trade associations are also involved in hunger and poverty issues. The Home Builders Institute, for example, has been one of the leading advocates for the Job Corps.

Local Anti-Hunger Organizations

Many local anti-hunger agencies publicize hunger issues to media in their communities. A survey of local food banks found that 71 percent attempted to influence media coverage. The average food bank was annually involved in nineteen newspaper or magazine stories and twelve television stories. Seventy-one percent of the stories were exclusively about the food bank, while 29 percent were about hunger and poverty in general. Twenty percent of the food banks urged specific policy changes as part of their media efforts.

A Survey of National Anti-Hunger and Poverty Organizations

National anti-hunger and anti-poverty agencies have perhaps the greatest capacity for publicizing hunger issues. Yet the vast majority of their publicized activities are focused on responding to hunger crises and raising funds, rather than preventing hunger crises.

In March and April 1993, BFW Institute conducted half-hour phone interviews with the media or public relations directors of the twenty-five largest charitable organizations focused on hunger, development, poverty, or low-income issues, including Second Harvest, Catholic Charities, CARE, and World Vision. Interviews were also conducted with the media or public relations directors of twenty-five of the most influential or visible hunger-related research, advocacy, or educational organizations, including Interfaith/Impact, the Center on Budget and Policy Priorities, and the Institute for Food & Development Policy.

Staffing. Approximately eighty-five full-time professional staff do media relations for these fifty organizations. This low number is surprising, given the amount of media attention devoted to feeding crises and hunger fund raising. Predictably, the largest anti-hunger organizations employ the largest media staffs. Surprisingly, half the largest organizations, with annual budgets between $10 million and $650 million, had yet to establish a media unit of more than two people. Most anti-hunger agencies are staffed to respond to media inquiries, not to initiate substantial issue-related media strategies.

Budget. Half the media directors reported having no set publicity budget. The remainder reported media budgets, excluding personnel costs, spread almost evenly along a wide range from $3,000 to $300,000. When personnel costs are included, a more accurate picture emerges as to the resources anti-hunger organizations devote to public relations. Fifty of the top anti-hunger organizations, with budgets totalling $3 billion, spend approximately $7.5 million on public relations, or

roughly 0.25 percent of all expenditures. It is fair to say that most anti-hunger organizations depend mainly on direct mail, newsletters, and paid advertising for external communication.

Collaboration. Forty percent of those surveyed reported collaborating with more than one other national anti-hunger organization on a media strategy. The Food Research and Action Center and InterAction were most frequently mentioned as partners in a collaborative media strategy.

Message. All totalled, 88 percent of the media efforts by these hunger organizations is devoted to fund raising and general public education on hunger. Only 12 percent is devoted to advocacy or influencing specific hunger legislation.

Target Medium. Anti-hunger organizations are primarily print-oriented in disseminating their messages. The majority of organizations surveyed devote the largest share of their media efforts to reaching newspapers. Only 15 percent identified television as the primary medium.

Strategies. Anti-hunger organizations make extensive, perhaps excessive, use of news releases. More than 75 percent of the organizations reported preparing at least one news release each month. In all, these fifty top anti-hunger organizations produced more than twenty-five hundred different news releases in 1992, an average of fifty per organization. Domestic anti-hunger agencies tended to make greater use of media events, charts, and graphs than their international counterparts.

Successful Tactics. Building and maintaining relationships with reporters was most frequently mentioned as an agency's most successful media strategy. Tying media strategies into the day's headlines, using eyewitness reports from those

Fifty of the top anti-hunger organizations, with budgets totalling $3 billion, spend approximately $7.5 million on public relations, or roughly 0.25 percent of all expenditures.

Fifty of the largest anti-hunger organizations together have the equivalent of only three full-time media staff devoted to the task of persuading television to cover public policy issues that affect hungry people.

visiting crisis regions, and taking journalists on site to crisis regions were also frequently mentioned. The media director of a large relief agency put it bluntly:

Disasters work. That's when the doors open. People say that you should think about cultivating media coverage other times, but I disagree. You should optimize your opportunities during emergencies.

Results. Only half of anti-hunger organizations measure their media results. The vast majority of those that do use a news clipping service and simply count the number of placements. A few of the larger organizations reported more extensive evaluative methods, such as measuring the equivalent advertising value of their coverage, or using polling and focus groups to measure the impact of their strategies on specific audiences.

Attitudes Toward Media Coverage of Hunger. Five common themes emerged from responses to the question, "Why, in your estimation, did hunger issues not receive greater coverage?" They include: hunger is old news, not sexy enough, too unpleasant, doesn't affect the average American, and doesn't sell newspapers. A number of media directors took issue with the question's assumption and expressed satisfaction about the amount of coverage hunger was receiving.

Future Strategies. Most media directors were hopeful that in the future they could devote more time toward attracting television coverage, increase their connections with public relations staff in other anti-hunger organizations, and increase personal contacts with journalists. Most media directors agreed that these efforts would be difficult to accomplish without greater

support by their organization for proactive public relations strategies.

The most astounding discovery from the survey is that fifty of the largest anti-hunger organizations together have the equivalent of only three full-time media staff devoted to the task of persuading television to cover public policy issues that affect hungry people. No magic bullet exists for creating an anti-hunger movement and reducing hunger. However, unless more energy is devoted to televising the anti-hunger message, the public will not even see the target.

Making the Anti-Hunger Movement Visible

Existing anti-hunger organizations should not only continue to address the immediate needs of hungry people, but should also help ignite an anti-hunger movement. Five challenges await anti-hunger activists in their efforts to draw media attention to the causes of, and solutions to, hunger. To help mobilize an anti-hunger movement that brings about social change, anti-hunger organizations and corporations should employ five strategies to dramatize an anti-hunger message creatively on television.

The movement must find a common message and vision. While there is frequent talk among anti-hunger activists about long-term development, public policy changes, and "teaching people how to fish, rather than giving them fish," these efforts are seldom highly visible. The public sees photos of people without fish, fund-raising campaigns to buy fish, and plane loads of fish being rushed into disaster areas. There is far less noticeable activity around helping people acquire fishing poles and ensuring them a place on the shore.

Most anti-hunger activists agree that the causes of hunger should be addressed. The problem lies in getting these activists, in practice, to emphasize that message as the most visible aspect public of communication. The current message being communicated is "feed hungry people," which evokes charitable responses. The anti-hunger movement must also present a call to "prevent hunger" and evoke feelings of passion.

The message of the anti-hunger movement should appeal to people's self-interest or to their deeply-held beliefs and convictions. It must also be a message upon which most actors in the movement can agree. However, it must go beyond a feeding message. Too often anti-hunger organizations have assumed that by simply showing enough pictures of hungry people, society will somehow understand the dynamics of preventing hunger. The message of the anti-hunger movement should be accurate as to the causes. The message must be presented in a way that allows people to understand the nature of the problem, and what needs to be done to solve it.

Part of the message is that hunger is human-made, not an act of nature or an ever-present tragedy. Similarly, because humans have the power to both cause and prevent hunger, it is necessary to ask which humans hold that power and inquire how they are using that power.

Greater collaboration would also help anti-hunger organizations unify their message and gain a more powerful voice in the media. While there seems to be very little collaboration on media strategies presently, a number of efforts show promise. Recent domestic anti-hunger campaigns have brought different organizations together around common media strategies. InterAction, the association of international relief and development organizations, is just forming a media working group. Oxfam America is in the process of establishing a speakers bureau for hunger experts from a wide range of organizations. Several suggestions emerged from the recent BFW Institute consultation on media coverage of the causes of hunger, including a monthly teleconference among media directors, or a common hunger daybook, which would regularly inform journalists about upcoming anti-hunger events.

The anti-hunger movement must take its message to television and to Hollywood. A social movement cannot succeed without television. Put simply, television will determine whether people will think about ending hunger. Television

> . . . is the Great Legitimator. TV confers reality. Nothing happens in America, practically everyone seems to agree, until it happens on television.[20]

The anti-hunger movement is still working on its capacity to present an anti-hunger message to television. It still relies heavily on paper rather than developing contacts and designing media opportunities. Unfortunately, the virtues of one's issue are rarely the most important requirement in gaining television coverage. According to a producer of CBS's "60 Minutes":

> When an idea (for news) comes in, my first reaction is always "Does anybody care? Is anyone gonna watch this?" It's not important in TV what you tell people. If you bombard them with a lot of facts in

"TV confers reality."

a dull fashion just to discharge your public duty, you perform no service at all. If you can entertain people, you can keep them close to the show and they'll come back next week.[21]

Not only does television determine whether people will *think* about ending hunger, it plays a significant role in determining what people *do* about ending hunger. Entertainment television, perhaps

Practical Steps For Anyone to Transform Media Coverage of Hunger

Become a local media activist. Editorial board meetings, letters to the editor, and op-eds in your local newspaper are key to influencing your members of Congress to support specific legislation for poor and hungry people. For example, Bread for the World and RESULTS have extensive networks for helping people publicize domestic and international hunger issues in their local media outlets.

Encourage the networks to create a development desk. Send letters to the major networks, especially CNN, to encourage them to assign at least one person to be a full-time "development correspondent" to report on long-term overseas hunger and development issues.

CNN's address is: 1 CNN Center, P.O. Box 105366, Atlanta, GA 30348. Telephone: (404) 827-1500

more than issue debates on "Nightline," plays a leading role in influencing public behavior and opinion. For example, when Fonzie got a library card on the TV sitcom "Happy Days," tens of thousands of children did the same thing.[22] According to Norman Fleishman:

Entertainment is the most powerful form of communication in the world. It throws your defenses to the winds, you're captured, you're part of it by definition. You go

someplace else and come back, whereas if somebody's lecturing or giving you facts in a documentary, your mind produces little responses. Somebody pushes, you push back. Entertainment isn't pushing, it's attracting – it takes you inside a new world.[23]

The environmental movement has been particularly successful in using entertainment to instill new values in society. People are far less tolerant of environmental polluters than they were ten years ago. Hollywood movies such as *The Medicine Man* and *Fern Gully* have helped people emotionally identify with the environmental cause. Environmental organizations have been successful in persuading some of Hollywood's biggest names – Meryl Streep, Robert Redford, Paul Newman, Sting, and Tom Cruise – to endorse their cause. Yet surprisingly, the potential constituency for an anti-hunger movement may be larger than that for the environmental movement. (See "Public Opinions," p. 71.)

Can television help create a "zero-tolerance" for hunger the same way it has created a "zero-tolerance" for environmental evils? An episode of "Star Trek: The Next Generation" modeled this view of the world. Captain Jean-Luc Picard informs a twentieth century businessman who has just been unfrozen,

A lot has changed in the past 300 years. People are no longer obsessed with the accumulation of things. We've eliminated hunger, want, the need for possessions. We've grown out of our infancy.

The End Hunger Network in Los Angeles is making headway in enlisting celebrities, screen writers, and producers in the fight to end hunger. In the late 1980s, the entertainment community arranged a week during which five network comedies featured hunger themes and provided toll-free numbers to call and offer help. In 1993, the End Hunger Network brought a group of stars to Washington to fast for a day with U.S. Rep. Tony Hall (D-Ohio). Hall's fast was a personal testimony to the continuing importance of hunger issues, following the demise of the House of Representatives Select Committee on Hunger.

The anti-hunger movement needs to dramatize its concerns by using celebrities, activities, untold stories, symbols, and events (C.A.U.S.E.) to galvanize public opinion. The media directors surveyed repeatedly expressed difficulty in placing long-term development and hunger policy stories on television. There is some reassurance in realizing that this was also the initial experience of the AIDS, environmental, and civil rights movements. A review of media coverage of other social movements in the United States in the last thirty years reveals that common strategies eventually emerged which succeeded in attracting mass media attention to complex issues. For example, in the case of the civil rights movement:

> *The sit-ins, the marches, the rallies, the Freedom Rides, the boycotts, the terminology used, the places selected and the time were all carefully manipulated to the advantage of the Movement, and King served as the impetus for them all. Methodically and systematically he and his entourage of followers masterminded campaigns that would change public opinion regarding the rights of blacks in America. . . .[24]*

More than half of the public relations directors of the fifty anti-hunger organizations interviewed named either Sally Struthers or the late Audrey Hepburn as the national celebrity or spokesperson they most readily identified with the issue of hunger. Both individuals have made enormous contributions in rallying public support to assist the victims of hunger crises. No individual, however, was consistently identified with anti-hunger issues.

It is revealing that national spokespeople from most social movements are not from Hollywood. More likely, they are prophetic individuals who have suffered under the particular social problem the movement seeks to eliminate. This suggests that an anti-hunger movement would benefit from a national spokesperson who has experienced poverty and hunger. For example, Audrey Hepburn's credibility as a spokesperson probably was due in part to her life being saved by a UNICEF program during the Dutch famine of the 1940s.

The public is fascinated with the protest techniques used by movements. Creative activities which challenge established powers make good television drama. Such activity can have an extensive media life as it is directed toward new and more powerful forces. Rep. Hall's hunger fast drew significant media attention. It was surprising that a member of Congress would fast for weeks. The fast had an element of protest and drama.

The untold story is the television special that usually becomes the topic of conversation around office water coolers the next day. It is the book that everybody is reading. Many movements have captured a place on the national agenda by presenting a previously untold story, causing a nationwide exclamation of "I didn't know

The anti-hunger movement needs to dramatize its concerns by using celebrities, activities, untold stories, symbols, and events.

As in other media dramas, the "untold story" does not receive national attention by accident.

things were *that* bad."

As in other media dramas, the "untold story" does not receive national attention by accident. When Hollywood has been involved, such as the "Maude" episode on abortion in November 1972, it has usually been the result of a lobbying effort by an advocacy organization. Likewise, almost every book version of the "untold story" is much more than a well-written manuscript. It is also a well-crafted media tour and publicity event.

Symbols are important in telling the story of a complex issue. Movement symbols serve as shorthand methods to represent solidarity with complex structural issues in a world where there is little time for explanation. Highly visible symbols also signal to the world that a social movement exists and is worthy of attention.

Mega-events are often needed to catapult a movement into the public eye. For example, *Newsweek, Time, Harper's, New York, Smithsonian, Sports Illustrated,* and *TV Guide* each published special issues coinciding with Earth Day 1990, and the networks presented special features on the environment.

Events are risky, as they require large investments of time and money and do not always succeed. For example, few people remember Drums Across America, a benefit concert for Native Americans which featured Stevie Wonder and Rita Coolidge. Publicity events can also backfire. In 1979, the media reported on the scars left by tractors on Washington, D.C., roads during Tractorcade, rather than on farm and agriculture issues promoted by the event.

Hunger, among social causes, has had its share of national media events. Generally, however, the drama of these events has been attuned to a feeding response as

opposed to demanding that the causes be addressed.

Anti-hunger activists should pool their creativity and publicity experience to help launch an anti-hunger movement. In particular, World Food Day, observed annually in 150 nations on October 16, provides the potential for a larger-scale event that would focus on the causes of, and solutions to, hunger.

Two factors become apparent in studying the C.A.U.S.E. approach for lessons in mobilizing a successful movement. First, successful movements usually generate controversy. And second, successful movements often identify a villain – an enemy who stands in the way of their mission.

The anti-hunger movement would benefit from a prophetic, controversial, and confrontational element. Very few people demonstrate anger about the millions of malnourished humans while the world has the capacity to feed everyone. Animal rights activists, in contrast, throw blood on fur coats because animals are dying. Greenpeace activists harass whaling ships. But massive numbers of preventable, hunger-related deaths have not morally enraged anti-hunger activists to take dramatic action.

Social movements must often hold a person or institution responsible to get the attention of those in power and to engage the interest of the public. During the oil spill off the coast of Alaska, public attention was rightly focused on Exxon as well as on the wildlife victimized by the disaster. Likewise, ACT-UP was able to encourage increased research into AIDS treatments by targeting Burroughs-Wellcome and the U.S. Food and Drug Administration with negative publicity.

During the crises in Ethiopia and Somalia, in contrast, most anti-hunger activists agreed that it had not been wise for the United States to have flooded the region with arms and ammunition in the 1980s, only to abandon it. Yet the same activists were not of one clear, audible voice in assigning blame for this human-made disaster. The recognition that specific people and institutions are responsible for most hunger-related deaths, and the willingness to hold them accountable, is necessary for eliminating the causes of hunger.

Anti-hunger organizations must develop their public relations capacity. The anti-hunger movement has barely begun to spend money on publicizing anti-hunger issues. The fifty anti-hunger agencies surveyed devote only $7.5 million each year to media relations, compared to the $1.5 billion Phillip Morris spends each year promoting its products. The Tobacco Institute and its public relations staff spend nearly $20 million a year trying to soften the fact that reportedly 350,000 people die annually of ailments linked to cigarette smoking.[25]

The same anti-hunger agencies employ just eighty-five public relations professionals, only ten of whom focus on changing U.S. government policies that affect poor and hungry people. In the context of the entire media and public relations industry, there are 150,000 public relations practitioners in the United States, or at least one for each of the 130,000 journalists.[26] In Washington, D.C., ten thousand public relations professionals court approximately five thousand journalists.[27] The U.S. Department of Defense has a public affairs budget of between $47 million and $100 million and between one thousand and three thousand information officers.[28] If one of the biggest anti-hunger issues of the past decade has been the federal budget battle between defense spending and human needs programs, anti-hunger publi-

cists have literally been outnumbered a thousand to one.

Few successful social movements, if any, capture the media spotlight by accident. There is as much competition to gain visibility on the national issue agenda as to be the nation's "cola of choice." It is not by accident that the nation often seems to care more about the fate of spotted owls and laboratory animals than malnourished children:

> *Public awareness is not an aspiration that you can only yearn for but is something that you buy. You pay in your time, your skill, and your budget – for consultants, printers, and other suppliers to communications professionals – and what you get for that is awareness.[29]*

Few stories make the news without a sizable public relations effort. One study of network news coverage found that nearly 70 percent of all stories were preplanned.[30] According to an editor of *The Wall Street Journal,* "Ninety percent of daily coverage is started by a company making an announcement for the record."[31] Anti-hunger activists can no longer afford the dreamy idealism that the simple virtue of their cause will attract media attention. More staff and money are needed to successfully publicize hunger issues.

The anti-hunger movement must enlist the help of corporations. Corporations are key to any serious attempt to address and publicize the causes of hunger. Anti-hunger activists need not only to draw attention aggressively to detrimental behavior, but also to court positive corporate involvement in seeking solutions. Unfortunately, anti-hunger activists often

Public awareness is not an aspiration that you can only yearn for but is something that you buy.

Yet even self-serving reforms are a beginning step toward social change.

view corporate partnerships as a liability, rather than a means of changing society by engaging its most powerful institutions.

Corporations can provide an influx of new funding to the anti-hunger movement. For example, Kraft General Foods financed the Food Research and Action Center's extensive examination of domestic hunger among children. Crest toothpaste found a natural link with Save the Children to promote a campaign to fund oral health and nutrition programs for impoverished children.

Corporate marketing and advertising efforts can dramatically increase public awareness of hunger issues. Recently, fashion advertisements featuring both handicapped and elderly people helped to reduce public stigmas and reshape social norms. Ben & Jerry's 1,000 Pints of Light campaign changed the flavor of President Bush's initiative by awarding pints of light frozen desserts to worthy community volunteers. A Trade, Not Aid marketing campaign by the cosmetic company The Body Shop has made it more fashionable to talk about trade and development.

Corporations are a powerful force in public policy decisions. For example, the Chamber of Commerce and many individual corporations have been fierce opponents of legislation to increase the minimum wage. On the other hand, the chief executives of AT&T, Bell South Corporation, Prudential Insurance, Honeywell, and Sky Chefs provided hungry people a great service when they testified before the House Budget Committee in 1991 in support of increased funding for the Special Supplemental Food Program for Women, Infants, and Children (WIC).

Many anti-hunger activists worry lest corporations use social issues only to benefit their corporate image. A corporate

polluter might make nominal contributions to an environmental group while continuing to damage the environment. Former Du Pont CEO, Irving Shapiro stated, "You'd have to be blind and deaf not to recognize the public gives a damn about the environment, and a businessman who ignores it writes his own death warrant."[32] Yet even self-serving reforms are a beginning step toward social change. Moreover, purity of motive should not be a precondition for anti-hunger activism, whether by corporations, donors, journalists, members of Congress, or citizen advocates.

Conclusion

Increased and improved media coverage of hunger is needed not for its own sake, but for its power to bring about social change. Numerous commentators have noted the nearly unavoidable relationship between media coverage and social change. According to Daniel Schorr, senior news analyst for National Public Radio, "If you don't exist in the media, for all practical purposes, you don't exist."[33] There is also a strong relationship between being on the media agenda and being on the political and legislative agenda. Over a hundred years ago, Abraham Lincoln observed that, "Our government rests on public opinion. Whoever can change public opinion can change the government." More recently, Theodore White explained:

No major act of the American Congress, no foreign adventure, no act of diplomacy, no great social reform can succeed in the United States unless the press prepares the public mind. And when the press seizes a great issue to thrust onto the agenda of talk, it moves action on its own — the cause of the environment, the cause of civil rights, the liquidation of the war in Vietnam, and, as climax, the Watergate affair were all set on the agenda, in the first instance, by the press.[34]

This chapter has emphasized the need to be proactive in developing dramatic strategies to heighten public visibility on anti-hunger issues. Presently, the anti-hunger movement is dwarfed by the feeding movement. Ending hunger requires that this relationship be reversed.

Journalists, anti-hunger activists, and members of the feeding movement are all essential to building an anti-hunger movement. In 1960, Edward R. Murrow produced a memorable documentary on migrant farmworkers titled "Harvest of Shame," which helped inspire a whole generation of activists for low-income people.

The tears hadn't yet dried in the CBS-TV screening room when Edward R. Murrow declared that the final scene was all wrong for his documentary on migrant farmworkers, "Harvest of Shame."

His colleagues were surprised. They had thought the effect of a young woman singing a sorrowful tune extraordinary. It tore at the heart. But Murrow didn't want to leave viewers feeling mere pity. He wanted anger. He wanted lasting concern. And he wanted viewers to understand the economic and

political forces that kept migrants sleeping on piles of straw and their school-age children toiling in the fields.

Repeatedly in the film he drew attention to the dearth of laws protecting their welfare. So, in the final frames, Murrow dubbed in the question, "Is it possible we think too much in terms of Christmas baskets and not in terms of eliminating poverty?" He then concluded, "The people you have seen have the strength to harvest your fruit and vegetables. They do not have the strength to influence legislation. Maybe we do. Good night, and good luck."[35]

Three decades later, a potential anti-hunger movement of millions of people awaits its call. Unfortunately, it is a social movement unaware of its own existence. It knows much about Christmas baskets but too little about legislation. Understandably it is fatigued with compassion and longs for lasting changes. Journalists and anti-hunger organizations have the capacity to ignite this movement with dramatic anti-hunger stories, and in so doing, to unleash great political power. ∎

Kraig Klaudt is external relations and advocacy officer, Tuberculosis Program, World Health Organization. He previously served as director of media at Bread for the World.

BFW media associate Marissa Buckanoff assisted in data collection for this chapter.

Journalists and anti-hunger organizations have the capacity to ignite this movement with dramatic anti-hunger stories, and in so doing, to unleash great political power.

Thirty Years of Anti-Hunger Advocacy

by Patricia L. Kutzner

Photo: Joseph Crachiola

Hunger advocacy in the United States began in the 1960s with a zeal to end poverty in the developing countries and, at home, the "war on poverty."

I n 1992, after members of Congress received more than 100,000 letters from constituents and local newspapers ran over one thousand articles in support of the Horn of Africa Recovery and Food Security Act, the legislation passed unanimously, despite the unpopularity of foreign aid and the prevailing "America first" mood of the country.

In 1993, as in 1992, the House of Representatives passed the Mickey Leland Childhood Hunger Relief Act that would end hunger in most households qualifying for food stamps. Also in 1993, for the first time, a president submitted a federal budget calling for full funding by 1996 for the Leland act.

These developments would be unthinkable in the present political climate of the United States aside from the hard work of anti-hunger activists carried on faithfully, win or lose, over many years.

Anti-hunger advocacy in the United States arose from two drives that began in the 1960s – a zeal to end poverty in developing countries that launched the First United Nations Development Decade, the Peace Corps, and U.S. Agency for International Development (AID); and, at home, the "war on poverty."

Background to World Anti-Hunger Advocacy

When the United Nations (U.N.) General Assembly declared the First Development Decade in 1960, the benefits of investment in modern, large-scale industrialization were widely expected to "trickle down" to eliminate poverty. B. R. Sen, of India, head of the Food and Agriculture Organization of the U.N. (FAO), pressed for investment in agriculture and rural development as a wiser course. FAO launched a worldwide advocacy movement of citizen volunteers called the Freedom From Hunger/Action for Development Campaign. Its objectives were to raise public awareness about rural poverty and development, collect private donations for grassroots self-help projects, and promote political will for official development aid to improve agriculture and rural development.

The American Freedom From Hunger Foundation (AFFHF) was weaker than its counterparts in some other countries. But in 1963, it hosted the First World Food Congress of the Freedom From Hunger/Action for Development Campaign. President Kennedy challenged the delegates:

> So long as freedom from hunger is only half achieved, so long as two-thirds of the nations have food deficits, no citizen, no nation can afford to be satisfied. . . .We have the means, we have the capacity to eliminate hunger from the face of the earth in our lifetime. We need only the will.

AFFHF started Young World Development (YWD), a youth program that sponsored 190 local "walks for development" between 1967 and 1970. In 1971, YWD organized an International Walk for Development Weekend in more than three hundred U.S. communities, involving a million walkers.

In the late 1960s and early 1970s, famines in Biafra and Bangladesh evoked massive outpourings of generosity. But it took the world food crisis of 1973-1974 to provoke a new wave of advocacy on behalf of hungry people worldwide. Bread for the World and several other anti-hunger advocacy organizations started at about that time.

Origins of Advocacy to End Hunger in the United States

Advocacy against hunger in the United States started in the mid-1960s. President Kennedy's concern about Appalachia and Michael Harrington's 1962 book, *The Other America,* drew political and public attention to hunger and poverty at home. The federal government significantly expanded food assistance programs for low-income families.

In 1965, the National Council of Churches of Christ in the U.S.A. (NCC, the umbrella organization of mainline Protestant denominations), the Presbyterian Church in the United States, the Ford Foundation, and the United Auto Workers union established an advocacy organization called the Citizen's Crusade Against Poverty. Also in 1965, public interest lawyers at Columbia University's Center on Social Welfare Policy and Law began litigation to establish the U.S. Department of Agriculture's (USDA's) obligation to fulfill the intent of federal food legislation. The U.S. Senate set up a Subcommittee on Manpower, Employment, and Poverty to oversee progress in the war on poverty.

In 1967, this subcommittee heard testimony about starving children in rural Mississippi. The Field Foundation sent a team of pediatricians to investigate.

That same year, the Citizen's Crusade Against Poverty enlisted twenty-five civic leaders as a Citizen's Board of Inquiry Into Hunger and Malnutrition in the U.S.A., funded by the Episcopal Church, the United Presbyterian Church USA, and six foundations. In mid-April 1968, the Citizen's Board released *Hunger U.S.A.,* with an introduction by Sen. Robert Kennedy.

At about the same time, *Their Daily Bread,* the report of a national women's Committee on School Lunch Participation,

The federal budget remains advocates' toughest political obstacle.

revealed widespread exclusion of poor children, whether by neglect or intent. The Field Foundation funded this investigation sponsored by Church Women United, the National Board of the YWCA, the National Council of Catholic Women, the National Council of Jewish Women, and the National Council of Negro Women.

Spurred by these reports and the riots which followed the assassination of Dr. Martin Luther King, Jr., the Senate unanimously adopted Sen. George McGovern's (D-S.D.) resolution for a Select Committee on Hunger and Nutrition to investigate the problems of hunger in the United States.

Also in spring 1968, millions of middle Americans who would never read the reports saw the terrible truths in their own living rooms when CBS showed its independent documentary, *Hunger in America*.

Advocacy efforts continued. The NCC established a Crusade Against Hunger to engage the leadership of mainline Protestant denominations and encourage action by local congregations. In New York, a National Council on Hunger and Nutrition replaced the ad hoc Citizen's Board, with Harvard nutritionist Jean Mayer as president and John Kramer as executive director. As chief counsel to the House Agriculture Committee a few years later, Kramer authored most of the far-reaching reforms enacted in the 1977 Food Stamp Act, including elimination of the purchase requirement that kept the poorest people from receiving food stamps, a longtime goal of advocacy groups.

In May 1969, President Nixon told Congress that "the moment is at hand to put an end to hunger in America itself. For all time." Privately, however, he instructed Secretary of Agriculture Clifford Hardin to "use all the rhetoric so long as it doesn't cost money."[1] Then as now, the federal

budget remains advocates' toughest political obstacle. The problem, Kramer told a Children's Foundation conference in 1977, is never that lawmakers do not want children to have enough to eat but that they want other things more.

Nixon asked Mayer to organize a White House Conference on Food, Nutrition and Health in 1969, hoping to get business involved in solving the hunger problem. Mayer drafted Patricia Young from the NCC Crusade Against Hunger to get church groups and grassroots organizations involved. When the White House Conference met in December, the priorities and recommendations from consumer and poor peoples' advocates conflicted sharply with those of the food industry. Nevertheless, in December 1969, Nixon re-emphasized a commitment to end hunger.

In 1970, start-up funding from the federal Office of Economic Opportunity (OEO) helped establish three new, permanent, domestic anti-hunger advocacy organizations – the Children's Foundation, the Food Research and Action Center, and the Community Nutrition Institute.

Many of the pioneer advocacy organizations no longer exist, or have moved on to other issues. The AFFHF, founded in 1961, closed in 1979, bequeathing its name and assets to Meals for Millions, a direct aid agency. The Citizen's Crusade Against Poverty evolved into the Center for Community Change, a technical assistance center for communities seeking federal funds. The Children's Foundation now focuses mainly on childcare issues. The seeds of anti-hunger advocacy which these and other groups planted, however, continue to bear fruit. The trails they blazed are now major highways for Americans exercising their political rights on behalf of hungry people.

A Movement on Two Tracks

Approximately twenty national organizations currently guide the anti-hunger advocacy efforts of hundreds of other organizations, many at the state and local levels. (See pp. 87-89.) They involve hundreds of thousands of U.S. citizens in understanding the issues, the policy-making process, and the strategies of effective advocacy. The ranks of anti-hunger advocacy often are reinforced by the allied efforts of those working on human rights, the status of women and people of color, workers' welfare and fair wages, environmental protection, sustainable agriculture, U.S. relations with particular developing countries, and other issues linked to hunger.

Since the origins of anti-hunger advocacy in the 1960s, domestic and world anti-hunger advocacy have proceeded on parallel, but usually separate tracks. They intersect when Congress reauthorizes the Farm Bill, which covers both the Food Stamp Program and overseas food aid. In 1978-1979, World Hunger Year united both arenas in lobbying to establish a Presidential Commission on World Hunger. Both collaborated again in 1984 under the leadership of Bread for the World to lobby for a House Select Committee on Hunger. But, so far, these convergences are exceptions rather than the normal process in U.S. anti-hunger advocacy.

Some organizations have worked in both arenas. These include World Hunger Year (WHY), co-founded in 1975 by Harry Chapin and Director Bill Ayres; World Hunger Education Service (WHES), this author's organization, founded in 1976 with national church support for *Hunger Notes* and "politics of hunger" leadership training; Clergy and Laity Concerned (CALC), formed in 1965 for anti-Vietnam War advocacy; Seeds, established in 1977 as publisher of *Seeds Magazine* "for Christians concerned about hunger;" the hunger programs of mainline Protestant denominations; many state and local anti-hunger advocacy groups; and AFFHF, Bread for the World, and Interfaith Action for Economic Justice.

All anti-hunger advocacy groups have found funding to be a recurrent problem. Funding for advocacy related to world hunger is especially hard to sustain. Foundation support is typically limited to one-time, short-term grants. Relatively few foundations are willing to fund activities which seek to change public policies.

During the 1960s and 1970s, the U.S. Agency for International Development (AID) was the chief source of funding for AFFHF's work, while member denominations of the NCC gave generous and repeated funding for hunger education and advocacy to a wide variety of state, local, and national organizations. But then a serious decline began, which further compartmentalized anti-hunger advocacy in the United States.

First, AID stopped funding development education by outside sources and AFFHF went out of business. A 1981 congressional mandate cosponsored by Sens. Joseph Biden (D-Del.) and Claiborne Pell (D-R.I.), put AID back into development education funding, but only of one-time seed grants for projects, few of which survived beyond the grant. AID's policy is being revised again as this is written.

For several years following the world food crisis of the early 1970s, special collections in churches and synagogues across the country created bountiful national budgets for world hunger programs which included issue analysis, leadership training, and advocacy. By the end of the

Approximately twenty national organizations currently guide the anti-hunger advocacy efforts of hundreds of other organizations, many at the state and local levels.

State and Local Anti-Hunger Advocacy

by Linda Eisenberg

During a recent state legislative session, an anti-hunger coalition met with one of its elected officials. The delegate chaired a powerful budget committee and had been "voting the state's financial interests" in supporting cuts in public assistance programs. But those votes were hurting many low-income constituents. Coalition members wanted assurance that future votes would satisfy basic needs for food and shelter.

Coalition members who participated in this meeting share many characteristics with anti-hunger advocates of the 1990s around the country, among them:

- They have been providing food for more than a decade to growing numbers of families with children, and to unemployed and working poor people; and

- They are lay leaders and clergy; urban, suburban, and rural; low-income and professional; poor and well-off; all willing to take time from daily tasks to volunteer in the political process.

Advocacy coalitions of the 1990s often focus their work on policy and budget issues in their state capitals. State funding for nutrition programs has been key to anti-hunger efforts since the federal cutbacks of the 1980s in food and other assistance programs for poor people.

Some of these coalitions began as efforts to coordinate and fund emergency feeding efforts during their rapid expansion in the early 1980s. Direct service providers grow increasingly frustrated as demand for their services continues to grow and the same people return repeatedly for food assistance. They have seen their temporary programs become institutionalized.

As they look for other food resources and refer people to the federal Food Stamp Program, school meals, or WIC, other frustrations often set in. For example, they find that an elderly retiree qualifies for only $10 a month in food stamps, and the application process is more complex and embarrassing than she or he is willing to endure for that amount. Or they find that the federal School Breakfast Program is not available locally because the school principal thinks it too disruptive to an academic program already struggling to educate disadvantaged children.

1970s, however, those special funds were dwindling or gone. Then came the 1980s' rapid increase in hunger and homelessness in the United States. Local congregations found their resources stretched to the limit by those in need in their own communities. With hunger funds by now greatly reduced, national religious agencies also turned almost entirely to the domestic arena.

In 1985, the recording of "We Are the World" by forty-five U.S. pop stars attracted mass attention and $58 million for Ethiopian famine victims (some of which the sponsoring group, USA for Africa, channelled to education and advocacy). Otherwise, though, world anti-hunger advocacy lost ground during the 1980s as measured by funding support, public attention, and number of active participants compared with the 1970s. Domestic anti-hunger advocacy, on the other hand, gained headway by every measure.

Today, only Bread for the World, with forty-four thousand members providing three-fourths of its approximately $3 million budget (including funds for the related educational organization, Bread for the World Institute), is able to maintain a program of both domestic and international anti-hunger advocacy. The Food Action Center, spun off from the National Student Association with foundation support in 1975 to promote advocacy leadership on college campuses, lasted only four years. CALC has vanished from the hunger arena, and Seeds is less active than before. Interfaith Action lost $90,000 (about a third of its budget) in contributions from religious agencies in 1988 alone. Now it is part of a new advocacy organization where hunger and international development compete with many other issues. WHES, with a greatly reduced program sustained by individual supporters since the end of major church funding, concentrates on hunger and poverty in developing countries, while keeping an eye on the domestic agenda. WHY's emphasis, after recovering painfully from the tragic death in 1981 of its co-founder and chief patron, the singer Harry Chapin, does the opposite. WHY's quarterly journal continues to have a comprehensive anti-hunger agenda, but all advocacy energy goes into a Reinvesting in America program, promoting the Medford Declaration, and the domestically-focused Campaign to End Childhood Hunger. Some anti-hunger organizations at the state and local levels used to work on both domestic and global hunger, but they now concentrate almost entirely on domestic issues.

The Nature of Anti-Hunger Advocacy

A lobbyist's viewpoint gains weight with a lawmaker when the message also says "I am a voter in your district." The Washington-based advocacy staff of the Food Research and Action Center (FRAC) or Bread for the World, for example, may be able to influence the content of legislation through discussions with members of Congress or their aides. However, legislators' estimates of voter support remain a more critical factor in the final outcome.

In its "softest" or most general form, advocacy says simply "Hunger must stop. It can be stopped, and you can make a difference. Get involved." The Hunger Project's advocacy is a good illustration. The Hunger Project began in 1977 with the initial goal of generating a "critical mass" of popular determination to end hunger.

Another example is the U.S. National Committee for World Food Day, initiated in 1981 by the Community Nutrition Insti-

And so the providers, already overwhelmed by disbursing food, information, referral, and other assistance, look increasingly to public policy solutions.

Coalition advocacy has become increasingly sophisticated in its ability to document needs and recommend solutions. In many states, coalitions get public policy attention by working with a governor's or legislature's task force on hunger or nutrition. Other coalitions participate in FRAC's Community Childhood Hunger Identification Project.

State advocacy efforts to expand the School Breakfast Program, obtain supplemental funding for WIC, or secure food stamp outreach funds are often helped by their affiliation with FRAC's National Campaign to End Childhood Hunger, focused on strengthening the federal child nutrition programs. These well-coordinated state-level wins have led to an impressive increase nationwide in the number of nutritious meals available to children in the United States.

At the same time that legislators are being sympathetic to children's nutritional needs, the economic base of many low-income families is under attack. In state capitals across the country, advocacy efforts are shifting increasingly toward welfare reform.

As the recession lingers, swelling welfare rolls contribute to budgetary pressure. Growth in public assistance expenditures, combined with enduring stereotypes about the "typical" welfare client, contributes to dramatic cuts in benefit levels and a range of proposed new criteria to qualify for public assistance. These include children's school attendance ("learnfare"), nonvoluntary community service when paying jobs cannot be secured, and even fingerprinting.

While federal food programs provide a vital nutritional floor for many Americans, the roles of federal and state governments in meeting basic needs are changing because of the federal deficit and state budgetary constraints. Anti-hunger advocates, like other Americans, are trying to understand, and influence, the new shape that government will take. Traditionally, advocates have argued for client rights while government has pressed for client responsibilities. Advocates are increasingly challenged to articulate the respective responsibilities of governments, at the local, state, and national levels, and individuals.

The United States has the resources to ensure every family *food security* – access to a diet that is nutritionally adequate and available through normal channels. As advocates seek to make food security for all a reality, they should keep a few common-sense principles in mind:

• People who work need to earn a wage that enables them to meet their needs;

• Parenting is a form of work, and society has an obligation to assure the well-being of every child;

• People who cannot work, because of age, disability, drug addiction, or over- or under-skill, also need income and opportunities adequate to meet their needs;

• Communities need policies that support keeping resources at home and managing them for their common benefit; and

• A sustainable agriculture system can preserve natural resources and produce nutritious foods to be consumed close to the source of production.

When we get "out of our boxes" in the way we think about hunger and poverty – about work, family, community, food production, and what we reward economically – we will succeed in getting an ample food supply onto the kitchen tables of all our families.

Linda Eisenberg is executive director of the Maryland Food Committee. The committee funds self-reliance projects and operates program partnerships with state and local agencies for delivery of food and nutritional benefits. It engages in public policy advocacy at the national, state, and local levels.

tute and World Hunger Education Service. The committee now includes 450 member organizations. Every year on World Food Day, October 16, the committee, coordinated by Patricia Young, encourages local groups across the United States to plan activities on themes relating to food and hunger. In 1984, the committee began also to produce an annual teleconference where panels of experts discuss hunger policy issues and reply to questions from audiences at nearly one thousand participating sites, mainly college campuses. "Soft" advocacy of this kind broadens the base of citizen support for policies that might be legislated some time in the future, but is quite different from "hard" advocacy – lobbying Congress or the president to seek the enactment and implementation of specific public policies.

Anti-Hunger Lobbies

Of all the advocacy organizations working on hunger, only three were founded as public interest lobbies – RESULTS, Bread for the World, and Interfaith Action/Interfaith Impact. Their supporters must forego income tax deductions, although each has an affiliated educational organization that receives tax-deductible contributions.

RESULTS

The newest lobby is RESULTS, founded in 1981 under the leadership of Sam Harris. Its members are trained to build political will for legislation by writing opinion articles for newspapers and communicating directly with policy makers, helping win significant gains for UNICEF's child survival campaign, AID microenterprise lending, and the rural poverty alleviation programs of the U.N. International Fund for Agricultural Development. In 1990, RESULTS mobilized 250,000 people in the United States and a million around the world at candle light vigils in support of the World Summit for Children. Policy implementation of the summit's goals is currently its main agenda. Above all, Harris stresses, RESULTS is about "healing the break between people and government."

Bread for the World

The oldest of the three lobbies is Bread for the World, "a Christian citizens' lobby" begun in 1973 by a committee of seven Catholics and seven Protestants. Rev. Arthur Simon was appointed executive director in January 1974. There were about four hundred dues-paying members when national recruiting began in mid-1974. By 1980, membership exceeded thirty thousand. In 1990, it stood at forty-four thousand, with 240 active groups organized by congressional district and one thousand affiliated congregations. Upon Simon's retirement in 1991, David Beckmann, a Lutheran pastor who had formerly worked on environmental and anti-poverty policies at the World Bank, became president.

Bread for the World's founders explained why they chose the organization's name, even though they recognized that hunger was a reflection of poverty and underdevelopment:

> *Precisely because we want to show the link between hunger and poverty, between hunger and injustice. . . . A tactical matter is also involved [in using] hunger as a key metaphor: (1) it singles out the most acute aspect of poverty; (2) it is nonideological; (3) there already exists a large, demonstrable constituency in the churches for assisting the hungry; and (4) the hunger problem, when pursued, leads people into the wider issues of poverty and justice. In short, if we are serious about reaching middle Americans for the cause of the underdeveloped countries, this is not a bad starting point.[2]*

Critics (including this author on occasion) sometimes charge that Bread for the World fails to challenge adequately the biases of middle America in order to end the causes of hunger. Feeding hungry people is not enough, critics say, unless it also addresses the political and economic structures at home and abroad that perpetuate systemic inequities.

Bread for the World's founders acknowledged "a strong tendency for people to favor policies that correspond to the level of their understanding."[3] But each year's campaign, known as an Offering of Letters, evokes many thousands of letters to the president and Congress. Campaign themes are chosen for obvious need as well as likely membership support and then interpreted in short background papers. Lawmakers from both parties know that Bread for the World's positions will not be viewed as too radical among their constituents, and they know many voting citizens will support these positions. The solutions Bread for the World advocates may at times seem naive to some hunger experts, but when the votes are counted, Bread for the World's position is often a winner.

Interfaith Action/ Interfaith Impact

The third direct anti-hunger lobby, the Interreligious Taskforce on U.S. Food Policy, evolved following the World Food Conference of November 1974. A major Working Session on World Hunger convened by

Lawmakers from both parties know that Bread for the World's positions will not be viewed as too radical among their constituents, and they know many voting citizens will support these positions.

the NCC gave high priority to influencing U.S. food policy. NCC's World Food Conference observer, Larry Minear, became development policy representative in Washington, D.C., for Lutheran World Relief and NCC's Church World Service. The Interreligious Taskforce, with strong support from NCC member denominations, was drawn from the Washington, D.C., staff of more than twenty Protestant, Catholic, Jewish, and ecumenical organizations. George Chauncey, director of the Washington Office of the Presbyterian Church in the United States, was the first chairperson. The initial operating budget of $52,000 provided by these agencies nearly quadrupled in four years.

By 1982, the taskforce had taken on a broader agenda of justice issues and changed its name to Interfaith Action for Economic Justice. In 1990, a merger with IMPACT (see below) formed Interfaith Impact for Justice and Peace, comprising a larger number of Christian, Jewish, and Muslim social justice agencies and advocates at the national, state, and local levels.

If Bread for the World has stressed Christian compassion in its anti-hunger advocacy, the stance of the taskforce and Interfaith Action (Bread for the World was a member of both) can be characterized as one of prophetic justice. Beginning in 1977, high-level members of the Carter admininstration actively sought the group's advice and courted its support. Its activity and influence grew steadily. Through IMPACT, policy papers of the Interreligious Taskforce reached fifty thousand religious leaders and advocates nationwide, and the organization was represented at major international conferences on hunger and development issues.

In 1982, when the taskforce became Interfaith Action, it established work groups on domestic human needs (including tax, health, and welfare issues), U.S. food and agriculture policy, and international development (including international economic issues), assisted by two or three full-time policy staff. Member agencies still provided about 90 percent of the budget, but this was becoming more and more difficult to sustain.

Rather than developing its own membership base, Interfaith Action, aided by denominational and NCC staff, strengthened its grassroots links through dialogue with local and regional groups close to the problems of economic justice. This strategy led to coordinated lobbying with state interfaith agencies and minority farmer organizations that won legislation aimed at preserving minority farmer ownership. The organization also held meetings around the country to hear local views about employment issues.

Multi-Issue Lobbies With a Hunger Focus

Three national faith-based organizations founded to lobby on broader peace and justice agendas have often worked on hunger: the Friends Committee on National Legislation (FCNL), established by Quakers in 1943; Network, established in 1971 by members of Catholic women's religious orders; and IMPACT, a grassroots interfaith lobby started in 1967 to support the war on poverty and oppose the war in Vietnam. IMPACT reached its peak membership of about ten thousand in the mid-1970s.

Research and Information As Advocacy

The primary task of most other advocacy organizations is to gather, analyze, and present information that aids policy-related thinking. These organizations seek to establish the facts, understandings, and fresh insights from which sound policy on the many interrelated aspects of hunger can emerge. In addition to the organizations already mentioned which maintain a combined domestic-international perspective, there are a number of important organizations working in only one of the two arenas.

On the international side, the Institute for Food and Development Policy, or Food First, founded in 1975 by Frances Moore Lappé and Joseph Collins, and the Development Group for Alternative Policies (Development GAP or D-GAP), founded in 1977 by former Peace Corps volunteers Fred O'Regan and Steve and Doug Hellinger, attempt to make international development efforts more supportive of self-reliance among poor and disadvantaged groups. The Center of Concern, founded in 1970 by North American Jesuits, was inspired by "Vatican II" to advocate international justice in solidarity with the world's poor people. The World Hunger Program at Brown University, started in 1985 with a grant from philanthropist Alan Shawn Feinstein, is the only U.S. world anti-hunger advocacy organization (as distinguished from direct-aid provider) that focuses more on nutrition intervention to ameliorate the effects of poverty than on poverty eradication itself.

Worldwatch Institute is best known for publications concerning the sustainability of world food and energy resources. It was founded in 1974 with Rockefeller Foundation support by Lester Brown, a former USDA international agricultural development expert.

The Overseas Development Council (ODC), established in 1969, is the oldest and most prestigious U.S. international development advocacy organization. The dual purpose of its founding members representing corporations, labor unions, universities, foundations, the news media, and civic groups, was to build U.S. understanding of global interdependence and to generate support for U.S. policies alleviating underdevelopment. Starting with major grants from the Ford and Rockefeller Foundations, the ODC's Board of Directors engaged Lester Brown as the first senior fellow and James Grant, a retired foreign service officer, as CEO (Grant left in 1980 to become executive director of UNICEF). Father Theodore Hesburgh, president of Notre Dame University, was elected council chairman in 1972.

In 1974, ODC lent a senior fellow, Martin McLaughlin, as executive director for the World Hunger Action Coalition based at AFFHF. That same year, ODC convened approximately one hundred Catholic, Jewish, Protestant, and Orthodox leaders in a landmark interfaith "Consultation on Global Justice." Following the World Food Conference of 1974, Hesburgh continued to rally consultation participants to lobby a reluctant President Ford for an increase in U.S. food aid to Africa and Asia. World food issues gradually faded from ODC's agenda during the 1980s, however.

In the arena of domestic anti-hunger efforts, an acknowledged advocacy leader is the Food Research and Action Center (FRAC), established with federal government funds in 1970 to improve the operation of federal nutrition programs by conducting research and providing legal counsel on behalf of recipients. Since 1986, FRAC has been directed by Robert Fersh.

The Center on Budget and Policy Priorities began in 1981 with a Field Foundation grant to analyze Reagan administration food policies. Director Robert Greenstein has established the center's influence as a reliable source of analysis on U.S. budget

When the Reagan admininstration's fiscal 1982 budget closed down CSA, this also ended the agency's Community Food and Nutrition Program.

issues affecting low-income people.

At Public Voice for Food and Health Policy, started with foundation support in 1982, Director Ellen Haas continued the research and consumer advocacy she previously directed for the Community Nutrition Institute. Haas became President Clinton's Assistant Secretary of Agriculture for Food and Consumer Services in May 1993.

The Center on Hunger, Poverty, and Nutrition Policy was started at Tufts University in 1991 by Professor Larry Brown, former chairman of the Harvard School of Public Health. He directed the research and advocacy efforts of the Physicians' Task Force on Hunger in America from 1984 to 1987 and is one of the principal authors of the Medford Declaration.

The Community Nutrition Institute (CNI) was a key center of advocacy on U.S. hunger and food policy from 1970 until 1982. Director Rodney Leonard, USDA food program administrator at the end of the Johnson admininstration, started CNI with a grant from the Office of Economic Opportunity (OEO) to publish a newsletter on federal nutrition policy from a low-income consumer perspective. CNI's activities soon expanded to include policy advocacy, training for food program admininstrators, and, during the Carter admininstration, technical assistance to local anti-hunger groups funded by the Community Services Admininstration (CSA, OEO's successor).

When the Reagan admininstration's fiscal 1982 budget closed down CSA, this also ended the agency's Community Food and Nutrition Program which, from 1972 to 1981, had supported a wide variety of local and national programs to improve nutrition assistance. After Congress restored the program in 1984, grants were restricted to local organizations.

Both CNI and FRAC had been major recipients of CSA support. The end of the agency meant a sudden and drastic reduction in the two organizations' budgets. At CNI, the only program surviving beyond 1981 was the *CNI Weekly Report* (now *Nutrition Week*). CNI had already been publishing the newsletter without government funds since 1973 after its board, incensed by OEO censorship during the Nixon admininstration, returned the balance of the original OEO grant.

FRAC, under Nancy Amidei's leadership from 1980 to 1984, survived by trimming salaries and staff, and intensely wooing private funding. In January 1983, FRAC began *Foodlines,* a monthly report on hunger news. By 1984, forty-one foundations, corporations, law firms, labor unions, and religious agencies were sustaining FRAC's vital advocacy work. Since 1982, the federal Legal Services Corporation has maintained FRAC's legal counsel service (about 5 percent of its budget), while private funding for research and advocacy now regularly exceeds $1 million a year.

Advocacy Coalitions

Cooperation critical to the success of advocacy is sometimes hampered by organizational turf battles and competition. Nevertheless, advocacy coalitions are more the rule than the exception.

The World Hunger Action Coalition of 1974 (WHAC), directed by ODC's Martin McLaughlin and chaired by AFFHF president Herbert Waters, included Church Women United, the National Board of the YWCA, several major private foreign aid agencies, the National Farmers Union, and many other religious and secular organizations. They lobbied for positive U.S. action at the World Food Conference, and secured

400,000 signatures on a petition urging Congress and President Ford to increase U.S. food aid and support a "new world food security system" and long-range improvement of agriculture in developing countries.

Subsequently, other coalitions worked on world hunger issues:

- The Infant Formula Action Campaign, initiated in 1977 by the NCC Center on Corporate Accountability, led efforts to establish an International Code of Marketing of Breastmilk Substitutes, which is monitored by the U.N.'s World Health Organization;

- Advocacy coalitions led jointly by Bread for the World and the Interreligious Taskforce gained a U.S. farmer-held grain reserve established in 1977, a U.S. Emergency Grain Reserve to backstop food aid supplies in 1980, and numerous food and development aid reforms to promote self-reliance, to better serve disadvantaged groups, and to advance the cause of human rights;

- In the 1980s, cooperative advocacy, often led by Bread for the World and RESULTS, won marked increases in U.S. foreign aid to Africa, the International Fund for Agricultural Development, the child survival programs of UNICEF and AID, the U.N. Development Fund for Women, and the International Training and Research Institute for Women;

- Interfaith Action and D-GAP led a coalition on developing country debt issues; and

- FCNL, a key member of Interfaith Action, led the formation of another very broad coalition to engage citizen involvement in the 1992 U.N. Conference on Environment and Development.

Stopping the "War on the Poor"

The most dramatic example of the power of coalitions comes from domestic anti-hunger advocacy in the 1980s. The first three rounds of food program cuts enacted by Congress in 1981 and 1982 reduced food stamp benefits approximately $1.5 billion in 1982, $1.3 billion in 1983, $2 billion in 1984, and $2.1 billion in 1985. The Special Supplemental Food Program For Women, Infants, and Children (WIC) and school nutrition programs fared better, but not well.

Then the initial shock passed. The domestic anti-hunger lobby recovered its morale, private funders renewed FRAC's strength, and advocates fought more vigorously than ever to preserve the remains of a severely weakened "safety net" for low-income people. Leaders from a wide range of organizations at state, local, and national levels developed strategies to combine their complementary strengths. Together they:

- Formed coalitions linking service providers and advocacy groups at all levels;

- Documented the facts of local hunger, such as "Hunger Watch U.S.A." surveys by Bread for the World members in twenty-seven towns and cities in 1983, and visits to twenty-five states by the Physicians' Task Force on Hunger between 1983 and 1987. Since 1987, most ambitiously, FRAC's Community Childhood Hunger Identification Project (CCHIP), designed by community nutritionist Cheryl Wehler, has continued this effort;

- Publicized facts from federal data analyzed by the Center on Budget and Policy Priorities;

Victory was especially sweet to domestic anti-hunger advocates when Congress passed the Hunger Prevention Act of 1988.

- Supplied firsthand testimony from local experience before congressional committees;

- Deluged Congress with voter messages;

- Carried out a media blitz using television and local and national newspapers (with more than eleven thousand articles and interviews generated by the Physicians Task Force alone); and

- Registered hundreds of thousands of new low-income voters, even as they waited in soup kitchen lines and welfare offices. This was the most extensive voter registration drive since the civil rights campaign of the 1960s. It was started in 1983 by the NAACP, joined by the League of Women Voters, the NCC, Interfaith Action, and many others.

In spring 1984, FRAC and the National Anti-Hunger Coalition of poor people's organizations and advocates in forty states (first convened by FRAC in 1979) launched a campaign called Feed American Communities Today. In 1987, FRAC began a series of annual conferences that drew each year more than four hundred advocates, service providers, federal food program admininstrators and recipients, legal services attorneys, state and federal policy makers, and students.

There were more coalition efforts. A Fair Budget Action Campaign banded together organizations from more than a dozen separate political movements, as did the March on Washington for Jobs, Peace, and Freedom in August 1983, commemorating the March on Washington led by Dr. Martin Luther King, Jr., twenty years earlier. Interfaith Action, working closely with the Center on Budget and Policy Priorities, launched a media and lobbying campaign in 1982-1983 under the motto "the poor have suffered enough." Bread for the World's 1987 letter-writing campaign, combined with actions by other organizations in the growing WIC coalition, generated sufficient support to secure a funding increase that allowed 150,000 more nutritionally-vulnerable women, infants, and children to enroll in the program in 1988. USA for Africa sponsored Hands Across America in May 1986, linking people in a human chain from coast to coast and generating $20 million in contributions for local efforts against hunger and homelessness.

Victory was especially sweet to domestic anti-hunger advocates when Congress passed the Hunger Prevention Act of 1988 and President Reagan, dropping his veto threat, signed it. Key supporters included Sens. Patrick Leahy (D-Vt.), chairman of the Agriculture Committee, and Edward Kennedy (D-Ma.), and Rep. Leon Panetta (D-Calif.), chairman of the House Subcommittee on Nutrition. The act included the largest increase in food program benefits since 1977, authorizing more than $4.5 billion from fiscal 1989 through fiscal 1993.

But the act, fully implemented, would restore only about 40 percent of the benefits lost to cutbacks earlier in the decade, even in combination with all other expansions in food assistance enacted since 1982.

During the 1988 presidential campaign, more than seventy-five thousand people signed petitions urging full funding for WIC. Nevertheless, President Bush's fiscal 1990 budget proposed a $21 billion cut in domestic programs, including WIC and other federal food programs. His fiscal 1991 budget proposed cuts of nearly half a billion dollars in these programs. Advocates geared up again.

At the beginning of 1989, Bread for the World, FRAC, the Center on Budget and

Policy Priorities, and WHY spearheaded a campaign for WIC's reauthorization and full funding. By May, congressional offices were deluged with candles from thousands of constituents repeating Bread for the World's motto: "Keep WIC Lit!" WIC was reauthorized and gained the biggest funding increase in five years, opening the program to 200,000 more beneficiaries.

Advocacy lost an inspiring congressional leader in August 1989 when Rep. Mickey Leland, (D-Tex.), chairman of the House Select Committee on Hunger, died in a plane crash in Ethiopia. The following February, to extend the gains of the Hunger Prevention Act, Representative Panetta, chairman of the House Budget Committee (in 1993, he became President Clinton's budget director), introduced the Mickey Leland Memorial Domestic Hunger Relief Act. Reintroduced each succeeding year, the Leland act finally received funding in the Budget Reconciliation Act for fiscal 1994.

Advocacy in the 1990s

The generosity of the U.S. political and private response toward hunger – in attention, concern, action, and money – rises and falls with the peaks and lows of "sudden" crises "discovered" by television, political leaders, religious leaders, and heroes of popular culture, then "resolved" and forgotten. The most remarkable achievement of organized anti-hunger advocacy in the United States is its persistence since 1970 despite the fickleness of public interest. Domestic hunger obviously holds a steadier place in the U.S. political agenda (and in the priorities of private giving) than does hunger and poverty in developing countries.

The roots of hunger crises are never sudden, of course. They always have a long history. And, since most cases of undernutrition in the United States, as in developing countries, stem from chronic lack of food and do not fit the crisis image anyway, people suffering from hunger are never hard to discover when anyone cares to look. The unsung heroes of anti-hunger advocacy are advocates and their supporters who continue to look at the hunger issue long after almost everyone else has turned attention to other issues, until the next wave of crisis excitement hits and hunger is "discovered" again.

There are perennial questions of strategy among anti-hunger advocates. How can advocates gain the most salutary possible influence on public policy? Is it through "numbers," how many people they can point to as supporters of their positions? Is it through "pragmatism," how "doable" the proposals are in an imperfect world? Is it through "wisdom," how ultimately beneficial the recommendations would be if put into practice? Far from being academic questions, these are the subject of many ardent and sometimes bitter debates among advocates.

Political advocacy has been most successful whenever advocates found allies among committed members of Congress, large numbers of organized voters lobbied in support, and the news media created the impression of broadly favorable public opinion. The story of domestic anti-hunger advocacy during the 1980s exemplifies how effective advocates can be when, collectively, they do not merely stand back and wait for "history" to favor their cause but go out and intentionally generate that history.

Sustainable advocacy needs a sustainable budget for permanent staff, newsletters, offices, mailing lists, and the other accoutrements of a regularly active organization.

The most remarkable achievement of organized anti-hunger advocacy in the United States is its persistence since 1970 despite the fickleness of public interest.

Sustainable advocacy needs a sustainable budget.

This, in turn, is most likely to be possible with a very broad base of funding sources, whether these be the forty-four thousand individual members of Bread for the World or the foundations, labor unions, businesses, and religious groups that account for most of FRAC's budget. The American Freedom From Hunger Foundation closed in 1979 after seventeen years, not because the need for such an organization ceased, but because not enough private money was found to replace the AID grants and contracts upon which AFFHF had depended.

"Band-Aids or Cures?"

How much effort to devote to programs that feed people now and how much to reserve for measures that will allow people to feed themselves over the long term is the constant dilemma for anti-hunger advocacy. Both the domestic and international streams of the movement wrestle continuously with this problem. Experience shows that it is far easier to muster political support for immediate, humanitarian action than for the painful, controversial changes in the distribution of economic and political power that may be required to end hunger's recurrence both within the United States and internationally. Sooner or later, most policy advocates yearn to address those deeply rooted causes, but a shrinking membership and fewer funds are the likely consequences of pursuing that path very far or very long.

There is always a risk of losing essential backing from "the troops" if an organization's staff tackles an issue or takes an advocacy position that is too far from where the members and funders are willing to go. Then the whole advocacy effort loses credibility and with it, the organization's future viability. Many observers of recent U.S. church history cite "too radical" advocacy – or the perception of it – as a major reason for declining social action and hunger program budgets in Protestant denominations formerly the mainstay of organizations like Interfaith Action and, during its years of greatest activity, WHES.

Advocates who focus on world hunger have tended to deal more with development and empowerment than domestic anti-hunger advocates, who have focused mainly on the federal food programs. When hungry people themselves are asked what they want, they always much prefer an opportunity to earn a living to programs of assistance.

Some advocates on the domestic anti-hunger side are calling for more emphasis on dealing with the causes of hunger. The "Medford Declaration to End Hunger in the U.S." prescribes two steps: full funding of existing federal food programs to "virtually eliminate domestic hunger by 1995," and "economic self-reliance for most American households by the year 2000." The second is to be achieved through measures "to increase the purchasing power of employed heads-of-households so that work raises families out of poverty." The declaration was drafted in 1990-1991 by WHY, FRAC, and the Center on Hunger, Poverty, and Nutrition Policy at Tufts University. It has been endorsed by hundreds of organizations with millions of members across the country.

The inspiration for the Medford Declaration came from a statement of priorities for reducing hunger in developing countries, "The Bellagio Declaration: Overcoming Hunger in the 1990s," produced in 1989 by twenty-three experts from fourteen countries convened at the Rockefeller Foundation Conference Center in Bellagio, Italy by the Brown University World Hunger Program. This declaration also focuses on both immediate and long-range action to lessen hunger, though the emphasis is on short- to medium-term efforts. Its four targets are to eliminate deaths by famine, cut malnutrition in half for mothers and small children, eradicate iodine and vitamin A deficiencies, and end hunger in half the poorest households. The first three, the experts agreed, can be done, as demonstrated in many places, by relatively inexpensive, practical methods. The fourth goal, moving into the economic causes of hunger, is more difficult to achieve.

Actions and policies that can end hunger without waiting to end poverty are now well understood. Where actions and policies are applied intelligently, sincerely, and with adequate resources, we have seen that they can do the job. Whenever families cannot care adequately for those too old, too sick, too young, or too disabled to meet their own needs, the larger society will always have that obligation. But only in a few places and for relatively short periods of time have governments had enough political will to apply the full resources required to end hunger.

"It is never that lawmakers want children to go hungry, but they usually want something else more." Public funds applied to end hunger cannot, at the same time, be applied to "something lawmakers want more." Even in the best of all likely worlds, therefore, anti-hunger advocacy must remain vigilant on behalf of disadvantaged groups. ■

Dr. Patricia L. Kutzner is executive director of World Hunger Education Service.

It is never that lawmakers want children to go hungry, but they usually want something else more.

The Road Not Taken — The United States Government and Hunger

by Marc J. Cohen

The WIC program is a cost-effective government response to the nutritional needs of low-income children in the United States.

In 1980, the Presidential Commission on World Hunger recommended that "the United States make the elimination of hunger the primary focus of its relationships with developing countries, beginning with the decade of the 1980s."[1] The commission also praised the federal Special Supplemental Food Program for Women, Infants, and Children (WIC) and the Food Stamp and School Lunch Programs as "very successful in addressing the problems of hunger and malnutrition in the United States." But, the commission noted, "inflation and fiscal austerity policies threaten the advances that have been made to treat the symptom of hunger."[2]

To counter this threat, the commission called for "a systematic effort to assess the nutritional status" of people in the United States, along with "a national policy of economic development, designed to foster balanced growth and full employment. . . ."[3] Giving such high priority to eliminating hunger proved to be "the road not taken" by U.S. policy makers.

This chapter describes U.S. government anti-hunger programs, and looks at the impact of programs and policies which do not have hunger reduction as their main purpose. It also outlines an anti-hunger advocacy agenda.

U.S. Programs and Policies Affecting Domestic Hunger

A "Map" of Public Hunger Reduction Programs

The U.S. government spends billions of dollars each year trying to alleviate hunger in the United States. Congress appropriated $39 billion for fourteen U.S. Department of Agriculture (USDA) food assistance

Table 1

USDA Food Assistance Programs

Program	Description	FY 1993 Appropriation ($ million)
Food Stamps	Coupons for low-income people to purchase food in retail stores	28,115
Nutrition Assistance to Puerto Rico and the Northern Marianas	Cash and coupons for low-income people to purchase food in retail stores	1,051
Food Distribution	Low-income families on Indian Reservations and in Pacific Island Trust Territories may choose to receive food commodities directly through this program or participate in the Food Stamp Program	81
School Lunch	Cash and food provided to schools and residential centers; low-income students may eat for free or at a reduced price	4,055
School Breakfast	See School Lunch	902
Summer Food Service	Free meals for children in low-income areas when school is out	216
Child and Adult Care Food Program	Cash and Commodities provided to day-care centers	1,331
Special Supplemental Food Program for Women, Infants, and Children (WIC)	Coupons for high-nutrition food, health screening, and nutrition education for low-income, nutritionally vulnerable pregnant and nursing mothers, infants, and children up to age five	2,860
Commodity Supplemental Food Program (CSFP)	Commodities for low-income elderly people and women, infants, and children; WIC participants may not also participate in CSFP	95
Special Milk	Milk provided to schools, summer camps, and child-care institutions without other federal food assistance; free milk for low-income children	15
Nutrition Program for the Elderly	Cash and commodities for senior citizens; served in senior centers or provided by meals-on-wheels programs	475
Commodity Distribution to Charitable Institutions	Commodities provided to soup kitchens, food banks, nursing homes, and others which do not participate in other federal food programs	32
The Emergency Food Assistance Program (TEFAP)	Commodities distributed to needy families	165

Source: U.S. Department of Agriculture

School meals raise nutrition levels, and the breakfast program helps children be alert in class.

programs in fiscal year (FY) 1993 (October 1, 1992 through September 30, 1993, see table, p. 100). One of every six people in the United States participates in these programs. In March 1993, the largest of them, the Food Stamp Program, enrolled 27.4 million people. Over half the recipients are children, and 87 percent are children, women, or elderly.

Several of these programs are particularly effective. Food stamps improve both the quantity and the quality of food consumed in recipient households. School meals raise nutrition levels, and the breakfast program helps children be alert in class. The childcare program improves the nutritional intake of low-income preschoolers. WIC enhances participants' nutrition; reduces low birthweight, infant mortality, and anemia; and saves the government Medicaid expenditures.[4]

In fiscal 1993, the U.S. Department of Health and Human Services (DHHS) provided food worth $700 million to senior citizens and to low-income children participating in the Head Start early childhood education program. DHHS also runs the $7 million Community Food and Nutrition Program, which assists communities in starting and coordinating food assistance programs. The Federal Emergency Management Agency granted $129 million to local food and shelter agencies in FY 1993.

USDA and DHHS also engage in extensive nutrition education, food safety, and nutrition-monitoring activities.

State governments are required to help pay administrative costs of food stamps and TEFAP. Some states and the District of Columbia voluntarily supplement WIC and school nutrition programs. Some states provide for the use of special WIC coupons at farmers' markets. This enhances recipients' ability to buy fresh fruits and vegetables.

Also, some states fund outreach for the food stamp and child nutrition programs, and have their own funds to assist private emergency food providers.

Other federal assistance helps poor people obtain health care, housing, utilities, legal services, drug and alcohol abuse counseling, and job training. Federal aid also provides income to poor families with children and low-income blind, elderly, and disabled people. The Earned Income Tax Credit reduces the tax burden on "working poor" families with children. Workers who lose their jobs may be eligible for federal unemployment compensation or other special assistance. The federal government spent $150 billion in FY 1992 on various low-income assistance programs. This was equivalent to 12.5 percent of federal spending and 3.9 percent of the gross national product.[5] Because these programs boost the purchasing power of poor people, they contribute to reducing hunger.

State governments administer most of the federal programs. With the exception of food assistance programs, benefit levels vary greatly from state to state, and many states require able-bodied poor people to work as a condition of receiving assistance. Some states and localities have their own general and emergency welfare funds which provide benefits to people ineligible for federal aid (e.g., low-income couples without children who have short-term disabilities).

Without the "safety net" of anti-poverty programs, hunger in the United States would clearly be even worse than it is today. Unfortunately, the programs have serious limitations.

Problems With the Programs

The federal government bases its definition of poverty, which determines eligibility for most assistance programs, as well as benefit levels of many programs, on a 1955 food consumption survey. It found that the average family spent one-third of its income on food. The official poverty line is defined as an income equal to three times the cost of food under USDA's Thrifty Food Plan, the most modest of several family food budget plans. It assumes that a family spends a dollar per person per meal each day. The 1993 poverty line is $14,343 for a family of four.

This definition presupposes a high degree of nutritional knowledge and time for careful shopping and food preparation. Food stamps are supposed to supplement the 30 percent of income which recipients use for food. Benefits provide an average of just seventy-five cents per person per meal per day. But low-income people often do not have convenient access to grocery stores. And the 30 percent of income assumption is increasingly unrealistic. The federal government reduced its spending on low-income housing programs by 70 percent between 1978 and 1991, contributing to a shortage of affordable housing. The U.S. Census Bureau estimates that 45 percent of poor renters spend at least 70 percent of their incomes on shelter. The remaining 30 percent must cover not only food, but health care, child care, and other necessities.

In 1989, the Urban Institute found that food stamp benefit levels were 24 percent below participants' actual average food expenditures. Families who receive food stamps frequently have to rely on food pantries and soup kitchens for part of their food needs.

Food stamps have other limitations. The program is an entitlement, so it is supposed to enroll all eligible people, regardless of cost. But limited outreach, inaccessible offices, and burdensome application procedures keep many eligible people from applying. The Urban Institute estimates that the actual participation rate may be as low as 51 to 66 percent.

Food stamps often are inadequate for homeless people, who are extremely vulnerable to hunger, because the stamps cannot be used for hot, ready-to-eat, or lunch counter items. Homeless people usually do not have access to cooking facilities, and so rely heavily on soup kitchens and shelters for food.[6]

Because WIC is so effective, it is popular with Democrats and Republicans, liberals and conservatives. Nevertheless, Congress has resisted making it an entitlement program because of competing demands on the constrained federal budget. In recent years, the program has received only enough funding to enroll 58 percent of those eligible.

Other programs have similar financial problems. School lunches are available at 90 percent of all schools and 98 percent of public schools, serving an average of twenty-four million children daily. Eleven million poor children receive a free lunch, and two million get lunch at a reduced price. But not all children attending schools with lunches participate in the program, and rising costs, along with a heavy paperwork burden, have forced many schools to drop out of the program. Only about half of the ninety thousand schools which offer federally-subsidized lunches also serve breakfast, and only one-third of the low-income participants in the lunch program also receive breakfast. The summer and day-care programs can serve only a fraction of the eligible low-income children.

Without the "safety net" of anti-poverty programs, hunger in the United States would clearly be even worse than it is today.

Low-skill jobs generally offer low pay, and often provide no health benefits. Therefore, it often makes more sense not to work and to receive federal assistance which includes health care.

Systemic Flaws

Beyond these program-specific issues, the U.S. social welfare system has serious flaws. First, it fails to lift its clients out of poverty. The median value of income support (e.g., Aid to Families with Dependent Children, or AFDC) and food stamps combined for a family of three is 72 percent of the poverty line.[7] A major reason is that AFDC, unlike Social Security, is not indexed for inflation. Between 1970 and 1991, the purchasing power of the median benefit declined by 42 percent.[8]

Second, the system is biased against work and families. A poor person who begins earning income from even a low-paying job quickly becomes ineligible for food stamps, even though the wages may not cover food needs. Moreover, a low-income single parent may be able to receive AFDC, WIC, food stamps, and Medicaid, which can help meet many family needs. Low-skill jobs generally offer low pay, and often provide no health benefits. Therefore, it often makes more sense not to work and to receive federal assistance which includes health care. These disincentive effects would be reduced if benefits were tapered off, rather than abruptly stopped, for recipients who get jobs.[9]

Some federal job programs emphasize training over job creation and placement. While upgrading poor people's job skills is critical, they need employment at an adequate wage.[10]

The federal government does not offer adequate direct child-care assistance or incentives to employers to provide such assistance. In contrast, states which have required AFDC recipients to work generally have provided them with additional child-care benefits. A recent law that requires most employers to offer workers unpaid family leave will help some welfare recipients get into the job market.

Third, the services that the federal government makes available to poor people lack integration, and this often causes great hardship. Recipients usually have to visit widely separated offices to obtain benefits from different programs for which they are eligible, and each program has its own application procedures and processes and its own bureaucracy, which sometimes seems hostile to the people whom it is supposed to serve. This administrative duplication is also costly.[11]

Hungry People Lack Clout

Ultimately, the critical issue is lack of political power. Hungry people often do not participate in the political process. When they do register and vote, they still cannot afford to gain additional influence through political action committees and high-powered lobbyists. Policy makers hear far more from representatives of major corporations, the labor movement, or well-organized, well-financed interest groups, such as the National Rifle Association and environmental organizations, than they do from hungry people.

So it is not surprising that between 1981 and 1983, programs serving low-income people bore 33 percent of the reductions in federal spending, even though these programs made up just 10 percent of the budget. In contrast, well-organized lobbies like farmers and western users of federal water were able to preserve their subsidies. Nor did Congress restrict or eliminate the mortgage interest tax deduction, because it benefits a broad range of middle- and upper-class voters. During this same time, corporations and wealthy individuals saw their tax burden reduced substantially and the military budget grew rapidly, to the benefit of the powerful "military-industrial complex."

Hundreds of thousands of people became ineligible or had their benefits reduced as a result of cuts in social service programs. Drastic reductions in federal low-income housing spending and other cuts, deinstitutionalization of mentally ill people, and the 1982-1983 recession (during which unemployment averaged nearly 10 percent) combined to re-create the problem of widespread homelessness, which remains serious today.

The economic growth of the 1980s failed to create "a rising tide which lifts all boats." The top fifth of income earners increased their share of total income from 42 percent in 1980 to 47 percent in 1990. The share of the bottom two-fifths shrank from 17 to 14 percent.[12]

Labor Market Trends

Inflation-adjusted median wages have fallen since the early 1980s. As manufacturers succumb to foreign competition or move abroad in search of cheaper labor, fewer U.S. workers hold high-paying manufacturing jobs. Employment growth is in the service sector, where wages are lower, benefits often unavailable, employment often temporary or less than full-time, and unions weak or nonexistent. Government trade adjustment assistance programs have proven an inadequate response. Failure to index the minimum wage to inflation means that many full-time workers have less than poverty-level incomes.[13]

Government alone cannot address these structural changes in the U.S. economy. Maintaining U.S. standards of living will require cooperative action on the part of public, private, and nonprofit institutions, including major investments in education and training. But government, through direct programs and incentives to employers, can do much to insure that "work pays." Recent legislation to expand the Earned Income Tax Credit and encourage job-creating investment in low-income areas are steps in this direction.

Rising Hunger and Poverty

By the end of the 1980s, 21 percent of all children in the United States were poor and therefore vulnerable to hunger. For African-American children, the figure is 46 percent, and for African-American children in female-headed households, it is 68 percent. By the end of 1991, more than 14 percent of the population lived in poverty, compared to 11 percent in 1973.[14]

Hunger is closely related to poverty. Low-income people suffer a higher incidence of undernutrition as measured by low birthweight, infant deaths, stunted growth, and vitamin and mineral deficiencies.[15] A study by the Center on Hunger, Poverty, and Nutrition Policy at Tufts University found that the number of hungry people in the United States rose 50 percent between 1985 and 1992 to thirty million. In June 1993, the center estimated, based on 1991 data, that twelve million children in the United States are hungry. The number of people in poverty also increased between 1985 and 1992 to 35.7 million.[16]

During the early 1990s, state and local governments addressed fiscal problems brought on by the recession with drastic reductions in low-income aid. These cuts were politically easier to undertake than raising taxes on the middle class and the wealthy.

An Agenda for U.S. Anti-Hunger Advocacy

Advocacy groups have put forth realistic proposals for changes in public policy to

Inflation-adjusted median wages have fallen since the early 1980s.

Failing to end hunger and reduce poverty has enormous costs.

reduce hunger in the United States. The most comprehensive is the 1992 Medford Declaration, which calls for adequate funding of federal food programs, thus eliminating outright hunger within a few years. Supporters of the declaration say that achieving this would cost the federal government an additional $10 billion a year, or less than 1 percent of total federal spending.

Anti-hunger advocates are also seeking stronger outreach efforts, which would involve private food assistance agencies, incentives for food retailing in low-income neighborhoods, more accessible transportation, improved program integration, reforms to make health care accessible to everyone in the United States, and an increased supply of affordable housing.

Bread for the World has endorsed the Medford Declaration, and has also initiated the Every Fifth Child Act to obtain increased funding for WIC, Head Start, and Job Corps. The name of the legislation is a reminder that every fifth child in the United States lives in poverty and faces hunger.

The Medford Declaration goes beyond the safety net, seeking to assure "economic self-reliance" through "market-based employment and training programs," child care, and tax incentives which reward work. Other policies which would support this objective include an increase in the minimum wage, indexed to inflation; expansion of community development banks and other sources of credit that will allow poor people to start microenterprises; and incentives for poor people to accumulate assets.

Funding all these initiatives will be costly. Some of the needed funds could come from reductions in military spending possible with the end of the Cold War. These can go beyond planned reductions

without threatening U.S. security.

Failing to end hunger and reduce poverty has enormous costs, including: productivity and creativity loss when humans do not achieve their full potential; continued declines in U.S. export competitiveness; rising medical costs to cope with the health consequences of hunger; and the costs of the crime, drug and alcohol abuse, and social and racial tensions that widespread poverty and declining economic justice inevitably breed.

U.S. Programs and Policies Affecting Overseas Hunger

For most of the period since World War II, the United States was the global leader in providing international development assistance, in terms of both resources and innovative programs and institutions. The United States has provided a total of $450 billion in aid to developing countries (including military, development, and food assistance) since World War II.[17] Yet this country presently devotes just 1 percent of federal spending and 0.2 percent of gross national product (GNP) to foreign aid (compared to the United Nations-endorsed target of 0.7 percent). The United States ranks nineteenth among the twenty leading donor countries in level of GNP devoted to overseas assistance. In 1989, Japan surpassed the United States as the largest donor of development aid in dollar terms. The United States is still the leading source of military aid.

Furthermore, U.S. trade, investment, debt, and monetary policies have a far greater impact on hunger and poverty in developing countries than the rather modest level of U.S. aid. The geopolitical calculations that guide foreign policy likewise have a tremendous impact on hunger.

Cold War considerations have tended to

overwhelm other objectives of U.S. relations with the developing world. For example, U.S. aid to the Philippines increased significantly in 1972 when anti-communist dictator Ferdinand Marcos declared martial law. U.S. policy makers traded aid for secure access to military bases that they believed would help contain the Soviet Union. Need or a recipient government's commitment to equitable, sustainable, and participatory development have had much less to do with aid allocations.

Meanwhile, the need remains critical. The Food and Agriculture Organization of the United Nations (U.N.) estimates that 786 million people in the developing world (20 percent of the total population) are chronically undernourished. And, according to the U.N. Development Program, 1.3 billion people live in absolute poverty, too poor to afford an adequate diet and other necessities.[18]

With the Cold War over, the United States must revise its foreign aid policy. Bread for the World has sought to shape this reform effort in 1993 with a campaign called Many Neighbors, One Earth – Transforming Foreign Aid. This effort seeks to make sustainable development – especially the reduction of poverty and hunger in environmentally sound ways – the leading purpose of U.S. overseas assistance.

Food and Development Aid and Hunger

Program "map." In recent years, the U.S. Congress has appropriated $20 billion per year for "international affairs." Seventy percent of this goes to "foreign assistance" programs. Table 2 (p. 108) shows the allocation of the $14.7 billion FY 1993 foreign assistance appropriation to a variety of major program areas.

Some of this aid has a loose relationship at best to reducing poverty and hunger. In addition to the obvious example of military aid, funds provided to the multilateral development banks promote economic growth in developing countries, often with little attention to what happens to the incomes of poor and hungry people.

Multilateral aid is provided to developing countries via international organizations. In FY 1993, multilateral development banks, including the World Bank and regional development banks for Africa, Asia, Latin America and the Caribbean, and Europe, received $1.6 billion in U.S. funds. The World Bank and the regional banks have affiliates which make loans to poor countries on easy terms.

In the 1980s, the World Bank and regional banks shifted from their 1970s emphasis on project loans intended to alleviate poverty to "structural adjustment lending." These loans are conditioned upon the recipient government's agreement to adopt economic policy reforms which reduce fiscal deficits, public spending, and regulation; lower import barriers; devalue currencies; and encourage increased exports. Such macroeconomic reforms are intended to help countries cope with balance of payments problems and stimulate economic growth.

But these reforms have had mixed results, and they have often entailed immediate hardships among low-income groups, such as reduced spending on health and nutrition, higher food prices, and production of cash crops for export at the expense of food crops for local consumption. The International Food Policy Food Research Institute has found that export cropping often leads to a decline in nutritional status, even if household incomes

In the 1980s, the World Bank and regional banks shifted from their 1970s emphasis on project loans intended to alleviate poverty to "structural adjustment lending."

increase.[19] Currency devaluation helps promote exports, but it makes imports suddenly more expensive. Higher prices for imported food, fuel, and fertilizer can have a severe impact on poor and hungry people. The multilateral banks have not always been careful that adjustment is carried out in ways which do not make poor people worse off, and they have seldom sought to tilt the benefits of adjustment toward low-income groups.

The banks continue to make development project loans as well. Some, in such areas as nutrition, health, agriculture, and urban development, benefit poor people. Others fund large-scale infrastructure projects, which have sometimes displaced people and harmed the environment.

A third of the $325 million contribution to other international organizations and programs went to the United Nations Children's Fund (UNICEF), which effectively assists poor and hungry children in developing countries, often during times of war. UNICEF has also played a leadership role in creating a global mass movement to support child immunization. BFW Institute's analysis of the contributions to international organizations – which also assist poor women in developing countries and promote environmentally sound development – is that, on the whole, this spending supports sustainable development and humanitarian relief.

Bilateral development aid. Most bilateral development aid, which the U.S. government provides directly to foreign countries, is channelled through the U.S. Agency for International Development (AID). AID initiates projects in such areas as agriculture, population, health, education, environment, and private sector development.

Approximately 25 percent of AID development funds are channelled through U.S. nongovernmental organizations (NGOs), such as CARE, Catholic Relief Services, World Vision, and Save the Children. Many of these agencies, in turn, work in partnership with local NGOs.

During the 1970s, AID's stated program emphasis was on meeting the basic human needs (for food, shelter, health care, and education) of the poorest people in developing countries. In the 1980s, the focus shifted to using aid as an instrument to encourage developing countries to achieve financial stability, market economies, and economic growth. In recent years, AID has stepped up efforts to expand foreign investment opportunities for U.S. businesses.

Economic Support Fund. The Economic Support Fund (ESF) promotes U.S. security and political interests. In FY 1992, 26 percent of ESF funds went to such development projects as infrastructure and health care. Many of these projects may have helped alleviate poverty and hunger. The remaining 74 percent included loans to help countries import U.S. goods, including food, and cash grants. Critics point out that these unrestricted grants free up recipients' funds for military spending. Israel and Egypt will receive 75 percent ($2.1 billion) of ESF funds in FY 1993. Most of this is not tied to specific projects.

Aid and Sustainable Development. Table 3 shows BFW Institute's analysis of the proportion of FY 1993 bilateral economic aid and ESF funds focused on sustainable development or humanitarian assistance. The grand total, $2.8 billion, is 36 percent of the $7.8 billion spent in these categories, and 19 percent of all foreign assistance. The AID total of $1.9 billion supporting sustainable development (including some ESF projects) represents 29 percent of the $6.6 billion which the agency administered.

The United States maintains a few bilateral aid programs outside of AID. They received $939 million in FY 1993, and 78 percent of that was focused on sustainable development or humanitarian assistance. The Inter-American Foundation and African Development Foundation provide seed money for grassroots anti-poverty projects in their respective regions. Appropriate Technology International targets its programs to poor people in poor countries. Much of the work of the Peace Corps focuses on education, rural development, and health programs targeted to poor and hungry people. The non-AID programs that are not poverty-focused include the Overseas Private Investment Corporation, which insures U.S. firms' investments in developing countries against political risks like nationalization, and the Trade and Development Program, which promotes U.S. exports to middle-income developing countries.

Food aid. Food for Peace, or Public Law 480 (PL 480), is the major channel for U.S. overseas food assistance. Title I of PL 480 is run by USDA and provides low-interest loans tied to the purchase of U.S. agricultural commodities. Titles II and III are grant programs administered by AID. The total PL 480 program level in FY 1993 was estimated at $1.7 billion.

Title II channels food through private voluntary organizations and the U.N. World Food Program to support refugee and other emergency feeding, long-term maternal and child health programs (serving eleven million people in thirty-nine countries in FY 1992), school nutrition programs (feeding nearly twelve million children in twenty-

Table 2

Foreign Assistance Appropriation Fiscal 1993

Program	Appropriation ($ billion)
Multilateral Development Banks	1.6 (11%)
Other International Organizations and Programs	0.3 (2%)
Bilateral Development Aid and Special Initiatives	3.2 (22%)
Other Bilateral Economic Aid (Non-AID)	1.9 (13%)
Food Aid	1.5 (10%)
Economic Support Fund	2.7 (18%)
Military Aid	3.5 (24%)
Total	**14.7 (100%)**

Source: Congressional Research Service.

Table 3

Bilateral Economic Aid Supporting Sustainable Development and Humanitarian Relief Fiscal 1993

Program	FY 1993 Estimated Obligations ($ million)
U.S. AGENCY FOR INTERNATIONAL DEVELOPMENT (AID; includes Development Fund for Africa)	1,878
Food Security and Agriculture	210
Child Survival and Health	586
Basic and Vocational Education	200
Environment and Energy	517
Democratization and Human Rights	216
Disaster Assistance	149
BILATERAL - Non-AID:	939
Appropriate Technology International	3
Inter-American Foundation	31
African Development Foundation	17
Peace Corps	218
Refugee Aid	670
Total	**2,817**

Source: "What Counts?"

seven countries), and food-for-work projects (employing nearly twelve million workers in thirty-eight countries) aimed at improving infrastructure and employing poor people. In FY 1992, the United States provided an estimated $710 million worth of food under Title II, including $320 million for emergencies. That total grew to an estimated $810 million in FY 1993, due to increased emergency needs in Africa.

Title III, created in 1990, provides commodity grants to governments of developing countries which experience food shortfalls and are committed to sustainable development. Recipient governments may use the commodities in feeding programs or to establish food reserves. Or, they may sell the commodities, but they must use the proceeds in ways which benefit poor people, such as child survival activities, measures to promote food security, environmental protection, and activities which generate income and employment. At least 10 percent of the funds from such sales must go to indigenous NGOs which work closely with poor people. Fifteen countries received $334 million worth of assistance under this program in FY 1992, and AID planned to provide $327 million worth of commodities to sixteen countries in FY 1993. As yet, the effectiveness of Title III in promoting sustainable development has not been assessed, although the law requires the U.S. General Accounting Office regularly to evaluate the program.

Military aid. FY 1993 military aid accounts for 24 percent of all foreign assistance, the same level as in the late 1970s. Military aid levels have declined since 1986, however, following rapid growth in the early 1980s. Military aid and ESF together accounted for 42 percent of all foreign assistance in FY 1993.

Most military aid ($3.4 billion) consisted of loans and grants tied to the purchase of U.S. equipment. A small portion ($43 million) funded training of foreign armed forces, and a still smaller allocation ($27 million), covered U.S. contributions to international peace-keeping operations. Eighty-eight percent of FY 1993 military aid

went to Israel and Egypt.

Past and ongoing U.S. military aid to the governments of El Salvador, Somalia, the Philippines, and Indonesia, and to insurgent groups in Angola, Afghanistan, Cambodia, and Nicaragua, has fueled conflicts and, in other ways, done much more harm than good to poor and hungry people.

Limitations of aid programs. Unquestionably, some U.S. aid programs have helped hungry people in developing countries. Every year, AID child survival activities help to save the lives of more than four million poor children in developing countries. These programs immunize poor children against measles, whooping cough, and other potentially life-threatening diseases. They teach parents to give their children simple, inexpensive salt tablets to prevent deadly dehydration caused by diarrhea. U.S. support for UNICEF funds similar efforts around the world.

U.S. emergency food aid has helped keep millions of people from starving in such places as the Horn of Africa, Southern Africa, Cambodia, and Bangladesh.

Programs funded by AID, the Inter-American Foundation, the African Development Foundation, and the International Fund for Agricultural Development have assisted poor farmers throughout the developing world to grow more food and improve their families' nutrition and health while protecting the environment.

International anti-hunger programs also have limitations. First, despite the end of the Cold War, strategic relationships and high profile politics tend to dictate the direction of U.S. assistance. The top ten recipients of U.S. aid in FY 1993 were Israel, Egypt, Turkey, the Andean nations (Peru, Colombia, and Bolivia, which receive large aid allocations for drug eradication), Eastern Europe, the former Soviet Union, Greece, El Salvador, the Philippines, and Nicaragua. Israel, Egypt, and Turkey alone received 40 percent of all foreign assistance. Several of the leading aid recipients are home to U.S. military facilities, and most are far better off than many countries in sub-Saharan Africa. While the level of need is great in Peru, El Salvador, and the Philippines, the governments have devoted more of their resources to counter insurgency efforts than to meeting poor citizens' basic needs.

Second, the level of U.S. assistance to developing countries has declined by about 20 percent since 1985. Mounting budget deficits and strong popular sentiment that the U.S. government should meet domestic needs before helping people overseas are factors in this decline. Security-related assistance has fallen faster than development aid.

The modest foreign aid budget offers few resources for deficit reduction or meeting domestic needs. And, since the developing world purchases 35 percent of U.S. exports, the well-being of people in the developing countries increasingly has a direct impact on the well-being of people in the United States. The businesses which produce these exports employ 2.5 million U.S. workers.[20]

Third, like many other donors, the United States requires much of the aid it provides to be spent on U.S. goods and services. U.S. food aid funds must be spent on U.S. agricultural products; many other food aid donors finance the purchase of food from developing countries. Roughly 90 percent of military aid and 50 percent of bilateral development aid is spent on U.S. goods and services. In many cases, it would be more beneficial

for countries to buy local technologies and services than to import from the United States.

Fourth, the current legislative mandate for most aid, the Foreign Assistance Act of 1961, has become encumbered with so many goals as to become unwieldy. The law establishes thirty-three major objectives for U.S. aid and requires hundreds of reports to Congress each year.

Fifth, AID's ability to carry out development programs declined drastically during the 1980s. The agency has cumbersome bureaucratic procedures. It has cut back on its own technical staff and "contracts out" an increasing proportion of its programs, with the bulk of the contracts allocated to a small number of firms. In recent years, a number of AID officials have been prosecuted for corruption.[21]

Impact of Other Policies on International Hunger

Other aspects of U.S. economic relations with the developing world dwarf the $14.7 billion foreign aid budget. In 1990, the United States shipped $123 billion in exports to developing countries, which, in turn, sold $186 billion in goods to the United States.[22] Presently, U.S. private investment in developing countries is running at about $9 billion per year.[23]

Trade

The U.S government insists that other countries reduce or eliminate their barriers to U.S. exports, but continues to maintain tariff and non-tariff barriers against developing country goods. These include quotas on textile imports. Textile manufacturing is a critical infant industry in many of the poorest developing countries, such as

Other aspects of U.S. economic relations with the developing world dwarf the $14.7 billion foreign aid budget.

Expanding the Boundaries
Of Trade Agreements

by Don Reeves

Many observers believe that growing international trade and the policies which govern it are critical factors in overcoming hunger and poverty in developing countries and providing jobs in the United States. People of good will disagree, however, about the overall costs and benefits of increasing trade. These disagreements are sharply focused on two trade agreements currently under negotiation: the General Agreement on Tariffs and Trade (GATT) and the North American Free Trade Agreement (NAFTA).

Congress granted the Clinton administration authority through April 1994 to complete the current round of global GATT negotiations. Since its founding in 1946, GATT has sought to reduce international trade barriers. This 114 nation body makes rules which generally set the standards for world commerce.

NAFTA would virtually eliminate trade restrictions among the United States, Mexico, and Canada. It becomes effective in January 1994 if all three nations adopt it. At this writing, NAFTA's adoption by the U.S. Congress hinges on the administration convincing Congress that NAFTA will advance environmental protection and labor rights.

Both sets of negotiations have expanded the boundaries of traditional trade agreements.

GATT

In the current round of GATT negotiations, underway since 1986, the wealthier nations, which have always dominated GATT, wish to expand the kinds of trade covered. They want more protection for foreign investments and intellectual property rights. In developing nations, banking standards and patent protection are not as clearly defined or as rigorously enforced as in the industrial world.

Poorer nations, whose share of world trade is increasing, have their own demands. They insist on freer access to industrial countries' markets for agricultural products such as sugar or tropical oils, for example, and labor-intensive manufactured products, notably textiles and clothing. GATT presently grants agriculture and textiles exceptions to rules for other products. Wealthy nations have favored their own farmers and manufacturers.

Bangladesh, and the United States is a major market.

The U.N. Development Program estimates that trade barriers in the industrial world cost developing countries $500 billion annually, almost ten times what they receive in aid. Just the Multi-Fiber Arrangement, which governs the global textile trade, costs developing countries more than they obtain in development assistance.

U.S. trade barriers sometimes contribute to increased hunger and social conflict in developing countries. Quotas on foreign sugar purchases, demanded by politically powerful, high-cost U.S. sugar producers, are one factor in the low incomes and high rates of malnutrition among landless peasants on the Philippine island of Negros. The livelihoods of these people depend on the sugarcane plantations that control 74 percent of the island's arable land and ship most of their produce abroad. The anti-government rebels of the communist New People's Army have been very successful in recruiting among poor people on Negros. Many people have left the island for the slums of Manila, construction work in the Middle East, or work in the sex and tourist trade in Hong Kong.[24]

Subsidies on U.S. exports of corn, rice, and wheat have hurt local producers in developing countries. For example, in Costa Rica, widespread availability of cheap U.S. grain has undercut local food producers, causing thousands of farmers to abandon their land.

The arms trade is another major U.S. export industry often directly contributing to hunger in the developing world. U.S. arms sales abroad totalled $135 billion in FYs 1981-1990, and the United States remains the world's leading arms exporter. Sometimes, the United States arms a number of hostile parties in a volatile region, e.g., the Middle East. In Somalia, where U.S. arms sales totalled $147 million for FYs 1981-1990, the impact of militarization on hunger has been especially gruesome.[25]

The United States continues to maintain Cold War-inspired trade embargoes against Vietnam and Cuba. These have contributed to hunger and poverty in both countries.

Investment

Investment by multinational corporations headquartered in the United States and other developed countries is a two-edged sword for developing countries. On the positive side, foreign investors have transferred technology, created jobs, and helped developing countries diversify their economies. In Taiwan, for example, foreign firms have played a key role in the country's shift from a primarily agrarian to a primarily industrial society with vastly improved nutrition and living standards, though at a high cost to the environment and human rights.

Too often, however, firms flock to developing countries in search of cheap labor and lax environmental and safety regulations. U.S. firms operating on the U.S.-Mexico border, for example, have contributed to a growing environmental and public health crisis. They often maintain unsafe and unhealthy workplaces, and frequently pay workers less than a dollar an hour. In Chile in the early 1970s, U.S. firms, such as ITT and Kennecott Copper, encouraged the Nixon administration's efforts to undermine the democratically-elected government, which had sought to nationalize their enterprises. And, U.S. firms operating abroad often do not cooperate with efforts by their local workers to exercise their internationally-recognized rights to organize and bargain collectively.

NAFTA

NAFTA is mainly a bargain between U.S. investors and Mexico's political leadership. It would eliminate most remaining tariffs (which are already reduced to minimal levels), some immediately and some over a five-to-fifteen-year period. The agreement would open Mexico to more foreign investment and lock in current favorable regulations. NAFTA would guarantee intellectual property rights and assure free movement of business representatives – but not workers – across borders.

Mexican-U.S. trade has mushroomed since Mexico's unilateral steps toward rapid industrialization starting in the mid-1980s. NAFTA supporters expect further growth in jobs and trade which will, on balance, benefit consumers and workers in all three nations. Critics question overall net gains, and stress the magnitude of inevitable job loss and adjustments – especially among low-wage, moderate-skill U.S. workers.

New Issues and Actors

Both the NAFTA and GATT negotiations have been marked by the presence of new actors and issues. Citizen groups from around the world, including those from NAFTA countries, have complained about lack of access to the processes and information about stands taken by their government representatives.

Working in national and international coalitions, these groups have raised questions about environmental issues, working standards and conditions, and democracy and human rights. Trade negotiators previously regarded such concerns as "unwarranted non-tariff trade barriers."

Critics of NAFTA have highlighted environmental and working conditions in Mexico's *maquiladora* factories. In these plants, half a million workers assemble imported components for duty-free re-export, chiefly to the United States. Workplace conditions are often unsafe or unsanitary. Workers are discouraged or prevented from organizing and are frequently abused, in spite of fairly liberal Mexican labor laws. Environmental damage is rampant both in factories and communities, even though Mexican environmental laws are likewise quite strong.

Environmental, labor, and public interest groups have convinced Congress and the administration that permitting such conditions to persist constitutes unfair trading practices.

Clinton's trade negotiating team has negotiated supplemental NAFTA agreements which would set up trilateral commissions on the environment and labor rights. Each commission would have authority to investigate complaints by governments and NGOs about poor enforcement of national laws. Congressional approval of NAFTA will hinge on the judgment whether labor rights are adequately protected, and whether the commissions' findings could be enforced. The establishment of trilateral commissions as part of a trade agreement would represent a major innovation in trade negotiations.

Whether or not NAFTA is implemented, Mexico and the United States have agreed to begin cleanup of horrible environmental conditions along the border. Mexican President Salinas has taken modest steps to enforce existing environmental and labor laws.

GATT has revived its moribund Commission on Trade and the Environment. A parallel group is meeting within the Organization for Economic Cooperation and Development, an association of twenty-four industrial nation governments. Both groups are discussing what environmental safeguards might be added to GATT.

It is clear that Congressional acceptance of a GATT agreement depends on at least modest environmental provisions.

Partly as a result of trade-related discussions, interest has revived in U.S. ratification of several pending human, social, economic, and labor rights conventions. These conventions, which have already been negotiated, will reinforce and provide guidance for clearer standards to protect the well-being of consumers and workers in trade agreements.

Don Reeves is economic policy analyst at Bread for the World Institute.

Debt

As of 1993, developing country governments owed the industrialized nations $1.7 trillion. The U.N. Development Program reports that payments on this debt were $60 billion in 1991. This exceeded the total aid from developed countries (approximately $50 billion).[26] The extent to which developed country governments and banks are willing to forgive past debts is critical. In 1991, the United States forgave $2.7 billion of poor countries' debt. This frees up resources which would have gone into debt service for potential use in sustainable development. Neither the Bush nor the Clinton administration, however, has been

willing to sign on to the Trinidad Terms proposed by the British government, which call for forgiving two-thirds of the debt of the poorest countries (mainly in Africa).

Realpolitik

U.S. international strategic calculations have a great deal to do with the scope of world hunger. During the Cold War, U.S. foreign policy makers' desire to counter and contain Soviet power was the overriding goal in nearly all decisions.

Humanitarian goals and the desire to assist Third World development often jibed with this objective. Massive development and military aid to Taiwan and South Korea in the 1960s helped contain communism in those countries and frustrate communist forces in neighboring countries.

By the same token, the United States sometimes withdrew or denied aid to real or alleged communist forces in developing countries. In the late 1970s, the country refused to provide emergency food aid to Vietnam following a series of devastating droughts and floods, effectively forcing hungry Vietnamese children to pay for the policies of their government. In the early 1970s, non-communist South Vietnam was the largest recipient of U.S. food aid.

An Agenda for World Anti-Hunger Advocacy

There is consensus that U.S. foreign aid needs to change but much less consensus about how it should change. Yet in today's interdependent world, the United States cannot ignore the problems of hunger, poverty, and environmental decay outside its borders. These problems, rather than the Soviet Union, now pose the greatest threat to U.S. security. Four of five people in the world live in developing countries. What happens to four-fifths of the world touches the lives of the other one-fifth in social, economic, political, and environmental ways. As one U.N. development program advisor has said, "Poor people can be stopped at borders, but poverty can't be stopped. Poverty travels in the form of drugs, terrorism, global warming, and AIDS."[27]

People in developing countries are unable to become consumers of U.S. goods and services on a sustained basis when they are engaged in a constant struggle to overcome poverty and hunger.

If eliminating hunger is to become the priority of U.S. relations with the developing world, other policy changes are needed:

- Timely and effective response to humanitarian crises, preferably through multilateral channels, and upholding the right to food over claims of national sovereignty;

- Refraining from the use of food as a weapon;

- Improvements in Agency for International Development staffing and management;

- Reduced U.S. barriers to developing country exports, including processed and manufactured goods, and efforts to encourage trading partners to uphold internationally accepted worker rights and environmental and occupational safety and health standards;

- Efforts to prevent U.S. agricultural exports from undermining local food pro-

ducers in developing countries, and to discourage other exporters from doing so;

- Taking the lead in seeking to reduce arms proliferation globally, and conversion of U.S. arms export industries to peaceful purposes;

- Seeking a global code of conduct for multinational corporations, requiring them to uphold labor, environmental, and workplace safety standards wherever they operate, and to refrain from interfering in politics in developing countries; and

- More extensive measures to forgive developing country debt, such as allowing repayment in local currencies which are used to fund poverty and hunger reduction efforts.

Stronger political support is essential if hunger elimination is to become a U.S. foreign policy priority. Surveys show that the U.S. public supports ending hunger overseas, but doubts that foreign aid does this. So, at present, there is little organized support for foreign aid outside of Washington, D.C. think-tanks, PVOs, and the land grant colleges and universities. Yet both the moral and the self-interested basis for such support ought to be clear. ■

Dr. Marc J. Cohen is research director at Bread for the World Institute.

In today's interdependent world, the United States cannot ignore the problems of hunger, poverty, and environmental decay outside its borders.

Africa

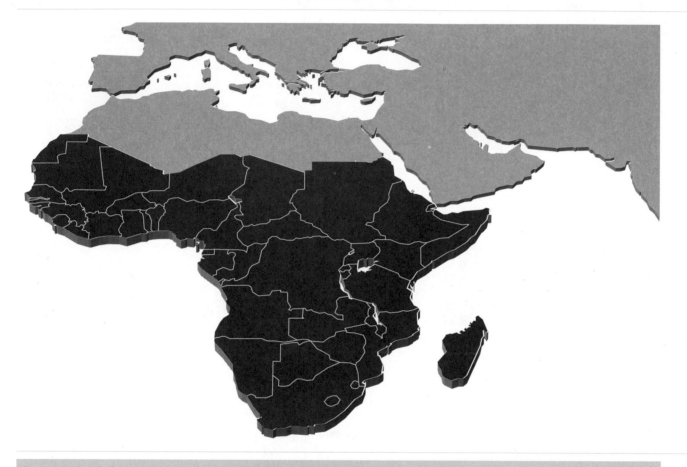

by Masimba Tafirenyika and John Prendergast

Overview

In Africa, the year 1993 was a continuation of a growing divergence between states which have collapsed or are in the process of collapsing and states which are attempting either political or economic reforms.

Civil conflict and a host of other factors conspired to aggravate the acute vulnerability of millions of Africans. State authority collapsed or deteriorated in **Somalia, Zaire, Liberia, Togo, Sudan, Angola,** and **Djibouti,** and in sub-regions of **South Africa, Mozambique, Rwanda,** and **Sierra Leone.** At the same time, though, many governments undertook economic reform programs, liberalized their political systems, or both. Countries moving in this direction included **Zimbabwe, Tanzania, Zambia, Ethiopia, Eritrea, Malawi,** and **Lesotho.** Despite reform efforts, whether political or economic, instability and economic deterioration almost universally prevailed.

Proliferating Emergencies

Complex humanitarian disasters in numerous African countries during the past year required innovative, comprehensive responses, both locally and internationally. The building of indigenous capacity to respond to ongoing or sudden disasters still has not advanced beyond a rhetorical priority of the United Nations (U.N.) agencies and other donors, even though the efforts and capacity of local people and

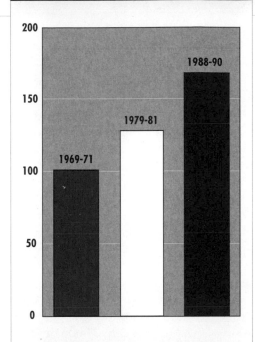

Graph 1

Chronically Undernourished Africans (Million)

1988-90

1979-81

1969-71

As Percent of Developing World Total

11% — 1969-71
15% — 1979-81
21% — 1988-90

Source: FAO and WHO

communities are of paramount importance in responding to recurring crises. But the menu of other options available to the international community for responding to these emergencies has expanded during the last few years, including such innovations as the West African military intervention in **Liberia,** the U.S. and U.N. intervention in **Somalia,** the move toward peace-keeping forces in **Angola** and **Mozambique,** and fresh approaches to delivering humanitarian assistance in conflict situations.

Armed Intervention

One of the most profound developments in the international response to humanitarian crises is movement toward establishing a human right to food. This principle often collides with other international principles, such as the inviolability of state sovereignty. Without the agreement of a sovereign government, the international community can reach vulnerable populations only through covert assistance, such as cross-border operations, or through armed intervention, which was considered for **Zaire, Sudan,** and **Angola,** but undertaken only in **Somalia** and, for other reasons, **Liberia.**

Case Study – Somalia

After nearly two years of increasing civil conflict, deteriorating food security, and little action, the international community finally reached consensus on a new initiative to stem the extraordinary loss of life in **Somalia.** In December 1992, the United States launched an unprecedented, multinational armed intervention in southern Somalia to secure and protect delivery routes for humanitarian relief supplies.

The conditions triggering the intervention included the most extreme looting and extortion ever witnessed by relief workers, the total absence of functioning government, and the nearly complete destruction of Somalia's infrastructure. The UN estimates that 300,000 to 500,000 Somalis perished between 1991 and mid-1993, the vast majority of them young children. Over two million Somalis were displaced, half as refugees in **Kenya, Ethiopia,** and other countries. Undernutrition rates among the displaced were estimated at nearly 75 percent.

Only when the media finally gave high visibility to this suffering was the international community shamed into action

Local control and transition to rehabilitation cannot be secondary considerations.

during the latter half of 1992. Prior to that, only the International Committee of the Red Cross and a few nongovernmental organizations (NGOs), such as Save the Children-UK, the International Medical Corps, World Concern, and Médecins Sans Frontières, were present in Somalia. Most of the humanitarian work undertaken was carried out by Somali NGOs and Somalis working for international organizations. The vast majority of the international organizations which later undertook major fund-raising and advertising campaigns for their Somalia programs were not present in that country before the troops arrived. Most conspicuously, the UN was largely absent from 1991 through mid-1992.

In addition to the media's role in focusing attention on the crisis, Sen. Nancy Kassebaum (R-Kan.), visited Somalia in July 1992 and called on the Bush administration to respond. Candidate Bill Clinton picked up the theme and used it to highlight perceived shortcomings in Bush's foreign policy. In August, President Bush launched an emergency airlift of food to Somalia. But with port access blocked and militia-merchant alliances using food as a weapon, the situation only worsened in many locales.

In response to intense U.S. pressure, the U.N. Security Council passed Resolution 794 in December, authorizing the deployment of U.S.-led forces to secure relief distribution access. At the operation's peak in early 1993, nearly thirty-five thousand troops from twenty-four countries were participating in the effort, which targeted eight major urban centers.

Some two million Somalis remained at great risk by mid-1993. The multinational military presence concentrated its efforts in a handful of major urban centers. Thus,

the various local militia groups had, for the most part, moved out into the country-side or across the Ethiopian and Kenyan borders, creating tremendous rural insecurity. More ominously, the U.S. diplomatic effort had focused on agreements between major warlords, and only later began to include elements of civil society such as women's groups, indigenous NGOs, and elders. When General Mohammed Farah Aideed was implicated in the deaths of two dozen Pakistani peace keepers, U.S. airplanes bombed areas in Mogadishu suspected of harboring Aideed's weaponry.

Aside from the two million Somalis who remained at risk, many more suffered from reduced strength and mental capacity due to severe undernutrition and constant bouts with dysentery, dehydration, hypothermia, anorexia, or muscle loss. Most families not affiliated with a major militia group have lost all of their assets and funds, making absolute dependency a certainty in the short term.

Two critical issues which the UN had not addressed adequately by mid-1993 were resettlement and capacity building. The UN assumed command of intervention forces from the United States in May 1993. The speed and efficiency with which the UN can assist in the restoration of people to their agricultural or pastoral ways of life is one key to the success of the intervention. Another is the extent to which international aid organizations strengthen the capacity of local Somali organizations to manage their own disaster response and reconstruction processes. One of the seldom-reported stories of the Somali emergency has been the primary importance and even greater potential of Somali individuals and organizations in participating in efforts for relief, rehabilitation, and reconciliation.

Local control and transition to rehabilitation cannot be secondary considerations.

Humanitarian and Human Rights Diplomacy

Another innovation during the last few years is the proliferation of diplomatic efforts to create space for emergency assistance in zones of conflict. These creative initiatives include safe passage agreements for relief supplies, safe corridors for civilian movements, demilitarized zones, refugee repatriations, and, in the absence of negotiated agreements, cross-border operations and targeted airdrops of humanitarian supplies. In all of these, local religious communities or NGOs often play critical roles in negotiation and implementation.

When a government or opposition movement is seeking international legitimacy, strong international protestations regarding human rights abuses can facilitate agreements on the humanitarian front. **Sudan** provides a good example of how human rights pressure and humanitarian diplomacy combined to enhance efforts to reach at-risk populations.

Case Study – Sudan

By the late 1980s, food was the primary weapon used by both the government and rebels in Sudan's civil war. In 1989, the UN negotiated an agreement between the warring factions which allowed the delivery of humanitarian supplies to both sides of the battle lines. It was called Operation Lifeline Sudan. It was sporadically effective, but then collapsed in 1992, due to a major government offensive and factionalism within the rebel Sudan People's Liberation Army (SPLA).

Entire subcultures are literally at risk of extinction in parts of southern Sudan. Denial or blocking of relief food is often only the last step in a descending staircase of terror which includes forced displacement, asset stripping, slavery, mining of agricultural lands, poisoning of wells, and bombing of market areas. For most southern Sudanese children who have never experienced peace, these degradations are perceived as normal facets of life.

By late 1992, mounting human rights violations spurred legislative bodies around the world to publicly condemn the combatants. International human rights law provided plenty of legal ammunition. The Geneva Conventions, ratified by 164 states, spell out clearly that all victims of war have the right to protection from murder, torture, and starvation. Article 3 of the conventions forbids the use of weapons against civilians. Chapter 7 of the U.N. Charter authorizes the security council to act if it determines that internal violence poses a threat to peace.

Reeling from growing international condemnation, the government and factions of the SPLA signalled their willingness to enter into negotiations with the UN over humanitarian access issues and with the Organization of African Unity regarding a peace process. Although the latter talks sputtered, two sets of talks in December 1992 and January 1993 led to the resumption of Operation Lifeline Sudan deliveries. The government and SPLA factions also agreed to give greater access and mobility to NGOs.

Access opened up to dozens of locations by plane, truck, barge, and train. Populations which had not been reached in more than a year were found to be in abysmal conditions.

The U.S. Centers for Disease Control undertook nutritional surveys in March

Sudan provides a good example of how human rights pressure and humanitarian diplomacy combined to enhance efforts to reach at-risk populations.

Famine Early Warning and the Politics of Hunger in Africa

by Celia Petty

Joint research by Save the Children Fund (UK) and the Institute of Development Studies, Brighton (UK) examined how four food aid donors – the U.S. Agency for International Development (AID), the European Communities, the British Overseas Development Administration, and the United Nations (U.N.) World Food Program (WFP) – responded to early warning information on African famines in 1990 and 1991.

This project examined the cases of **Sudan, Ethiopia, Mali, Chad,** and **Kenya.** The findings suggest a need for policy changes, which anti-hunger advocacy could help secure:

- Donors generally put resources for emergency relief, long-term rehabilitation, and famine prevention in separate budgets, despite the need to integrate these efforts. In addition, donors need to collect information for food security planning, as well as on famine early warning.

- Present famine monitoring relies too much on post-harvest crop assessments, which can lead to late responses. Donors need to link food aid allocations to assessments carried on throughout the growing season by WFP, the Food and Agriculture Organization of the UN, and others.

- Donors should become more flexible about the use of emergency food aid. Allowing relief agencies and recipients to sell some or all of the food can support the revival of local economies and improve food security.

- Donors should provide resources on a multi-year basis to countries facing endemic food emergencies and they should also pre-position emergency food supplies in these countries. Implementation of such a policy, however, would depend on good bilateral relationships.

1993, and the findings were shocking. In the southern Sudanese towns of Kongor, Ame, and Ayod, severe undernutrition rates were found to be 84 percent, 81 percent, and 75 percent, respectively. Mortality rates, measured as an "annual accrued death rate," are normally about fifteen deaths per one thousand people annually. In Ame, the figure was 234 per one thousand; in Ayod, 276 per one thousand. "It is a silent famine, the most silent of the major humanitarian crises around the world today," proclaimed James Kunder, director of the U.S. Office of Foreign Disaster Assistance (OFDA), after a visit in February.

U.N. efforts at humanitarian diplomacy continued throughout spring 1993. One of the most interesting initiatives was an attempt by the new Operation Lifeline leadership to negotiate demilitarized zones. These are productive areas with no strategic significance where people can farm or graze their animals, and no armed faction is allowed. The idea is to begin to restore the subsistence agro-pastoral economy of southern Sudan, which for centuries averted large-scale famines, and to re-empower local community structures, especially churches. An agreement was brokered by U.N. staff and U.S. Ambassador Donald Peterson at the end of May 1993 to demilitarize a forty-five-mile radius around Kongor, Waat, and Ayod, collectively known as the "starvation triangle." At the time of this writing, other areas were being negotiated.

Peace Keeping and Conflict Resolution

In 1984, the then U.N. Secretary-General, Javier Perez de Cuellar, observed that peace keeping is an expression of international political consensus and will. If that consensus or will is weak, uncertain, divided or indecisive, peace-keeping operations will be correspondingly weakened.

Less than a decade later, international peace-keeping missions in countries such as Angola and Cambodia have become test cases of the U.N.'s capacity to solve regional conflicts in the post-Cold War world. Since the 1991 U.N. deployment of troops on the Iraq-Kuwait border, approximately six missions are attempting to carry out the world body's services as mediator, peace keeper, election monitor, and food relief distributor. African operations include **Angola, Mozambique,** and **Somalia.**

While the end of the Cold War has provided the international community with the opportunity to resolve regional conflicts, the absence of political consensus and funding shortfalls often bog down U.N. peace missions and threaten further to damage the credibility and future influence of the UN.

Case Study – Angola

Angola has been torn by deep political animosities and ravaged by years of fighting that has claimed up to 500,000 lives. Tens of thousands of people have been maimed, leaving Angola with the world's highest number of amputees per capita and more than two million refugees in a country of ten million people. The infant mortality rate, at 127 per one thousand live births, is one of the highest in sub-Saharan Africa. Angolans can expect to live only forty-six years. Only a quarter of the population has access to health services. Estimates of damage to the infrastructure are well over $30 billion.

Unfortunately, the much-heralded 1991 Angola peace accord turned into a monumental disappointment. The opposition National Union for the Total Independence of Angola (UNITA) resumed fighting following its electoral defeat by the ruling party in September 1992. Despite the declaration by the UN and other international observers that the elections were free and fair, UNITA leader Jonas Savimbi insisted that voting was rigged. By February 1993,

- Donors should decentralize decision making in response to early warning information. Decisions made on the spot are more likely to be timely and appropriate. Significant political and institutional barriers stand in the way, however, both at the recipient and donor government level.

- Major bilateral donors should support greater multilateralism in food aid. WFP's International Emergency Food Reserve is regularly under-filled, and bilateral interests continue to influence emergency food aid distribution, leading to inequities.

Although this research project focused on food crises in emergencies and considered response options in the context of existing institutional structures, the sponsoring agencies were constantly aware of the macroeconomic environment that determines food security in Africa. The lack of government funds for such basic inputs as seed and fertilizer means that the rural economy across most of sub-Saharan Africa is undercapitalized and underdeveloped.

Ultimately, famine prevention requires the development of national wealth in famine-prone countries. This means substantial investment in peasant farming systems, including such basic measures as appropriate fertilizer input, pest control, and improved infrastructure. But rural, poor people are not presently a high priority of bilateral donors. Food security in the Southern Hemisphere also depends on a fairer international trading system, with lower barriers to developing country exports in industrial country markets and lessened Northern producer subsidies. Concerted advocacy by humanitarian, development, and anti-poverty organizations can help bring about such changes.

Dr. Celia Petty coordinates policy development at Save the Children Fund (UK).

U.N. World Food Program (WFP) officials warned that Angola faced a disastrous famine, with starvation threatening up to three million people. Philippe Borel, WFP director of operations, warned that "the second quarter of 1993 looks like being very hard. We will have to prepare for a disaster." Crops planted in January for harvest in April were totally disrupted by renewed fighting, and relief distribution was also affected. The government estimates

With a famine looming, it would be tragic for the UN to abandon a "bleeding" Angola at this critical hour.

that about 276,000 tons of food will be needed to feed two million refugees, displaced persons and returnees from neighboring countries.

There is evidence that the Angolan crisis has exhausted the U.N.'s capacity to act decisively. U.N. Secretary-General Boutros Boutros-Ghali threatened to reduce the organization's presence in Angola and pull out completely if no progress toward a cease-fire was made by spring 1993. This was after UNITA had inflicted considerable damage by systematically attacking U.N. posts and threatening its personnel with death if they refused to quit the country. By February 1993, UNITA had captured U.N. vehicles and equipment worth about $7 million and forced the world body to abandon about forty-five of its sixty-seven bases inside Angola.

With a famine looming, it would be tragic for the UN to abandon a "bleeding" Angola at this critical hour. Instead of withdrawing, the UN should:

- Strengthen its presence and extend its mandate in Angola;

- Press both sides, particularly UNITA, to adhere to the letter and spirit of the Bicesse Peace Accords of 1991; and

- Ban foreigners from supplying arms to either party in the conflict.

Moreover, any pullout should be temporary; the UN will need to come back to address a "famine as devastating as that in Somalia," according to WFP. The international community has an obligation to ensure that all parties in Angola follow the acceptable route to power – the ballot box.

In May 1993, as a recognition of the legitimacy of the September 1992 elections, the United States abandoned its previous support of UNITA and extended diplomatic recognition to the Popular Movement for the Liberation of Angola government.

Case Study – Mozambique

The possibility of a replay of the Angolan debacle in **Mozambique** is causing much anxiety to the war-weary people of this southern African country of fifteen million people. They have known no peace for more than a decade. The opposition, Renamo, was a creation of Ian Smith's **Rhodesia** (now **Zimbabwe**) and was later bolstered by South Africa. Renamo had waged a protracted war against the FRELIMO government, accusing it of implementing socialist policies. The war ended in October 1992 with the signing of a cease-fire agreement in Rome.

The UN was assigned to maintain peace, protect humanitarian relief, and supervise war-ravaged Mozambique's first multi-party elections scheduled for late 1994. Despite repeated assurances that the costly mistakes made in Angola will not be repeated in Mozambique, the UN has been slow to implement the peace agreement. Although the UN approved a contingent of approximately seventy-five hundred military and civilian observers under a $331 million budget, deployment was delayed by about eight months after the peace accord.

A positive outcome of the cease-fire has been the opening up of Renamo-controlled areas to relief agencies for food distribution. The International Committee of the Red Cross, WFP, and scores of other relief agencies are now able to get food to previously inaccessible places. Notwithstanding the drought that engulfed the entire southern Africa region in 1992, many parts of Mozambique have received enough rain to ensure a reasonable harvest. However, even with prospects of a good harvest, Mozambique faces a food deficit of 1.1 million tons this year, according to the Southern African Development Community's Regional Early Warning Unit.

So far the government and Renamo have adhered to the peace accord except for an initial flurry of post-accord skirmishes. If peace holds, more food aid will be distributed to an estimated four million people – about one-fourth of the total population – who are displaced both internally and externally. Even if lasting peace develops, Mozambique will continue to depend on food aid for a long time, given the social dislocation caused by almost two decades of war. Reconstruction efforts are already under way. The country is also wrestling with the challenges of resettling millions of peasants, including about 1.8 million returnees who have been living in neighboring countries as refugees.

Reconstruction and Reform

Many countries have either emerged or escaped from major civil conflict, and are embarked on reconstructing or reforming their economies. **Namibia, Ethiopia,** and **Eritrea** are engaged in major post-war reconstruction efforts. Dozens of countries, including **Zambia** and **Zimbabwe,** are implementing economic reform, or structural adjustment programs, usually in tandem with the International Monetary Fund and the World Bank.

Post-War Reconstruction

Peace agreements and cease-fire accords bring a host of opportunities and challenges in the area of post-war reconstruction. Strategies developed during periods following peace accords have a major impact on whether conflicts are renewed. Inequitable distribution of resources or limits on economic and political participation can re-ignite conflicts.

Case Study – Eritrea

The war between successive **Ethiopian** central governments and independence-seeking **Eritreans** was the longest ongoing war in Africa until the Eritrean victory in 1991. After an internationally supervised referendum established Eritrea's independence in April 1993, post-war reconstruction began in earnest. The various departments throughout the Eritrean government are charged with moving the country from dependency to self-reliance.

One major challenge facing Eritrea is how it handles its structural food deficit. With 75 percent of the population relying in some way on food aid, Eritrea is vulnerable to dependency-perpetuating relationships with donor governments and aid organizations. Agriculture and pastoralism provide livelihoods for 80 percent of the population. The Eritrean government stresses that the key to food security lies in enhancing the productivity and asset base of farmers and herders.

A drastic decline in the oxen population since 1987 has reduced the ability of farmers in the highlands to produce anywhere near their potential. One innovative response has been the establishment of oxen banks to pool and increase availability. Direct food handouts have been eschewed in favor of food-for-work programs. Grain markets and local production are to be stimulated by cash for work, internal purchase, and food monetization schemes. Already, roads and irrigation systems are being built, water catchments are being improved, trees are being planted, and hillsides are being terraced, although the scale of these undertakings is seriously constrained by a lack of

Even if lasting peace develops, Mozambique will continue to depend on food aid for a long time, given the social dislocation caused by almost two decades of war.

Recovery for Zimbabwe will be a prolonged and agonizing experience.

resources. Much of the work is done voluntarily or in exchange for food.

Again, building local capacity is a critical component of future political and economic development. Only indigenous organizations are allowed to operate in Eritrea. During the latter half of the thirty-year war, the Eritrean Relief Association organized all relief and rehabilitation activities in areas not controlled by the government. Civilian departments of the Eritrean People's Liberation Front organized the population at the local level and implemented development programs. Eritreans gained valuable experience, and post-independence policies should maximize the use of this knowledge and institutional capacity.

Economic Reform Programs

About forty African countries are currently implementing economic reform programs supported by international financial institutions such as the World Bank and the IMF. Results from these reforms have been mixed. While economic indicators have improved in some adjusting countries, virtually all have recorded sharp deterioration in social conditions.

Case Study – Zimbabwe

The influence of a crippling drought, growing unemployment and rising inflation made 1992 **Zimbabwe's** most difficult year since independence in 1980. The drought that afflicted Zimbabwe was the worst in this century, and came after a decade of poor rainfall, resulting in severe shortages of food and water. The crop failure rate for communal and small-scale farmers, who account for more than half of agricultural production, ranged from 80 to 100 percent. The drought struck another blow to the economy, already reeling

under the on-going IMF/World Bank-supported structural adjustment program.

Timely action by local people, the government of Zimbabwe, and aid donors helped assure that the drought did not lead to famine.

Recovery for Zimbabwe will be a prolonged and agonizing experience. In 1992, for example, GDP fell by an unprecedented 9 percent, while the forecast for 1993 is less than 1-percent growth. Although 1993 rains have been good, the Regional Early Warning Unit projects a food shortfall for 1993-1994. The deficit is expected to be met from 1992-1993 imports.

High unemployment, rising inflation, and deteriorating living standards are among the consequences of austere economic reforms and the severe drought. About 1.2 million of Zimbabwe's population of ten million are without jobs. More than six thousand posts were abolished in the civil service, and the government plans to increase the number of lay-offs to thirteen thousand by June 1993.

In attacking the budget deficit, the government re-introduced school fees and health-care charges. These user charges have contributed to increasing school dropouts and rising infant mortality. Toward the end of 1992, there was an outbreak of cholera, the worst ever to hit Zimbabwe. It was initially confined to camps hosting **Mozambican** refugees, but later spread throughout most parts of the country, including the capital, Harare.

Although a Social Dimension Fund was set up to mitigate the adverse effects of adjustment on poor people, only a handful have benefitted so far from its meager resources. On the other hand, military expenditures, which in the past have taken a large chunk from the national budget, are expected to decline if a lasting peace develops in neighboring Mozambique. Zimbabwe has been spending more than $6 million a month guarding the Beira and Limpopo corridors, its trade routes to the sea.

In its 1993 report, *Zimbabwe: A Policy Agenda for Private Sector Development,* the World Bank, Zimbabwe's biggest aid donor, calls on the government to transform the country into a full-fledged market economy, including the privatization of deficit-ridden state companies and relaxation of restrictive exchange controls. Recommended measures include:

- Allowing foreign firms 100 percent profit remittances (as in **Zambia**);

- Less government involvement in wage negotiations; and

- Streamlined rules on transport, agricultural marketing, and redundancy in government operations.

Even through recovery will be protracted, the government calculates that an end to drought, reductions in inflation, substantial aid and support from the international community, and growing export demand will all contribute to recovery.

Nevertheless, within Africa questions still remain regarding the effectiveness of adjustment programs in the face of their unsatisfactory record. A decade of adjustment programs has so far failed to produce a single example of an African country that has achieved self-sustaining economic growth.

Recent statements from World Bank officials suggest that an overhaul of current strategies in the bank's dealings with Africa is in the pipeline. These include:

- A relaxing of the existing stringent conditions that require cuts in civil service staff;

- Reducing the number of Western technical expatriates working in Africa;

- Greater use of African consultants in formulating projects; and

- More involvement of Africa-based Africans in drawing up policy framework papers and country reports.

Bank reviews of adjustment programs in Africa have clearly stated that the programs, which seek economic stabilization and growth, have not worked well. The latest shifts in the bank's focus may be steps toward a welcome change in objectives to promoting equitable, sustainable, and participatory development in Africa. ∎

Masimba Tafirenyika is a visiting Third World research associate at the Center of Concern. He has also worked as research coordinator for the Southern African Research and Documentation Center in Harare, Zimbabwe.

John Prendergast is research associate at the Center of Concern, co-coordinator of the Coalition For Peace in the Horn of Africa, and co-organizer of the Catholic Taskforce on Africa.

A decade of adjustment programs has so far failed to produce a single example of an African country that has achieved self-sustaining economic growth.

Asia-Pacific

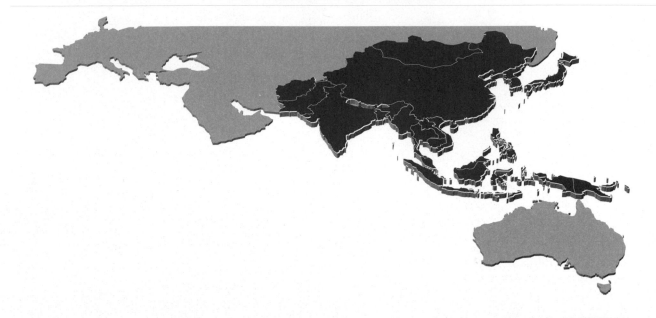

by Marc J. Cohen

Overview

Asian and Pacific countries have made steady progress in reducing poverty and hunger over the past two decades. The World Bank reports that in many nations, the *proportion* of the population living in absolute poverty has declined significantly. Between 1970 and 1990, the absolute poverty rate in **China** fell from 33 to 10 percent; it fell from 60 to 15 percent in **Indonesia**. The *number* of people living in absolute poverty fell from 275 million to 100 million in China and from 70 to 27 million in Indonesia. **India's** poverty rate dropped from 48 percent in 1977-1978 to 25 percent in 1992, but the number of poor Indians increased to 210 million because of population growth.[1]

A number of countries that had depended on food aid achieved self-sufficiency, including **India**, **Indonesia**, and **Vietnam. Bangladesh's** basic grain production kept pace with population growth during the past decade.[2]

Hunger has declined in the region. (See graph 1, p. 126.)[3]

For the purposes of analysis, BFW Institute defines South Asia to include Afghanistan, Pakistan, India, Bangladesh, Nepal, Bhutan, Sri Lanka, and the Maldives. Southeast Asia includes Burma (Myanmar), Thailand, Malaysia, Singapore, Indonesia, the Philippines, Brunei, Cambodia, Laos, and Vietnam. East Asia consists of Hong Kong, Macau, China (including Tibet), Taiwan, Mongolia, North and South Korea, and Japan. This chapter also looks at the independent nations of the South Pacific.

Progress against hunger in the region stems not just from rapid economic growth in East and Southeast Asia, but also from government anti-poverty policies. The governments of **Thailand** and **Indonesia** have undertaken aggressive village health and nutrition interventions, and have reduced child malnutrition in both relative and absolute terms. In Thailand, for example, the proportion of underweight children fell from 36 to 13 percent between 1982 and 1990. Many Asian countries have made substantial public investments in agricultural development. In South Asia,

Graph 1

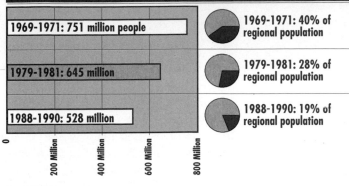

Slow Steady Progress. . . Chronic Undernutrition, Asia-Pacific

1969-1971: 751 million people

1979-1981: 645 million

1988-1990: 528 million

0 | 200 Million | 400 Million | 600 Million | 800 Million

1969-1971: 40% of regional population

1979-1981: 28% of regional population

1988-1990: 19% of regional population

Source: FAO/WHO

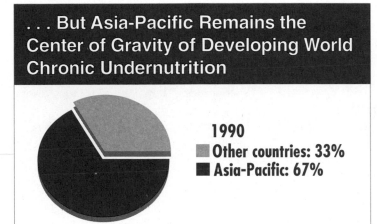

. . . But Asia-Pacific Remains the Center of Gravity of Developing World Chronic Undernutrition

1990
Other countries: 33%
Asia-Pacific: 67%

Source: FAO/WHO

governments have maintained social programs even as they have cut spending and privatized state companies.[4]

Nevertheless, hunger remains a serious problem throughout the region, which is home to two thirds of the world's chronically undernourished people and nearly 80 percent of the underweight children. In **India**, nearly half the adult population regularly consumes an inadequate number of calories.

Vitamin and mineral deficiencies - "hidden hunger" - are likewise heavily concentrated in Asia and the Pacific: half of the world's anemic women are found in South Asia, while over 50 percent of the people suffering from iodine deficiencies live in **China** and **India**. More than 80 percent of the children at risk of vitamin A deficiency, which can cause blindness, live in the region. Nearly half of all cases of goiter,

an enlargement of the thyroid gland caused by a lack of iodine, are found in Southeast Asia, as are 70 percent of the cases of iodine-deficiency cretinism.[5]

A number of factors led to short-term increases in hunger within the region during 1992 and the first half of 1993, as noted below. Yet there were some hopeful signs as well: 370,000 **Cambodians** returned home from years in refugee camps (see pp.129-132); the **Philippine** government obtained some debt relief and opened peace talks with its armed opponents; **Vietnam** continued to produce bumper food crops; and the **Indian** government resisted pressure from aid donors to abandon its public food distribution system.

Children and Hunger

More than half of the world's underweight children under the age of five years are found in South Asia. The proportion of the sub-region's children who are underweight fell from 68 percent in 1975 to 62 percent in 1990. In **Bangladesh**, the figure is 65 percent, the highest in the world. Because of high population growth, the absolute number of underweight children in South Asia increased from 91 million to 108 million. The United Nations (U.N.) Subcommittee on Nutrition (SCN)

Progress against hunger in the region stems not just from rapid economic growth in East and Southeast Asia, but also from government anti-poverty policies.

Many South Asian families provide girls less food, health-care, and education than boys.

considers this "probably the biggest nutritional problem in the world."[6]

Malnutrition persists among South Asian children despite declining poverty rates in **India** and **Pakistan**, gains in per-capita food production throughout the sub-region, large-scale child survival programs in **India** and **Sri Lanka**, and progress in reducing the percentage of the population with inadequate diets. Many South Asian families provide girls less food, health-care, and education than boys.[7] Shahla Zia, a Pakistani women's rights activist, says, "[D]iscrimination tends to start at birth."[8]

Women and Hunger[9]

Poor nutrition in children, and especially girls, tends to carry across the generations, as poor women tend to have inadequate diets into adulthood. Poor maternal nutrition and lack of prenatal care leads to low birthweight babies who are at increased risk of malnutrition and disease. Likewise, when girls are not sent to school, it increases the risk that their children will be malnourished. In **Pakistan**, uneducated women are three times more likely to have malnourished children than women with at least a primary education.

Preliminary SCN data on malnutrition among women of childbearing age indicate that 60 percent in South Asia and 45 percent in Southeast Asia are underweight due to malnutrition. This makes them more likely to have low birthweight babies and die in childbirth. Early pregnancy increases these risks and contributes to stunted growth in mothers. Eighteen percent of Asian women give birth by age eighteen; in **the Philippines**, 24 percent of the women ages fifteen to nineteen years give birth.

The risks are heightened by high rates

of anemia – 64 percent among these women in South Asia and 48 percent in Southeast Asia. Anemia also reduces work capacity and learning ability, while increasing susceptibility to infection. Ironically, success in boosting food grain output has contributed to high and apparently rising rates of anemia among South Asian women, as farmers have abandoned cultivation of iron-rich vegetables such as beans and lentils in favor of rice and wheat.

For poor women of childbearing age, there is heightened "social vulnerability" to malnutrition. They often work long hours in agricultural or, increasingly, factory jobs. They then have additional responsibilities for child care and obtaining family energy and water supplies. Their lack of discretionary time means that they often miss meals and face exhaustion, poor appetite, and poor nutrition.

Fifteen percent of the women ages fifteen to forty-nine years are of short-stature (due to poor nutrition) and at risk of dying in childbirth in both South and Southeast Asia. In South Asia, over 30 percent of babies are born with low birth-weights. This is the highest regional figure in the world. In Southeast Asia, the figure is 15 percent, and in **China** it is 9 percent. Regionally, the prevalence of low birthweight is declining, however.

Militarization and Conflict

The end of the Cold War does not seem to have reduced the level of violence or military spending in the region. In **Afghanistan**, conflict along ethnic and factional lines continued following the defeat of the communist government by Islamic rebels in April 1992. Shelling of Kabul displaced over half a million people.

Armed groups controlled access to food in the city. The situation of sixty thousand refugees from Tajikistan was described by relief personnel as "hungry, cold, and . . . miserable."

In the Afghan countryside, fourteen years of fighting left farms abandoned, irrigation works destroyed, and inputs and spare parts in short supply. Millions of mines sown at random throughout the country have disabled one of every six Afghans. Those still able to farm find that opium poppies fetch a better price than food crops, even though staple food prices tripled in 1992 due to shortages. While some food moved across the border from Pakistan, supplies proved erratic.[10]

In **Burma (Myanmar),** the government increased military spending by 10 percent in its 1992-1993 budget. Military spending is now 35 percent of the total. Authorities continue to subject ethnic minority populations to violent counter-insurgency campaigns. According to UNICEF, this conflict has contributed to rates of severe malnutrition among children under the age of three years that are comparable to those in Sudan.[11]

In **Sri Lanka**, military spending accounts for 12 percent of the government budget and 4 percent of GDP (compared to 4 percent and 1.5 percent before the beginning of the civil war in 1983). This means that resources are not available for food production and poverty alleviation. The war has also disrupted agriculture and damaged infrastructure. These costs are likely to increase in the future, and the country's dependence on external food aid is likely to rise. The combined effects of war, poor weather, and financial pressures have led to reduced food consumption among poor people. Twenty-five percent of the population is too poor to afford a

minimally adequate diet.[12]

Armed conflict continued in the **Philippines**. The 1993 budget raised military spending 19 percent and cut health and social services, although 70 percent of Filipinos remain in poverty.[13]

Uprooted People[14]

The Asia-Pacific region hosted 2.7 million refugees at the end of 1992, including 1.6 million **Afghan** refugees in **Pakistan** and 245,000 **Burmese** Muslim refugees in **Bangladesh**. Another 838,000 **Afghans**, **Burmese**, and **Pakistanis** lived in "refugee-like" situations in **Pakistan**, **Thailand**, and **Bangladesh**, respectively. Millions more people were displaced within their own countries, including one million Filipinos; 600,000 Sri Lankans; 500,000 to one million Burmese; 280,000 Indians; and 199,000 Cambodians.

About 1.5 million **Afghans** repatriated from Pakistan during the year, joined by 300,000 from Iran. Refugees and relief workers reported that the Pakistani authorities pressured some refugees into leaving by cutting off their food rations. The Pakistani government denied this allegation.

India similarly repatriated twenty-three thousand Sri Lankans involuntarily in 1992. In many instances, the authorities denied refugees food until they agreed to return home.

By early 1993, eighty thousand ethnic Nepalese had fled from alleged official harassment and discrimination in Bhutan to camps in Nepal. Nepal has no laws conferring refugee status, and landless citizens objected to the allocation of land to refugee camps. Refugees crowded into camps with poor sanitation and life-threatening health conditions, and depended on food aid for survival.

The end of the Cold War does not seem to have reduced the level of violence or military spending in the region.

Seed the Killing Fields

by Chanthou Boua

Vast destruction has been wreaked on Cambodia. It started in 1970 with the civil war between the Khmer Rouge, then nominally headed by Prince Norodom Sihanouk, and supported by China. U.S. bombing devastated Cambodia's countryside. During six months in 1973, the United States dropped more bombs on Cambodia than fell on Japan during World War II.[1] Many villages and towns were razed. The bombardment ravaged inhabitants, draft animals, equipment, and farm land. Pictures of malnourished Cambodians hit the world's television screens in early 1979 after the Khmer Rouge, who had ruled Cambodia since 1975, were ousted by a Cambodian movement backed by Vietnamese forces.

When the Khmer Rouge took power, they implemented rigid, forced collectivization, evacuating the cities and turning virtually all Cambodians into peasants. The regime knocked down schools and places of worship. Most buildings, bridges, and roads lay in ruins.

These policies caused at least one million deaths among a population of 7.5 million. It is estimated that half died of starvation, exhaustion, and illness, while the other half (mostly men) were executed. City people and the Muslim and Vietnamese minorities suffered the most. The Khmer Rouge nearly obliterated intellectuals and the educated among city dwellers, including teachers, nurses, students, and government officials.

The regime sought to expand irrigation systems, but put inexperienced functionaries in charge of these efforts. They paid little attention to the natural lay of the land and sources of water. This reduced the amount of cultivated land. According to a 1992 World Bank report, by 1979, only about 30 percent of the rice land farmed in the 1960s was still cultivated.

A Nation of Women

When Vietnamese forces ousted the Khmer Rouge, they found that most of the surviving adults were women. In rural areas, women comprised up to 65 percent of the adult population, and as much as 75 percent of the able-bodied population. Women headed 35 to 40 percent of the households, and often had to raise several young children of their own and sometimes orphans of relatives as well.

Change in Communist Asia

Vietnam has privatized much of its economy. This has boosted production and exports of food. But marketization has led to greater income inequality. Parts of the country which do not produce adequate food may be experiencing malnutrition, due to lack of infrastructure and poor marketing systems. The Vietnamese government estimates that two million to four million rural people have inadequate food supplies between harvests. Tribal highland people live in extreme poverty.[15]

Market-oriented reforms in **China** have also led to increased inequality. In the southern coastal regions, export manufacturing has led to double-digit growth rates. But in impoverished inland regions incomes are half those on the coast, and seventy million people languish in absolute poverty. Many of them do not consume an adequate diet. Rising food prices and stagnant incomes have hurt people in poverty areas.[16]

In **Mongolia**, the effort to move from central planning to a market economy has so far been unsuccessful. The country previously depended heavily upon aid and trade relations with the Soviet Union, and has yet to find new long-term donors and trading partners. Rice, the staple of the local diet, is not grown locally, and the country has little foreign exchange for imports. Food production fell, due to shortages of inputs and spare parts, as well as a severe winter. Since early 1991, staple food prices have risen by a factor of fifteen to twenty. Nearly 300,000 women, children, and people in large, single-parent families were in need of food aid in early 1993.[17]

The loss of Soviet economic patronage has likewise affected food security in **North Korea**, creating shortages of fuel and other agricultural inputs. In addition, the country is suffering from soil depletion and other ecological problems. Food production may have declined, and has clearly declined in per-capita terms, as rice yields have levelled off. The government has urged people to eat only two meals a day, and per-capita consumption is estimated to be 75 percent of requirements. People are likely to be thin and somewhat hungry, but there does not appear to be extensive malnutrition. The government has made food imports a high priority, with arms sales to Iran and Iraq providing much of revenue for the purchases.[18]

Non-Communist Asia and The Pacific: Adjustment, Growth, and Equity

Indonesia's economy has grown by an average of 7 percent per year in real terms for the past twenty-five years. Average farm incomes are $230 per year, however, making rice too expensive between harvests for many rural households.[19]

Similarly, in **Thailand**, impressive growth rates have not benefitted all citizens equally. The number of people living in absolute poverty between 1970 and 1990 remained at nine million, despite 7 percent economic growth per year. Malnutrition and landlessness remain widespread in the north and northeast of the country. In the northeast, home to 37 percent of the population, average incomes are 38 percent of the national average.[20]

India's fiscal 1994 budget raises prices of food and fuel and reduces fertilizer subsidies. In 1992, farmers in the conflict-torn Punjab had refused to sell grain to the government's food reserve because of below-market procurement prices. Much of the benefits of subsidies on food and fertilizer have not, in any event, gone to the poorest consumers and farmers, although the food

Cambodia moved from a self-sufficient nation to a country perennially short of food. Because of the Vietnamese occupation, the United States imposed an economic embargo, and encouraged other nations to join. Cambodia was also the only developing country refused development aid from the UN and its specialized agencies.

This trade and aid boycott hurt Cambodians in all walks of life, and greatly hampered reconstruction efforts. It placed a heavy burden on women, especially in agriculture. The embargo restricted sales and donations of agricultural inputs and equipment. During the 1980s, U.S. NGOs could not provide development aid, and had to obtain licenses to send "humanitarian assistance," such as food and medicine. The resulting shortages contributed to sporadic hunger and high mortality among children under five years.

When I visited Cambodia in the mid-1980s, I met Mrs. Mean, a thirty-six-year-old widow. She was struggling to raise three young children. The Khmer Rouge had murdered her husband and many other men of the village in 1977. In the rice-growing season, she left for the field with her children (there was no village school) at 4:00 or 5:00 a.m. She usually returned home only at sunset. Then she had to fetch water, cook dinner, feed pigs, perhaps patch the children's clothes. She did not go to bed until 8:00 or 9:00 p.m. Mrs. Mean also raised fruit and vegetables to earn money for clothing for the children and other necessities. Once, when the rice harvest fell short, she left the children with relatives and looked for work in the district town. When I met her, she was selling dried fish along a roadside. She told me,

Before the [rule of the Khmer Rouge], and when my husband was around, I did not have to do this sort of work. My family could easily live off farm produce and that was the only work which we did all year long.

She blamed the poor harvest on the lack of draft animals and the shortage of men for the heavy work.

Civil War

Since 1979, civil war has raged, with the Khmer Rouge seeking to return to power by force. The fighting drained scarce resources, including human resources, from efforts to rebuild the country.

The State of Cambodia government, which took power with the backing of Vietnamese forces, managed to return Cambodia's social, cultural, and economic life to a respectable level, however poor. Cambodians could again send their children to school, earn a living, buy their food in markets, and practice Buddhism. In the second half of the 1980s, many Western NGOs working in Cambodia and some scholars pleaded for diplomatic recognition of this government and restoration of international aid, but to no avail.

U.N.-Sponsored Peace Process

Following the pullout of Vietnamese troops in 1989, the State of Cambodia government, facing desperate economic straits, agreed to peace talks with the Khmer Rouge and two smaller noncommunist opposition groups. At no stage did the five permanent members of the U.N. Security Council (the United States, United Kingdom, France, the Soviet Union, and China), who brokered the negotiations, try to exclude the Khmer Rouge.

In October 1991, nineteen nations and the four Cambodian factions signed the U.N. Agreement on Cambodia, which called for disarmament, repatriation of nearly 370,000 refugees from Thailand (many had lived in the camps since 1979), and democratic elections. The economic embargo finally ended in January 1992.

The signing of the agreement did not bring in much badly needed aid, however. By May 1993, donors had pledged $880 million in assistance, but had sent only $25 million.[2] Most of this supported repatriation and development activities in opposition-controlled zones.

The refugees have returned home, and their repatriation has been called a "success." But returnees face scarcities of land, work, housing, and food.

Foreign investment has gone mostly into service industries, such as hotels and restaurants, catering to twenty-two thousand U.N. personnel. The number of prostitutes increased from six thousand in 1991 to thirty thousand in early 1993, according to NGO workers. Medical sources believe that 10 percent are infected with the AIDS virus. Most small industries that were sold to foreigners have closed, leaving workers unemployed and the economy heavily dependent on imports.

Violent conflict continues. The Khmer Rouge signed the peace accords, but quickly refused to cooperate. Khmer Rouge attacks on

consumption of rural poor people has improved.[21]

Natural Disasters And Poor Weather

In mid-September 1992, the worst flood in a century hit **Pakistan**, displacing one million people and causing $2 billion in damage. Irrigation works and export crops were devastated. In recent years, Pakistan has relied on earnings from these crops to cover the cost of substantial imports of wheat, the staple food.[22]

A second year of drought in 1992 in **Nepal** led to the worst grain crop in five years. The government sought to encourage farmers to plant food rather than cash crops (reversing the policy of the preceding two years), but over 400,000 people faced a short-term food emergency.[23]

In June and July 1993, monsoon flooding in **India**, **Bangladesh**, and **Nepal** killed one thousand people and left four million homeless. Rice crops in India's main production areas, Punjab and Haryana, were severely affected.[24]

In January 1993, tropical cyclone Nina left thousands of people in the South Pacific nations of **Fiji**, the **Solomon Islands**, and **Tuvalu** in need of emergency food and other assistance. In June, cyclone "Prema" caused extensive damage in **Vanuatu**.[25]

Future Prospects

Although the region as a whole has reduced hunger over the past twenty years, there are worrisome trends, as the Asian Development Bank notes:

In light of the region's high population growth, increased urban sprawl, and rampant environmental degradation, there are signs that hunger problems could loom unless action is taken by Asian nations and international development agencies.[26]

This means that by the year 2030, Asia will have to produce 60 percent more rice with fewer resources if population continues to increase by 2 to 3 percent per year. South and Southeast Asia have reached agricultural yield limits at current levels of technology, with little ability to expand cultivated area.[27] Without concerted action by governments and NGOs, these trends could threaten the region's capacity to support its people. ■

Dr. Marc J. Cohen is research director at Bread for the World Institute.

villages escalated. In recent years, the warring factions have laid ten million to twelve million land mines in provinces along the Thai border. These have injured and displaced many rural people, further disrupting food production.

In the three months leading up to the May 1993 election, the Khmer Rouge killed 131 people. These included Cambodian and ethnic Vietnamese villagers (the Khmer Rouge claimed the latter were covert troops) and U.N. peace keepers. The Khmer Rouge refused to keep their promise to disarm and boycotted the election.

The 90-percent voter turnout demonstrated the Cambodian people's strong desire for peace and political pluralism. This was a blow to the Khmer Rouge, but the election outcome was not. Their longtime ally, the royalist party of Prince Norodom Ranarridh (son of Sihanouk), won the largest bloc of assembly seats. According to Sihanouk, now the country's head of state, the royalist party has been infiltrated by "Khmer Rouge. . .tasked with eliminating true royalists." The Khmer Rouge control much of the royalist army as well.

Despite the U.N.'s $3 billion peace-making operation, the Khmer Rouge are greater threat than ever. Since the signing of the peace agreement, they have increased their military strength and profited from selling off Cambodia's natural resources to Thailand. They are trying to muscle their way into the elected coalition government, and are closer to returning to power than at any time since 1979.

The international community should help prevent this from happening by providing support to the new government to enable it to ward off the Khmer Rouge and improve the livelihoods of the Cambodian people. A positive step in this direction is legislation introduced in the U.S. Congress in 1992 and reintroduced this year which would assist Cambodia in collecting evidence so that the Khmer Rouge leaders can be tried for the crimes against humanity which they committed when they ruled Cambodia.

Chanthou Boua, a native of Kompong Cham Province in Cambodia, is an associate of the Asia Resource Center in Washington, D.C.

Former Soviet Union,
Central and Eastern Europe

by Sharon Wolchik

Overview

The collapse of communism and the break-up of multi-ethnic states continue to constrict food supplies and cause other hardships for people in the former Soviet Union and Central and Eastern Europe. Conditions vary widely within this vast region. Hunger is most widespread in situations of armed conflict, notably in former **Yugoslavia**, **Armenia**, **Georgia**, and **Tajikistan**. On the other hand, several countries in the region have had the benefit of good harvests, and countries in Central Europe have the advantage of relatively advanced economies.

Former Soviet Union

Hunger was most prevalent among the successor states to the Soviet Union in 1992 and 1993 in those countries that experienced significant levels of civil strife and war. Armed conflict continued to have a serious impact on food supplies in **Georgia**, and in **Armenia** and **Tajikistan**, which requested food and humanitarian assistance from former Soviet states and other governments.

The economic disruptions that have accompanied efforts to introduce economic reform and unsettled political situations continued to create food supply problems in the **Russian Federation**. The increased cost of agricultural inputs, the impact of land reform, and uncertainty about agricultural policies contributed to lower than average supplies of food. Inflation, weak systems for marketing and distributing food to processors, and growing unemployment decreased purchasing power and limited access to available supplies for many population groups.

Similar problems affected food supplies in other members of the **Commonwealth of Independent States** (CIS – former Soviet Republics other than Georgia and the Baltic States of Estonia, Latvia, and Lithuania). Government agencies continued to have difficulties procuring adequate supplies of grain.

Central and Eastern Europe

There are important variations in the extent of food shortages and hunger in Central and Eastern Europe. Problems with the food supply are most widespread in **former Yugoslavia**, where war ravaged **Bosnia-Hercegovina** and created large numbers of refugees, and in **Albania**, where a large proportion of food supplies continued to come from abroad in 1992 and 1993. Food supplies in **Bulgaria** and **Romania** continued to reflect poor economic performance, high inflation, and agricultural problems.

In **Poland**, **Hungary**, **the Czech Republic**, and **Slovakia**, where the re-establishment of market economies is well underway, decreasing production and a decline in purchasing power resulted in shifts in consumer spending and changes in the types and amounts of food many people consumed. The liberalization of prices and end of food subsidies increased the prices for agricultural and other goods. These trends created difficulties for vulnerable groups, including pensioners and large families, but hunger was not a widespread problem. Early signs of economic recovery are also encouraging in Poland, Hungary, and the Czech Republic. The break-up of the Czechoslovak Federation has delayed recovery somewhat in Slovakia.

Foreign Assistance

International aid and humanitarian assistance continued to be important in securing the food supply and averting famine in several parts of the region. This aid was particularly critical in war-torn areas, such as **Bosnia-Hercegovina** and **Tajikistan**. In Bosnia-Hercegovina, the dire situation of inhabitants of Sarajevo and other besieged cities led to international relief efforts, and in early 1993, U.S. airdrops of food supplies. Serbian interference with United Nations (U.N.) aid convoys, sniper fire on civilians trying to reach relief supplies, and difficulties in reaching targeted groups decreased the effectiveness of these measures to alleviate starvation and malnutrition among Bosnian Muslims.

International organizations also provided aid to alleviate food shortages in drought-plagued **Moldova**.

Assistance from the United States and

other nations to **Russia** and other states in the region to support the re-creation of market economies and buffer the effects of unemployment was supplemented by humanitarian aid. Russia's ability to buy grain from several nations, including Canada and Australia, was hampered by payment arrearages. The U.S. government suspended credits to Russia for wheat purchases in late 1992 in reaction to Russia's failure to pay interest on its debt, although donations of wheat continued. In an effort to bolster political forces supporting reform in Russia, the Clinton administration proposed a new U.S. aid package of $1.6 billion in early 1993. Approximately $700 million in credit was to be targeted for purchase of commodities and food products. The proposal also included $194 million in food grants.

Country Updates

Successor States of the Soviet Union

Russian Federation

Russia's grain harvest was approximately 20 percent greater in 1992 than in 1991, but remained below very high 1990 levels.[1] Although basic foods are available, skyrocketing food prices, which grew almost twice as fast as wages in 1992, created hardships for vulnerable groups. The U.S. Department of Agriculture estimates that Russians spend an average of 60 percent of their income on food.[2] In 1992, pensioners spent nearly 80 percent.[3] Pensions were increased again in early 1993, but many older citizens continue to find it difficult to afford adequate food.

Russians spend an average of 60 percent of their income on food. In 1992, pensioners spent nearly 80 percent.

In Ukraine, food prices increased by ten to twenty times in 1992, while real wages fell by one-half to one-third.

Malnutrition is also a problem for the 28 percent of the population Russian officials estimated to be below the poverty line in February 1993.[4]

Most other population groups have been able to cope with higher food prices by spending more of their total incomes on food. However, there have been important changes in diet. The State Statistical Committee indicated that citizens consumed 25 percent fewer milk and dairy products, 15 percent less meat, and 30 percent less fruit in 1992 than in 1991. Certain foodstuffs, including meat, are available primarily in higher-priced private markets.

Although hunger is not widespread, people are eating unbalanced diets. They are also consuming poor quality and, at times, contaminated food. Much of the food supply reflects the overuse of agricultural chemicals, toxic wastes, and widespread water pollution. Together with other aspects of the ecological crisis that developed during the communist period, this situation has resulted in health problems and a decrease in longevity.[5]

European Republics

In **Ukraine**, food prices increased by ten to twenty times in 1992, while real wages fell by one-half to one-third. The situation of pensioners, whose pensions in October 1992 equalled only a third of the price of a typical basket of consumer goods, continued to worsen. Lack of agreement with Russia on fuel prices resulted in shortages and decreased agricultural production.[6]

The grain harvest improved somewhat in **Belarus** in 1992, but the country still had to import grain for both bread and

livestock feed. There are no widespread shortages of food. However, the country's previously high levels of per-capita consumption declined significantly as the result of price increases.

Trans-Caucasus Republics

Violent conflicts disrupted food production and distribution in **Armenia, Azerbaijan,** and **Georgia. Armenia**'s war with Azerbaijan over control of the enclave of Nagorno-Karabakh led to critically low Armenian food supplies. Fighting and blockades disrupted grain imports. Fruits and vegetables were plentiful, but the supply of grain, most of which must be imported, was very low. Prices for many foodstuffs, including meat, dairy products, and bread, increased much faster than minimum salaries, which doubled over the course of 1992. Food prices continued to increase in 1993, climbing on average 150-200 percent by March.[8] The conflict reduced the land planted in grains in **Azerbaijan**.

Central Asian Republics

Civil war led to severe hunger in parts of Tajikistan. In other Central Asian nations, efforts to create market economies led to higher food prices and hardship for low-income households.

Tajikistan's 1992 grain harvest was better than that of 1991, but civil war led to conditions of near famine in the Kulyah region and serious shortages elsewhere. Refugees fleeing the strife also created serious food supply problems in the capital, Dushanbe. The war dramatically reduced the government's ability to export crops such as cotton to pay for grain imports.

Baltic States

Negative economic developments in Russia continued to have repercussions in the Baltic States, which remain dependent on Russia. Severe drought also reduced grain and fodder crops. In **Lithuania**, increased energy prices, disruptions in trade, and resulting declines in agricultural and industrial production were reflected in 50-percent increases in food prices in early 1993.[9] In **Latvia**, the cereal harvest was approximately 20 percent lower in 1992 than in 1991. Latvian officials note that the daily food intake of the poorest third of the population fell by 12 percent by early 1992. Price increases in 1992 further decreased food consumption.[10] Drought also reduced the **Estonian** harvest in 1992. U.N. officials indicate that resulting problems with livestock production and increased prices led to a 22-percent decrease in meat consumption and a 30-percent reduction for milk.[11] The collapse of exports of these products to the CIS states led to smaller livestock herds in all Baltic countries.

Central and Eastern Europe

Former Yugoslavia

Citizens in **Bosnia-Hercegovina** continue to suffer acutely from the disruption of food supplies caused by civil war and the policies of "ethnic cleansing" used against Muslims by Serbs. The office of the U.N. High Commissioner for Refugees indicates that there are over two million refugees, including 1.8 million from Bosnia. Ten percent of the population of Bosnia-Hercegovina was moderately malnourished by November 1992. U.N. officials estimated that 1.6 million people were at risk of hunger in Bosnia-Hercegovina in early 1993 and reported scores of deaths from cold and hunger in isolated Muslim cities in eastern Bosnia. Due to a relatively mild winter, as well as international assistance, there were fewer deaths than anticipated, but food supplies remain critically low in many areas. International relief efforts have been plagued by shortages of funds and equipment; fighting has also disrupted or blocked the delivery of aid.

As a result, the Food and Agriculture Organization of the UN estimated that international aid provided less than one-half of the minimum food requirements of the population in late 1992.[12] In early 1993, the United States began airdrops of food to besieged cities in eastern Bosnia, including Srebrenica, Kamenica, Zepa, Goradze, and Konjevic Polje. However, it is unclear how much of the food aid actually reached the population most in need of it.

The population of **Croatia** also continued to suffer from the impact of war. Inflation averaged 30 percent a month in late 1992 and early 1993, and real incomes decreased by 80 percent over a two-year period. Shortages of agricultural inputs and the impact of drought on the 1992 harvest resulted in serious food shortages. The estimated 600,000 refugees in Croatia have further boosted demand for food.[13]

The economic dislocations caused by the break-up of Yugoslavia also led to a 9-percent drop in industrial production in **Slovenia**. Drought followed by severe hailstorms led to a sharp decrease in the 1992 harvest.[14]

Macedonia's population suffered from the impact of hyperinflation and economic dislocations as well. By late 1992, the total value of a typical market basket was 50 percent greater than the average wage. One-third of the economically active population was not able to satisfy its basic living requirements without assistance.[15]

The estimated 600,000 refugees in Croatia have further boosted demand for food.

The diet of most Romanian families has deteriorated.

War and international sanctions had a negative impact on the food supply of **Serbia** and **Montenegro** (the only republics remaining in the Yugoslav Federation). Decreased grain production in Serbia due to drought and the impact of international sanctions led to bread, flour, and meat shortages. Hyperinflation, evident in the 16,690-percent increase in the price of milk and 16,127-percent increase in the price of bread between January 1992 and January 1993, further limited access to food. Fertilizer shortages due to sanctions and excessive rains are also expected to reduce Serbia's 1993 harvest.

Sanctions have drastically reduced foreign trade in Montenegro. Retail prices in 1992 were reported to be 22,663 percent above those in 1991. Over 50 percent of the labor force was unemployed in early 1993.[16]

Balkan States

Hunger was widespread in **Albania** in 1992. The economy of the poorest nation in Europe suffered drastically from the collapse of communist rule and disruption of production that followed. Economic hardship and political uncertainty pushed large numbers of Albanians to seek to leave their country in 1990 and 1991. U.N. officials indicate that drought, lower plantings, and reduced inputs led to another lower-than- average harvest in 1992. Bread and other foods in state stores are rationed, and most citizens cannot afford goods in private shops. Government officials estimate that 25 percent of the labor force is unemployed.[17]

The Italian government led the international humanitarian food aid effort, Operation Pelikan, in 1991. Nongovernmental organizations from several countries, including the United States and Germany,

also participated. Aid from groups in Italy and other European countries, the World Bank, and International Committee of the Red Cross continued throughout 1992 and is still critical in meeting food needs.

Living standards also declined markedly in **Romania.** In 1992, over 50 percent of the population lived below the poverty line.[18] Unemployment increased; as in other countries in the region, women have been hardest hit. The plight of approximately 200,000 people who do not receive unemployment compensation is particularly difficult.

Other factors contributed to reduced food supplies: privatization of agricultural land, which resulted in the proliferation of small farms; the advanced age of most agricultural workers; and the sizeable areas of land left untilled. Shortages of many foods, including bread, milk, and other dairy products, as well as fuel, occurred in many parts of Romania in the winter of 1992-1993. The government imported substantial amounts of grain, butter, and powdered milk in 1992.[19] Food price increases of 1,360 percent between October 1990 and December 1992 limited consumption.[20] Inordinately cold weather, coupled with the impact of drought in 1992, created serious problems in supplies of drinking water. As in the rest of the region, elderly people, women raising children alone, and others on fixed incomes have suffered most from this situation. The diet of most Romanian families has deteriorated. These conditions prompted mass protests by unions in early 1993.

Bulgaria, which initiated radical market reforms in early 1991, experienced the largest drop in industrial production in Central and Eastern Europe by 1992. The elimination of subsidies for food and most other goods led to five-fold price increases in 1991. This was not offset by wage supplements or the doubling of minimum pensions. Unemployment rose to approximately 14.8 percent by December 1992.[21] Pensioners comprise approximately 40 percent of the adult population. They faced a serious decline in living standards despite symbolic, one-time payments designed to offset inflation in early 1992. The 1992 harvest was a quarter less than that of 1991 as the result of lower plantings and the impact of uncertainty about land ownership, drought, and problems obtaining inputs.[22]

Central Europe

In the Czech Republic, Slovakia, Poland, and Hungary, there is little hunger. However, high prices and the economic dislocations associated with the shift to market economies reduced consumer demand. Increased prices for agricultural inputs also had a negative impact on agricultural production.

In **Poland,** dry weather contributed to lower than average harvests of cereals, potatoes, and feed crops, and led to increased grain imports. There were signs that Poland's economy was beginning to recover from its decline in 1992. However, positive trends in industrial output and success in keeping inflation near the forecast level did not prevent numerous strikes for higher wages in mining and other industries. Unemployment ranged from 12 to 14 percent in 1992, and contributed to unrest and dissatisfaction with the government.

Unemployment levels also continued to increase in **Hungary**, reaching 13.6 percent in January 1993. Although the economy showed positive developments in 1992 and early 1993, many workers have used up their one-year eligibility for unemployment benefits. Fears about shortages of bread, fueled by sizeable price increases in late 1992 and early 1993, were dismissed as groundless by agriculture officials in February 1993.[23] However, food prices rose 36.7 percent from February 1992 to February 1993.[24]

The food supply and overall living conditions of **Czech** citizens were influenced by favorable economic developments in 1992 and 1993. With a yearly average inflation rate of 11 percent in 1992 and an unemployment rate of approximately 3 percent in early 1993,[25] they continued to enjoy a higher standard of living than most others in the region. Larger than expected price increases as the result a new value-added tax strained the overall budgets of many families in 1993, however, and unemployment is expected to reach 5 percent.

Slovakia suffered more from policies designed to re-create a market economy. Unemployment, which reached 15 percent in early 1993,[26] threatens the living standard of many families. Dissatisfaction with the government's strategy of economic reform was one of the factors that contributed to the break-up of the Czechoslovak Federation, and the current Slovak government will face renewed protest if living standards decline further. ■

Dr. Sharon Wolchik is professor of Political Science and International Affairs at The George Washington University in Washington, D.C., and is associated with the university's Institute for European, Russian, and Eurasian Studies.

In the Czech Republic, Slovakia, Poland, and Hungary, there is little hunger.

Latin America-Caribbean

by BFW Institute

Overview

The worst drought in sixty years sharply reduced food production in impoverished
northeast **Brazil** in 1993. The Brazilian federal
and state governments provided assistance to six
million people, but that aid did not assure minimum
subsistence, and those assisted were only about half
of those in need. Even in times of normal weather,

thirty-two million Brazilians (more than 20 percent of
the population) have incomes below $120 per year,
the level needed to buy food and other necessities.
The richest 20 percent of Brazilians earn thirty-two
times as much as the poorest 20 percent, creating a
gap larger than in Bangladesh.[1]

Loss of aid and trade as a result of the collapse of

Graph 1

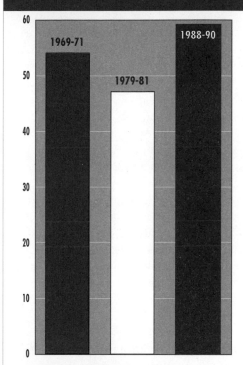

Chronically Undernourished Latin Americans (Million)

1969-71
1979-81
1988-90

As a Percent of Developing World Total

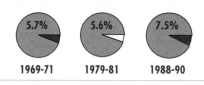

5.7%	5.6%	7.5%
1969-71	1979-81	1988-90

Source: FAO and WHO

the Soviet Union continued to have a severe impact on the food situation in **Cuba** in 1992-1993. Shortages of agricultural inputs, particularly fertilizer, reduced food and cash crop output. Basic food, medicine, fuel, and other goods are in short supply. The U.N. World Food Program (WFP) provided emergency food aid to 150,000 people affected by a damaging storm in March 1993. Floods in May and June displaced another forty thousand people. Nutritional deficiencies contributed to health problems, including forty-two thousand reported cases of vision disorders.[2]

In **Haiti**, political crisis continued to ravage the economy, agriculture, and social indicators in 1992-1993. Unemployment and inflation reached double-digit levels, capital left the country, and hunger and malnutrition were widespread. At least seventy thousand people depended on emergency food aid from WFP. The embargo imposed by the Organization of American States against the country's de facto military government increased food costs and decreased agricultural production (due to shortages of inputs). Grain production for 1993 was forecast to decline slightly.

In **Peru**, grain production was expected to decline sharply, due to poor weather, austerity policies, and violent conflict. The government's stringent economic policies helped reduce inflation from 7,600 percent in 1990 to a still high level of about 100 percent in 1992. But this limited access to food for much of the urban population, and lack of access to credit meant that it was difficult for farmers to produce food.[3]

War in Guatemala escalated between 1978 and 1982, with staggering results.

Land, Corn, and The Search for Peace In Guatemala

by Phil Anderson

People of Corn

As José Antonio sits in his newly constructed hut of plastic sheets stretched across wooden poles taken from the dense rainforest of northern Quiche, he reflects with emotion and amazement upon his return home after ten years of exile. His sixteen-year-old daughter, Natividad, listens attentively as she prepares corn tortillas over the fire. At age three, she ran messages back and forth between mother and father as they hid in the jungle from an advancing army that was destroying villages and crops and massacring civilians. Though conditions in the new settlement of "Victory, 20 of July" are very basic since their collective return two months earlier, José and family express joy and thanks to God at being back in their homeland.

Rooted in the volcanic soil of Guatemala are the *Hombres de Maíz*, the people of corn. The sacred Mayan creation stories of the *Popol Vuh* intertwine life, food, earth, and mystic meaning for Guatemala's five million indigenous people.

This harmonic vision is marred by the legacy of five hundred years of colonization – conflict over control of land. The sacredness and intimacy of land for the indigenous people clashes with the "modern" view of land as a commodity which can be bought and sold, and used to grow crops for distant markets, with gains going to owners or marketers whose hands never touch the soil.

For the Indian people of Guatemala, the struggle for cultural and spiritual survival and resistance to domination has meant war, hunger, and forced dislocation. For much of the period since 1960, a civil war centered around issues of land, culture, ethnicity, and economic power has engulfed Guatemala.

Other Central American countries experienced similar conflicts, particularly Nicaragua and El Salvador. In each of these nations, the United States supported unrepresentative governments on Cold War grounds. U.S. weapons, training, and other assistance added greatly to the suffering of poor and indigenous people. Their centuries-old aspirations were ignored; self-reliance efforts were beaten down. Guatemala's conflict received the least media attention.

War in Guatemala escalated between 1978 and 1982, with staggering results:

- 440 Indian villages destroyed;

- More than 100,000 dead, the vast majority civilians;

- Seventy thousand widows and 250,000 orphans;

- One million internally displaced people; and

- More than 200,000 Guatemalan refugees in other countries.

Those most affected by this war were the "people of corn" – the Indian people of the highlands, twenty-two ethnic groups of Mayan descent. Pursued primarily by their own government's soldiers, they fled where they could, some as far as

Europe, Australia, and Canada. Several tens of thousands reached the United States, most without documentation. Some fled to other Central American countries, mainly to southern Mexico.

About forty-seven thousand officially-recognized Guatemalan refugees have lived for a decade in Mexican settlements assisted by the United Nations High Commissioner for Refugees (UNHCR). Mexico informally acknowledges the likely presence of nearly twice that number who are not recognized to be refugees. Within Guatemala, as the midpoint of widely varying estimates, an additional 150,000 people are still internally displaced.

Return to the Land – National Re-Encounter, With Dignity

Santiago Antonio Martínez, his wife María, and their ten-year-old son Marcos carried sacks of corn and beans as gifts with them as they walked the two hours along the abandoned and muddy road into Santa María Tzeja. This was their first time back in the area after fleeing twelve years earlier. They had survived a year living in ravines and below the jungle canopy, hiding from the military, and living on roots, wild herbs, and honey, before they reached the Mexican side of the border and the safety of a refugee camp. Now, as they walked along, they recalled a military battle here, their previous cornfield over there, and the place where they left several loved-ones' bodies as they stayed a few minutes ahead of the army. As they reached their old village, a brother emerged from a house a

stone's throw away. They both thought the other had died in the battles. Joy overcame them as they embraced. Santiago blessed his nieces and nephews with the sign of the cross on the forehead, in traditional "campesino" fashion.

The desire to return to Guatemala burns fervently in the hearts of many refugees. The elders want to see their homeland again, and to be buried eventually in the land of their ancestors. Parents of children born in Mexico, or whose children were very young when forced into exile, want their children to identify themselves with the culture and land of Guatemala. Many young people are adapting to Mexican

The desire to return to Guatemala burns fervently in the hearts of many refugees.

In 1993, Guatemalan refugees began to return home.

Prospects for permanent settlement in Mexico are dim.

life. Some are attracted by the life of Caribbean resort cities, such as Cancún, where they find menial jobs in the tourist industry or as domestic servants for wealthy Mexicans. The attraction of fancy clothes, night life, and "gringo music" alienates them from traditional cultural roots.

Prospects for permanent settlement in Mexico are dim. Guatemalan refugees will never gain title to Mexican land. Often, in order to remain on land on which they have squatted for years, they have worked without pay, so as to avoid forcible eviction. Prices are low for crops grown in the region, and income doesn't keep up with inflation. If one is to live poorly, refugees often say, it is better to live in one's own country with the possibility of providing a future for one's children.

The Arias Peace Plan for Central America of 1987 gradually and precariously fostered a "firm and lasting" peace in the region. The end of the Cold War has stripped away elements of international distraction, making possible national and regional solutions.

In 1988, the Guatemalan refugees in Mexico began to organize for their journey home. The return was postponed several times due to continued violence and repression in Guatemala.

Throughout Central America, peace making efforts have included refugee repatriation and resettlement of internally-displaced people. CIREFCA (the Spanish acronym for the U.N. International Conference on Refugees in Central America, created in 1988) has provided the regional and international framework and mechanisms for dialogue on repatriation, as well as programs to assist non-recognized refugees and internally-displaced persons. UNHCR, in contrast, can only assist officially-recog-

nized refugees, and its authority diminishes rapidly once refugees reach their home country.

CIREFCA meetings have included all the governments of Central America, donor countries, nongovernmental organizations (NGOs), and displaced people themselves. CIREFCA's mandate terminates in 1994. Then, the U.N. Development Program will assist repatriated refugees. The return of Guatemalan refugees benefits from the experiences of more than twenty thousand Salvadoran refugees and several thousand Nicaraguans who returned home from Honduras. Other refugees have been repatriated from Costa Rica and Panama. Tripartite commissions between countries of origin, countries of refuge, and UNHCR were set up in each case. Mechanisms of dialogue were set up among refugees themselves, UNHCR, country representatives, and NGOs.

In January 1993, 2,480 refugees formed the first bloc to return home after formal agreements had been negotiated between their representatives and the Guatemalan government. Support from the international community added confidence regarding their safety. The returnees were greeted triumphantly throughout their journey home by thousands of well-wishers who greeted them with fireworks, marimba bands, flowers, and symbolic offerings of corn or clothing. The mass return of refugees was a sign of hope for peace and national reconstruction. Now, they face the arduous task of creating new communities out of the jungle.

1993 – Year of Peace For Guatemala

Father Nayo, village priest, recited reverently the names of loved-ones killed in the massacres of Ixcan Grande in 1982. This Good Friday ritual near the site of those events sent shivers through the crowd of family members who had survived. Fifty meters away, soldiers from the same military base kept a watchful eye. Remembering the death of Jesus on the cross and the death of loved-ones by bayonet, bullets, and fire, Father Nayo's prayers invoked the miracle of resurrection, newness, and peace on earth.

Guatemala became the focus of increased international attention in 1993. It remained the only country in the region formally at war. Also, the United Nations declared 1993 the International Year of Indigenous People, and the Indian people of Guatemala and the entire world were honored by the naming of Rigoberta Menchu Tum, a Quiche Mayan Indian of peasant origin, as Nobel Peace Prize Laureate.

Peace negotiations between the Guatemalan government and the insurgent Guatemalan National Revolutionary Unity (URNG), begun in 1990, intensified in early 1993. A Guatemalan Catholic Bishop, Mons. Rodolfo Quezada Toruno, has served as the principal mediator, assisted by the Lutheran World Federation. Dialogue has taken place among civilian sectors, including business, universities, labor, churches, and grassroots and Mayan organizations. The UN maintains an observer role in the discussions.

Prospect for the Future

Continued repatriation and resettlement of refugees and displaced people will depend on the availability of land, the state of the economy, continued progress toward peace, and respect for human rights. Speculation on land prices has inhibited the return of some refugees, and poverty and subsistence living are the rule in rural areas. Except for the pervasive presence of the military, much of rural Guatemala is devoid of government services. Many people migrate to the cities even at risk of long unemployment or work that pays starvation wages. Young women are drawn into the newly-created, foreign-owned "sweat-shops" *(maquilas)*, where work hours are long and there is no right to unionize.

But an attempted *coup d'état* in mid-1993 was turned around by strong pressure from democratic and civilian sectors of Guatemala and the international community. The failure of this *coup* was a major historical shift in Guatemala, away from the pattern of the last forty years, and perhaps toward a climate conducive to negotiated peace with dignity. Only such a prospect, which recognizes and begins to rectify fundamental inequities, will enable Guatemala to address the abysmal disparity between the rich and the vast majority of Guatemalans who are poor, and permit recovery of the vision of *Hombres de Maíz*. ∎

Rev. Phil Anderson, a BFW regional organizer based in Minneapolis, spent six months in 1993 working with refugees returning to Guatemala.

Middle East

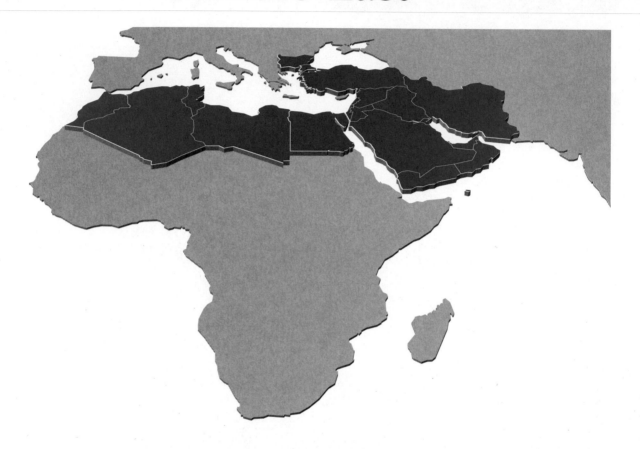

by Daniel U.B.P. Chelliah

Overview

Much of the Middle East is still reeling from consequences of the 1991 Persian Gulf War – loss of jobs and property, infrastructure damage, displacement of five million people, and environmental pollution caused by burned oil wells and spills in **Kuwait.** Most nations remain under dictatorial political leadership.

Tensions continue between Kuwaitis and Iraqis, Iraqis and Kurds in northern **Iraq, Iraqis** and Shi'ite Muslims in southern Iraq, and Israelis and Palestinians. Within the Maghreb countries of North Africa and in **Egypt, Saudi Arabia, Syria, Jordan,** and **Turkey,** the struggle between Islamic fundamentalist movements and the regimes is gaining momentum. Some of the

countries in the region, such as **Egypt, Jordan,** and **Morocco,** depend heavily on foreign aid. Other countries, such as the **United Arab Emirates** (UAE), **Libya, Turkey,** and **Iran,** do not. Food imports are on the rise in the region. Tourism, a major source of hard currency, has fallen off following terrorist acts by Islamic fundamentalists against Westerners. Efforts to maintain law and order divert resources from development. Food production, welfare programs (such as health and sanitation, and maternal and child care) and participation of citizen groups in welfare and development activities suffer greatly because of the uncertain political atmosphere.

There are pockets of acute hunger in the Middle

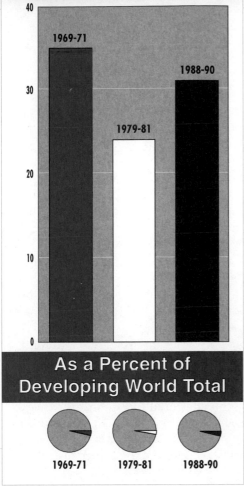

Graph 1

Chronically Undernourished Middle Eastern People (Million)

40

1969-71

1988-90

30

1979-81

20

10

0

As a Percent of Developing World Total

1969-71   1979-81   1988-90

Source: FAO and WHO

East, and with the exception of **Turkey** and **Iran,** all of the countries import over half their food supply. **Kuwait, UAE,** and **Bahrain** import more than 95 percent.

Acute Hunger

Iraq

Despite favorable weather, cereal production declined sharply in 1992, mainly due to a reduction in area sown and shortages of seeds, fertilizers, insecticides, and spare parts. The harvest will cover only one-fifth of 1992-1993 needs. Five million

tons of grain will need to be imported to maintain consumption at adequate levels. It is unlikely that this level of imports will be achieved, so hunger in Iraq will increase.

Food price levels on the open market remain well beyond the purchasing power of a large section of the populace. As a result, nutritional levels continue to deteriorate. The death rate among Iraqi children under age five tripled after the Gulf War. A study conducted by Alberto Ascherio of the Harvard School of Public Health and other studies found that, after the war, the risk of death for infants less than one month old had nearly doubled. According to a follow-up study by Miriam M. Shahin in 1992, the death rate for older children was four or five times higher than it had been. The children interviewed are "probably the most traumatized children ever documented." Researchers blamed the increased death rate on intestinal diseases caused and aggravated by sewage problems combined with diarrhea, dehydration, malnutrition, and lack of access to health care.

Northern Iraq

Approximately three million Kurds still suffer from the consequences of the war. Their long-term well-being depends on a stable political resolution of their status. Their short-term survival depends on a continued international presence, including adequate protection by allied aircraft. Without this, the Kurds would probably flee their villages as they did in 1991.

The United Nations (U.N.) sanctions, which prohibit items other than food and medicine from entering Iraq, hinder the Kurds' attempts to reconstruct their villages. Baghdad's internal embargo worsens the situation. Lifting the international

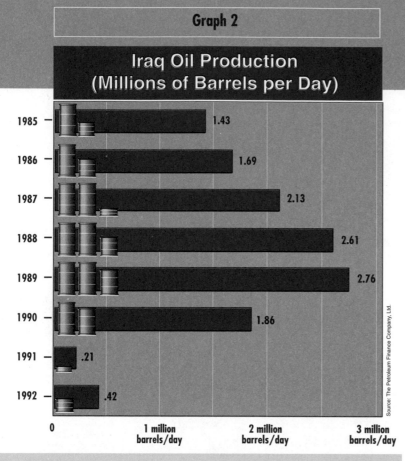

Graph 2

Iraq Oil Production
(Millions of Barrels per Day)

Year	Value
1985	1.43
1986	1.69
1987	2.13
1988	2.61
1989	2.76
1990	1.86
1991	.21
1992	.42

| 0 | 1 million barrels/day | 2 million barrels/day | 3 million barrels/day |

Source: The Petroleum Finance Company, Ltd.

Meeting Agricultural Needs

Agriculture is a major economic sector in northern Iraq, providing income and sustenance for large numbers of Kurdish people, especially those trying to resettle in destroyed villages. In the context of the Iraqi government embargo, local agricultural production can also help to keep down food prices in urban areas.

Aid agencies working in northern Iraq argue that basic agricultural needs — seeds, fertilizer, fuel, equipment, and pesticides — should be considered an integral component of emergency aid. If these needs are not met, the cycle of food dependency will be reinforced, and more food aid will be required.

The restoration of full production, particularly of fruit and livestock, will be a long process, made more difficult by land mines scattered over fields and pastures near the northern border, and land disputes caused by dispossession following a Kurdish uprising against the Iraqi government. External aid donors can have only a minor role in political settlements. They could, however, provide agricultural inputs on a stable basis, for several seasons if necessary. Such assurances would reinforce Kurdish families' resolve to stay on the land and their efforts to become more self-reliant.

sanctions on the three northern Kurdish provinces of Iraq might ease their plight somewhat.

The autonomous Kurdish regional government established in 1992 is having extreme financial difficulty. With kerosene too expensive for most people and international relief supplies slow in arriving, most of the few trees that survived Iraq's scorched earth policy have been cut for firewood. Shortages of fertilizers, pesticides, and diesel fuel frustrate Kurdish efforts to restore food self-sufficiency. (See "Meeting Agricultural Needs.")

For the foreseeable future, Kurdish survival will depend on international aid flows. Although the UN and some nongovernmental organizations (NGOs) hope to get enough supplies to vulnerable groups to prevent malnutrition, Kurdish officials say deaths from starvation appear inevitable.

International Intervention. While both the UN and NGOs are attempting to help negotiate a resolution of the Iraqi-Kurdish conflict, most of their activities involve providing relief and distributing agricultural inputs.

U.N. humanitarian operations face numerous obstacles. According to the U.N.'s Memorandum of Understanding with the Iraqi government, all U.N. missions outside Baghdad are to be accompanied by a government official. Due to procedural delays and security problems, the UN is finding it difficult to send staff into the Kurdish areas.

The U.N.'s Department of Humanitarian Affairs appealed for $500 million for its 1993-1994 Plan of Action to provide assistance to war victims throughout Iraq. So far, donors have pledged only $50 million, including a U.S. contribution of $15 million.

Inadequate resources greatly aggravate health conditions, especially among children.

Turkey

Widespread rains in Turkey promise a good wheat harvest in 1993. The 1992 wheat crop was lower than the record harvest the year before, but exceeded domestic needs.

Due to lack of institutional infrastructure, Turkey finds it difficult to achieve equitable food distribution in the southeast. Infant mortality rates are high in this area, due to low income, illiteracy, and lack of medical facilities.

Jordan

UNICEF studies indicate that unemployment in **Jordan** remains at about 34 percent since the Gulf War. Among war returnees, the rate is 83 percent. Remittances from workers in **Kuwait** were a major source of income in **Jordan.** As a result of the war, these remittances have fallen considerably, and a population of half a million, mainly women and children, are unable to cope with increasing food prices. Shortages of major staple items such as powdered milk, baby food, and rice cause nutritional deficiencies among children.

A recent survey of the nutritional status of preschool children by the Ministry of Health and UNICEF concludes that the incidence of chronic malnutrition is 16.1 percent among boys and 15.7 percent among girls; the figure for acute malnutrition is 1.9 percent and 1.3 percent, respectively.

Other surveys indicate that the population living in absolute poverty, which cannot afford food, shelter, and medical care, has increased from an estimated 3 percent of the total population to 5 per-

Nongovernmental Organizations in Iraq

As of December 1992, only CARE had signed agreements with the Iraqi government and UNICEF to work both in government-controlled areas and in the northern part of Iraq controlled by the Kurds. The agency is facilitating transport and distribution of food from the U.N. World Food Program to some 750,000 beneficiaries.

Oxfam UKI, which has signed an agreement with UNICEF, is working in the areas of health, water, and sanitation in one hundred villages in the north and is rehabilitating more than one thousand schools in the south.

Other groups working in northern Iraq have not signed an agreement with the government, and have no staff in government-controlled areas. (Staff, equipment, and supplies enter through Turkey.) Among these groups, Save the Children Fund (UK) has been improving access roads. Save the Children also assists with repairing shelters and distributing food for displaced people, with funds from Irish Concern. The Mines Advisory Group and Christian Aid are involved in de-mining. Other groups active in the north include Médecins Sans Frontières (MSF), Medico Internationalis, Handicap International, and Caritas. Security continues to be a major concern; there have been numerous bomb and grenade attacks.

In government-controlled areas, CARE provides daily meals for primary and preschool children in the neediest parts of Iraq. The Quakers continue to supervise distribution of fertilizers and pesticides in the south. The Middle East Council of Churches supports small-scale, income-generating projects through local churches.

cent since the Gulf crisis.

Jordan has agreed with the International Monetary Fund to implement a structural adjustment program. In the short term, it is likely to worsen the situation of poor people, because it calls for decreased subsidies on bread and farm inputs. The plan does not provide for the needs of those population groups which will be most adversely affected.

Israel and the Occupied Territories

Continuing tension between Israelis and Palestinians nearly ended the U.S.-initiated

Middle East peace process, and has constrained the ability of the U.N. Relief and Works Agency for Palestinian Refugees (UNWRA) to carry out relief and development activities for 2.7 million people. Women and children have been most seriously affected. (See table 1.) In 1992, according to UNICEF:

- The infant mortality rate among the refugees increased to thirty-seven per one thousand live births;

- Fifty percent of those admitted to camp clinics suffer from respiratory and diarrheal ailments;

- Inadequate sanitation led to a high incidence of infectious diseases; and

- Malnutrition and anemia are on the increase among children.

Due to the tensions created by the *intifada,* the Palestinian uprising against Israeli occupation of the West Bank and Gaza, and decreased nutritional levels, children suffer both physical and psychological problems. School closings, shortened school days, and reduced ability to concentrate in class are undermining a generation's basic education.

Regional Food Situation

Iran supports nearly 1.5 million Afghan refugees. The U.S. Committee for Refugees reports that the 750,000 refugees in the eastern provinces live in extremely difficult conditions. The women and children are highly anemic and suffer from malnutrition and disease.

Though **Yemen** increased its cereal production in 1992, it will need to import 1.4 million tons of wheat, about 94 percent of its needs, while trying to assimilate 1.5 million citizens who worked in **Saudi Arabia** before the Gulf War. Most of the returnees are jobless and without income; consequently their families suffer from low calorie intakes.

Egypt's cereal production increased substantially in 1992-1993, but imports are forecast to increase by 16 percent over the previous year. Egyptian government policies support high-value export crops, leading to reduced production of food for local consumption.

Increased foreign financial assistance followed Egypt's participation in the Gulf War. A combination of debt forgiveness, debt rescheduling, and other external aid has improved the country's macro-economic situation. But these benefits have not yet improved poor communities'

Table 1

Selected Studies of Palestinian Childhood Anemia

Year	Area	Age (months)	Sample Description	% Anemic
1984	West Bank & Gaza Camps	0-35	Refugee Children	50
1987	Ain Al-Dyuk	0-59	Village Children	59
1989	Jabalia	0-59	Village Children	63
1990	West Bank	0-35	Camps	58
1990	Gaza Strip	0-35	Camps	70

Source: Jacqueline Sfeir, Children of War Conference Documents, 1992.

access to food. "Discontent seethes from the mud-brick villages of the Upper Nile to the putrid slums of Cairo, all breeding grounds for growing Islamic insurgency. . . ."

The question is raised in Washington and Cairo repeatedly as to whether the United States has had its priorities right for the $2.1 billion a year it gives to Egypt. The aid does little to reduce the poverty, hunger, and dissatisfaction that fuel Islamic radicalism. Meanwhile, a growing population will continue to generate increased food needs.

Conclusion

Though some of the region's countries increased their food production in 1992, overall, the Middle East still faces food shortages. Hunger is an increasing problem for many Middle Easterners. The greatest stress comes from five million displaced people and refugees within the region who depend on welfare.

Political tensions, continuous foreign occupations, and the threat of war have led governments in the region to buy $35 billion in weapons since the end of the Gulf War. Many of these arms purchases are at the expense of agriculture and social services, thus jeopardizing regional peace. Preaching peace, the great powers have in fact stepped up their arms sales into the region exponentially.

Unrest, poverty, and hunger will likely increase if internal political solutions and international agreements for peace in the region are not achieved in the near future. Frustrated low-income groups may try to find solutions to their problems of hunger and poverty in ever more politicized religious fundamentalism. ■

Daniel U.B.P. Chelliah is coordinator, Refugee Affairs, at BFW Institute.

Table 2			
Estimates of Average Percentage of School Year Lost			
	1987-1988	**1988-1989**	**1989-1990**	**1990-1991**
Gaza	35%	47%	35%	43%
West Bank	75%	50%	50%	35%

Source: UNRWA Statistical Report, 1991.

North America

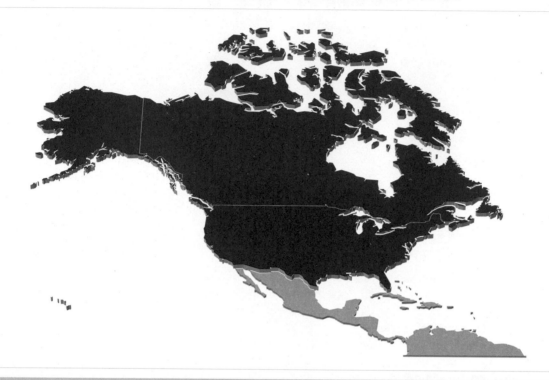

by Patricia Ann James

United States

More Hunger

Until recently, the U.S. government did not collect direct data on hunger and nutritional status in the United States. No data are as yet available from recent government nutrition monitoring. As a result, studies of hunger in the United States must rely on secondary indicators, such as poverty statistics, food stamp participation, and use of emergency food providers. Numerous studies have linked hunger to unemployment, underemployment, and the cost of life's basic necessities. These indirect indicators suggest that hunger worsened in the United States during the second half of 1992 and early 1993, due to a sluggish economy, public policy decisions, and long-term labor market changes.

In the first half of 1992, over twenty-five million people participated in the Food Stamp Program. The number increased by an average of 200,000 each month beginning in October 1992 and reached a record of 27.4 million in March 1993, before dropping slightly to 27.35 million in April. (See graphs 2 and 3, pp. 153-154.) The U.S. Department of Agriculture (USDA) calculates that the Food Stamp Program currently serves just 59 percent of those eligible.[1]

The U.S. Conference of Mayors reported that between November 1991 and October 1992, requests for emergency food assistance in major cities rose 18 percent over a year earlier.[2]

The Tufts University Center on Hunger, Poverty, and Nutrition Policy projected a rise in the number of hungry people in the United States in 1992 and 1993, due to economic conditions. Using 1991 data, the center had estimated that thirty million people in the United States were hungry (defined as "not always

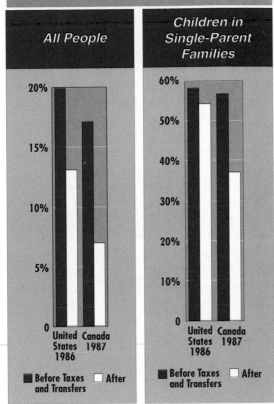

Graph 1

Impact of Tax and Social Welfare Policies on Poverty

All People

20%
15%
10%
5%
0

United States 1986   Canada 1987

■ Before Taxes and Transfers   □ After

Children in Single-Parent Families

60%
50%
40%
30%
20%
10%
0

United States 1986   Canada 1987

■ Before Taxes and Transfers   □ After

Source: Smeeding

having enough to eat"), including twelve million children under the age of eighteen. This compares to a finding of twenty million hungry people in 1985.[3] Other researchers have arrived at more conservative estimates of the number of hungry people in the United States.[4]

On the local level, a study by the University of California-Los Angeles found that 27 percent of the residents of a poor Latino neighborhood in South Central Los Angeles do not have enough money to buy food. Their families go hungry an average of five days each month. Median household annual income is about $16,000, less than half the Los Angeles County average. The typical family in this neighborhood spends 36 percent of annual income on food. In the affluent suburb of Lakewood, the figure is 12 percent.[5]

In spring 1993, Rep. Tony Hall (D-Ohio) staged a twenty-one-day fast to protest the demise of the House Select Committee on Hunger, which he had chaired. The committee helped Capitol Hill stay focused on hunger-related issues. Rep. Hall's fast led USDA to hold a national forum on U.S. hunger in Washington, D.C., in June 1993, with additional regional meetings planned. The World Bank agreed to hold a forum on global hunger. Members of Congress established a Congressional Hunger Caucus, and Rep. Hall also set up a nongovernmental Congressional Hunger Center.

Increased Poverty

From the late 1940s to the mid-1970s, the country's economic growth benefitted both poor and middle-class people alike – the rising economic tide truly raised most boats. Overall poverty rates fell from 40 percent in 1949 to 11 percent in 1973. "The 1980s was a decade of uneven tides" – people with lower incomes benefitted least while those in the higher brackets made the greatest gains to date.[6] The years 1973 through 1993 saw slow economic growth, rising poverty, and increasing gaps between rich and poor people, as well as between rich and middle-class people. (See graph 4, p.155.) Three recessions occurred between 1980 and 1991. At the same time, the federal government dismantled some social welfare programs and curtailed others.

These policy choices and economic fluctuations, along with declining wages for low-income workers, seriously weakened the ability of many families to achieve and maintain economic security. The 1980s saw a major change from past economic trends as unemployment rates

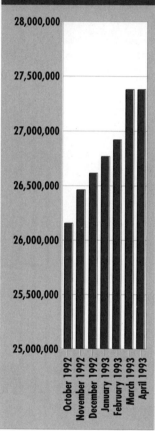

Graph 2

Food Stamp Program Participation October 1992- April 1993

28,000,000

27,500,000

27,000,000

26,500,000

26,000,000

25,500,000

25,000,000

October 1992
November 1992
December 1992
January 1993
February 1993
March 1993
April 1993

Source: USDA

remained unusually high, above 6 percent, for periods of economic growth.[7]

The 1989-1991 recession had an especially harsh impact on children. A 5-percent drop in median family income impoverished nearly two million additional children. By 1991, 21.8 percent of all U.S. children lived in poverty.[8] An estimated 300,000 more children fell into poverty during 1992.[9]

Labor Market Changes

In 1992-1993, record numbers of workers have been unemployed for so long they have exhausted their benefits. As a result, the government no longer counts them in the unemployment statistics. Others are working longer and harder for wages that leave their families struggling to survive at or below the poverty level.

Demand for white-collar, female, and educated workers has lessened in recent years. This placed "downward pressure on the wages of workers who had previously escaped wage erosion."[10] Between 1987 and 1992, white-collar wages fell by 2.1 percent. Wages for college-educated workers fell by 3.1 percent between 1987 and 1991. Entry-level wages for college graduates declined 9.8 percent. Nevertheless, education continues to provide workers with a wage premium. Semi-skilled and unskilled workers have seen their wages drop by double-digit rates.

The number of manufacturing jobs that provide high pay for skilled or semi-skilled work has fallen sharply. Every

industrialized economy faces this problem. Technological advances increase productivity while requiring fewer workers. International competition partly drives this trend. Many companies have moved their operations overseas in an effort to lower labor costs. It may be several decades before structural unemployment is solved – far too late for today's hungry Americans. The U.S. Department of Labor reports that job growth to the year 2005 is most likely to occur in service industries, where many positions are low-paid and lack health benefits and job security.

The State of Working America, a report by the Economic Policy Institute, paints a bleak picture of a work force emerging from a recession worse off than it was a decade ago:

By 1989, family income actually began to decline, and by 1990, average family income adjusted for inflation had dropped 2 percent, approximately half the gain won in the previous decade.[11]

The government reports that in 1991, the average worker's earnings failed to keep up with inflation for the first time in nine years. Economists have attributed the decline in incomes and the increase in joblessness in part to changes in international trading patterns, cuts in defense production, rising business costs due to new taxes, health care costs, and a global recession that affects export-related jobs.[12]

Impact of the 1990s Recession

The Economic Policy Institute says that the recession of the early 1990s differed from earlier recessions in a number of important ways:

The recent recession lasted at least twenty-two months, twice as long as the average length of earlier downturns . . . the recent recession involved roughly the same amount of permanent (versus temporary) job loss – a rise of 1.6 percent – as in recent, heavier downturns.[13]

The 1990s recession also involved "an unusually large rise in white-collar unemployment coupled with historically slow growth in white-collar employment."[14] As the economy recovered, employment did not increase as rapidly as after other postwar recessions. Unemployment actually increased by 0.7 percent from March 1991 to September 1992.[15] Secretary of Labor Robert Reich commented in early 1993:

In the last four recessions an average of 44 percent of the workers got their old jobs back. In this recession, only 14 percent are getting their old jobs back.[16]

The slowing of U.S. economic growth and the stalling of the unemployment rate at seven percent have shaken the faith of many Americans in the "recovery."

The U.S. growth rate climbed to 4.7 percent during the last quarter of 1992, but in the first quarter of 1993, growth fell below 1 percent. By the end of April 1993, state jobless claims for benefits surged to 380,000 – the highest level since December 1992. In addition to nine million unemployed workers, an additional 6.5 million part-time workers were seeking full-time employment. Government reports in April 1993 showed a sharp increase in unemployment claims, declining consumer confidence, and a decrease in business purchasing.[17]

Additional evidence of the recession's lingering impact came in job cutbacks by major firms and the findings of public opinion polls. IBM is laying off thousands of workers. Sears closed its century-old catalogue business and is cutting fifty thousand employees. Defense contractors are "downsizing:" United Technologies is laying off eleven thousand workers, Boeing is trimming its workforce by ten thousand, and McDonnell Douglas is letting go eighty-seven hundred employees in 1993. Xerox, Kodak, and General Motors all have shrunk substantially, along with many mid-size and small businesses that will either fail to grow, contract, or go under. Some analysts believe that this restructuring will eventually energize the U.S. economy.

In the short term, however, the process takes an unprecedented toll on the U.S. worker. Robert Solow, Nobel Laureate economist from MIT, said:

The immediate danger is not from the lay-offs themselves, but from the fact that millions of people will read about them and begin fearing for their own situations. It could have a psychological effect on consumer confidence.

Added Labor Secretary Reich, "Where is the market for your product if you don't employ people who can buy the product?"[18] In May 1993, the National Federation of Independent Businesses reported that U.S. job creation on a seasonally adjusted basis had been negative for eleven quarters. Further, most new jobs seem to be coming from small, start-up firms, suggesting that the major, blue chip firms – which generally offer higher pay – are not expanding.[19]

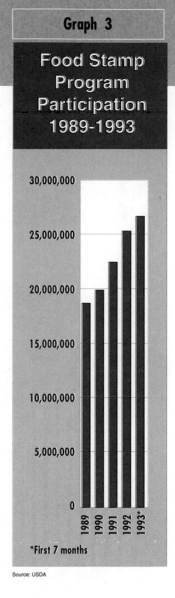

Graph 3

Food Stamp Program Participation 1989-1993

30,000,000

25,000,000

20,000,000

15,000,000

10,000,000

5,000,000

0

1989 1990 1991 1992 1993*

*First 7 months

Source: USDA

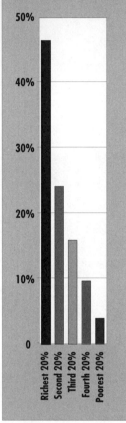

Graph 4

U.S. Income Distribution 1991

50%

40%

30%

20%

10%

0

Richest 20%
Second 20%
Third 20%
Fourth 20%
Poorest 20%

Source: U.S. Census Bureau

The Impact of Public Policy

Rather than offsetting these tendencies in the labor market, the government's tax and social welfare policies have made things worse. As the incomes of the rich were soaring, their taxes were cut, but as the incomes of the poor and middle class fell, their social benefits were cut. Faced with fiscal crises, many states have slashed or frozen public assistance benefits. Other states have been unable to implement programs designed to help families and poor children because of inadequate funding.

When Sonia Blutgarten spent $20 for cake mix and party favors to celebrate her sons' birthdays, it meant she could not afford to do eight loads worth of wash. The fat sacks of dirty clothes crowded the corridor of her shabby apartment for months while she squirreled away a dollar here and a dollar there to finance a trip to the laundry. For Ms. Blutgarten, a twenty-nine-year-old mother of two, such trade-offs are a fact of life, part of the day-to-day calculus of supporting herself, six-year-old TeAndré and four-year-old Kehnan on a $663 monthly welfare check, plus $168 worth of food stamps. . . . Even with current benefits, the fourth most generous among all states, Ms. Blutgarten rarely reaches the end of the month in the black, despite careful budgeting and much juggling of priorities, after she has paid her $400 rent and her $60 utility bill. She rides an hour and a half on the bus every couple of weeks to buy four packs of toilet paper at $.69 each, less than half of what it costs at the local supermarket. She has

been rationing an inch of window cleaner left behind by a previous tenant because there will be no more when that is gone. And things are getting worse for Ms. Blutgarten, a high school dropout. State budget cuts are expected to reduce services by MediCal, the state health plan for the poor, which has been whittled down in recent years. And city budget cuts in San Francisco forced up the price of a monthly transit pass from $35 to $40. Ms. Blutgarten is one of three welfare mothers who a few months ago sued the California Department of Social Services, accusing the department of failing to comply with federal regulations requiring states to reevaluate welfare benefits every three years.[20]

There are no simple cures for these hardships. Increased investment in education and training, research and development, and infrastructure offers the best hope for increasing productivity while also raising wages. Policies are needed which increase take-home income for working families, provide a safety net to tide over needy families in difficult economic times, and in other ways improve family economic security. The need to reduce the federal budget deficit makes it difficult to implement such initiatives, however.

The Tufts University Center on Hunger, Poverty, and Nutrition Policy in early 1993 analyzed child poverty trends and government social and economic policy choices. The analysis suggests that child poverty is closely linked to government social and economic policy.

It may be possible to virtually eliminate child poverty during the first decade of the new century under certain combinations of policy and economic conditions. If recent economic patterns repeat themselves, and if the federal and state governments do not implement strong anti-poverty measures, the number of children living in poverty in the United States could exceed twenty million within the next twenty years.[21]

Canada[22]

Poverty and hunger trends in Canada parallel those in the United States. Like the United States, Canada is one of the richest industrialized nations in the world. Yet, among this group of nations, it has one of the worst poverty rates among children and families. However, during the 1980s, Canada's social programs had a greater poverty-reducing impact than those in the United States. According to economist Timothy Smeeding, in the mid-1980s, U.S. tax and social welfare policies reduced poverty rates by 6.8 percentage points, whereas Canadian policies led to a reduction of 10.1. For children in single-parent families, the U.S. programs reduced poverty by 3.9 points, compared to 19.5 in Canada.[23] (See graph 1, p.152.)

During the 1980s one in six Canadian children fell below the poverty line. The beginning of the 1990 recession caused these figures to rise. In 1990, 16.9 percent of children under eighteen lived in poverty. By 1991, the figure rose to 18.3 percent.

The same period saw a growing polarization of family incomes between rich and poor. The poorest 40 percent of Canadian families had a smaller share of total income in 1990 than in 1980. At the same time the richest 20 percent of families gained significantly at the expense of other Canadians.

Canada does not have a federal program comparable to the Food Stamp Program in the United States. Social assistance (welfare) payments are intended to allow sufficient money to cover the cost of food.

Hungry Canadians also rely heavily on a privately-funded system of food banks. These food banks operate or supply over 1,200 grocery programs and 580 meal programs in 436 communities in all provinces and territories. According to the Canadian Association of Food Banks, more than two million people (7.5 percent of all Canadians), including 700,000 children, were expected to receive food assistance at least once in 1993. Since the first food bank opened in 1981, the number of food banks and the need for them have increased dramatically. This growth is a reflection of increasing unemployment and the number of single-parent families and the working poor who rely on food banks for assistance.

Campaign 2000 is a movement of Canadian NGOs to end child poverty by the year 2000. The campaign points out that it is vital that the federal government take a leadership role in crafting public policies to combat poverty. However, the most recent federal budget offers no policy innovations or reforms in the areas of child benefits or family support. According to the Caledon Institute of Social Policy, current federal tax and benefit policies will lead both welfare and working-poor families to fall further below the poverty line between 1993 and 2000. ■

Patricia Ann James was a domestic policy analyst at Bread for the World.

Western Europe

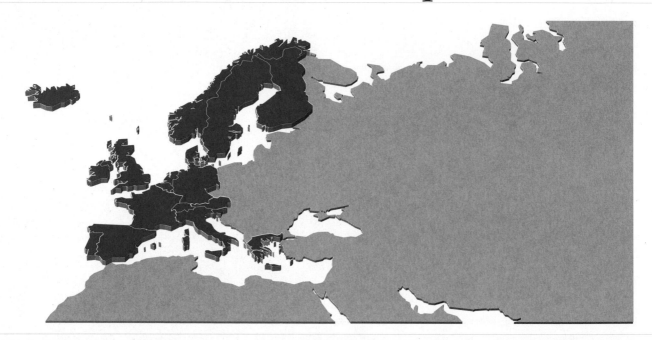

by A. Cecilia Snyder

Alarm is spreading: 17.4 million people are now unemployed in the twelve countries of the European Community, or 10.3 percent of the work force, up from 14.6 million at the beginning of the year.[1]

Overview

While European Community (EC) hunger and poverty problems are not as severe as those elsewhere, loss of jobs and a worsening immigration problem are taking their toll on Western European countries. As of December 1992, it was estimated that at least fifty million out of a total 345 million Europeans were living in poverty (defined by the EC as anyone earning less than half the EC average).[2] By July 1993, that number had increased to eighty million. In addition to soaring unemployment, homelessness has skyrocketed (three million people in 1992 and growing).[3] The re-unification of **Germany** and the collapse of the Soviet empire have drastically altered the smooth path EC Commission President Jaques Delors foresaw for European unity.

Monetary union, believed to be possible by 1996, is not even a consideration until at least 1999. Inflation rates, public-sector debt, and budget deficit percentages for over half of the member states are outside of the conditions set by the Maastricht Treaty of 1991.

Adding to this problem are the increasingly large numbers of refugees and asylum seekers who have been flooding into European countries at an alarming rate. In 1992 alone, over 700,000 immigrants (mostly from former Yugoslavia) crossed over into **Germany** and other EC member states. This new population is frequently blamed for worsening conditions, and ethnic and racial tensions have increased dramatically since 1991.

Unemployment

Beginning in mid-1990 in the **United Kingdom** and **Ireland**, increased unemployment had spread to most other parts of the community by 1991, and is projected to be at 11 percent by the end of 1993. Since 1990, slow economic growth has resulted in a drop in job creation. In contrast to average growth of

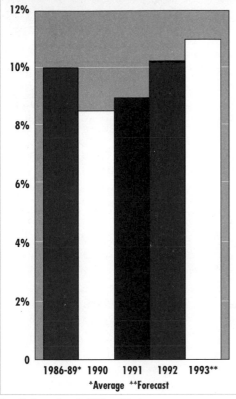

Graph 1

European Unemployment Rates 1986-1993

12%

10%

8%

6%

4%

2%

0

1986-89* 1990 1991 1992 1993**

*Average **Forecast

Source: The European Community, *1993 Economic Report*

over 1.5 percent between 1986 and 1990, employment numbers remained flat in 1991. Although growth is slowly resuming, increased employment numbers do not necessarily lead to a proportional decrease in unemployment. A large segment of the population, mostly women, make up what is termed the "hidden labor supply" – workers who are not counted officially as part of the labor force. As employment becomes available, therefore, this extra work force will compete with the twelve million unemployed on record for a limited number of jobs.

Unemployment compensation schemes vary widely among the member states, most of them involving a combination of unemployment insurance (payments based upon previous wages) and unemployment assistance (a guaranteed minimum level of income).[4] These systems, however, are not designed to reduce long-term unemployment, but only to provide replacement income.

Poverty and Social Exclusion

Long-term unemployment, along with unstable family structure and flawed social policies, are cited by the Commission of the European Communities as the primary causes of the "new poverty", also called "social exclusion."[5] The complexity and multifaceted nature of poverty require the definition to include other aspects in addition to low income. Housing, health care, and education all play a role in determining who will be able to participate fully in society and who will be excluded.

Homelessness has been on the rise since 1991. As of July 1993, there were nearly 630,000 homeless people living in both the United Kingdom and France. Germany's homeless population is 1.3 million.[6]

Individual member states, in an attempt to control budget deficits and inflation, have already taken steps to cut back on social welfare programs. In July 1993, **Germany's** cabinet approved a $12 billion reduction in social spending, and the **Dutch** parliament passed a strict new law to prevent abuse of disability payments. Since March 1993, **France** has cut its health-care spending by $6 billion.

Governments within the EC can no longer afford to spend a major part of their budget on social welfare. The community as a whole is therefore trying to develop new funds to combat poverty. Current forms of action, however, are generally limited and indirect with regard to poverty and social exclusion. For example, programs such as the European Regional Development Fund and the European Social Fund are intended to

Food Banks in Europe

by A. Cecilia Snyder

"Un belge sur cent a faim"[1] – one of every one hundred Belgians is hungry – is the sound bite from a brochure of the Belgian Federation of Food Banks. Although Belgium and its neighbors are relatively wealthy industrialized nations, stagnant economies and consequent unemployment have led to the establishment of seventy-five food banks in the European Community (EC), nine of which are in Belgium.

Inspired by the success of food banks in the United States, Bernard Dandrel established the first European food bank in Paris in 1984. By 1992, there were fifty-seven food banks operating in France alone. Spain, Italy, Portugal, Greece, and Ireland have all followed suit. Plans are under way to open banks in the Netherlands, Germany, and Great Britain.[2] Food banks are non-profit organizations, and rely heavily on financial and other donations. Supply and distribution of the food donations are free, and the staff consists of volunteers. Office equipment is usually donated, and operating expenses are covered by a third-party payment, usually tax-deductible cash gifts.

Most of the organizations belong to a national federation that coordinates the collection and distribution of food donations. These national groups in turn belong to larger coalitions, such as the European Federation of Food Banks. The federation provides support and information to its members, as well as a voice in the fight against hunger.

European food banks do not distribute food directly to hungry people. Like their U.S. counterparts, they distribute food to various charities which subscribe to principles established by the national federation. These local agencies provide needy people with food assistance in the form of groceries (e.g., meals-on-wheels) or meals (e.g., soup kitchens).

Most donations (64 percent) to the European Federation come from private businesses which provide surplus food that would otherwise go to waste. Official EC surpluses of butter, grain, fruits, and vegetables account for another 30 percent of donations.[3]

The food bank movement, like other anti-poverty and anti-hunger movements, shows no signs of slowing down. There is a growing need in Europe for real, lasting changes on all levels of society. Food banks are a positive sign that Europeans are beginning to recognize and respond to the needs of poor and hungry people in their community.

A. Cecilia Snyder is a research assistant at Bread for the World Institute.

provide financial support for the development of disadvantaged regions. However, these funds often do not directly assist the most disadvantaged groups and are often not easily accessible in many deprived areas.

New funds, billed as more encompassing and expansive, include the Poverty Three Program, which will provide over 55 million European Currency Units (ECUs), U.S.$63 million, on forty projects over a five-year period (1989-1994).[7] The projects experiment with different strategies for combatting poverty and social exclusion. However, the effectiveness of these programs will not be known until comprehensive evaluations are conducted.

Most recently, the community has developed a "cohesion fund" to help countries with a gross domestic product (GDP) per person below 90 percent of the EC average. As of 1993 these countries are **Spain**, **Portugal**, **Ireland**, and **Greece**. Between 1994 and 1997, the community is planning to spend 15 billion ECUs (U.S.$17 billion) on the cohesion fund and another 140 billion ECUs (U.S.$160 billion) on regional funds (for areas where the income per person is less than 75 percent of the EC average).[8] Until assessments are made, it will not be clear what impact these funds have had on the disadvantaged regions of the member states and on poor EC residents.

Emigration and Immigration

Immigration from North Africa and Eastern Europe increased to about three million in 1992, compared to one million in 1985. **Germany** has had to absorb the highest number of refugees, nearly 440,000 in 1992 (49.5 percent of the EC total).[9]

Refugees are among the poorest people in the EC, and are among the most intensely affected by hunger and malnutrition. Although hunger is not as severe or widespread as in other parts of the world, it still remains a problem for the poorest people of the EC. Previously unknown direct service organizations, such as food banks, are cropping up in **France**, **Belgium**, **Ireland**, and **Spain.** (See p.159.) Worsening economic conditions, in addition to new asylum laws, have a serious impact on refugees and asylum seekers.

Currently, **Germany** provides the most government assistance to asylum seekers of any EC member state. Asylum seekers are entitled to housing, clothing, food, medical care, and schooling for children. In addition, a social allowance is provided that averages about U.S.$325 a month per adult and U.S.$195 a month per child. In 1991, Germany spent almost $5 billion on public support for immigrants. But because federal subsidies are not covering the costs outlayed by German states, it is expected that there will be cutbacks in these assistance programs.[10]

Because of space shortages, refugees have been temporarily housed in public facilities. Asylum seekers have also been allowed to work in jobs for which Germans are not available since 1991, at wages set by national labor-management contracts.[11]

With rising inflation and unemployment, immigrants are feeling the frustration of unemployed Germans. Resentments have caused a number of violent attacks from Neo-Nazi and other hate groups. Political pressure, particularly from the former East German population, has led to a reform of the asylum system. On July 1, 1993,

Germany revoked its constitutional guarantee to an asylum hearing. Other countries in the European Community are also considering changing their asylum laws. **France** is seeking to restrict the number of applicants for asylum, and **Denmark** has imposed constraints and quotas on the numbers of asylum seekers that will be allowed into the country.

Conclusion

The European Community is not severely affected by hunger and poverty problems. However, faltering economies and subsequent job loss have affected the most vulnerable groups in the member states. There is a growing need for direct service organizations, but the attempt to respond to this need is hampered by national government budget cuts and welfare reforms. Refugees and asylum seekers face both poverty and unemployment, as well as resentment from populations in their host countries. The European Community is taking steps to spark economic growth, but it remains to be seen if these measures will indeed lead to recovery. ■

A. Cecilia Snyder is a research assistant at Bread for the World Institute.

Graph 2

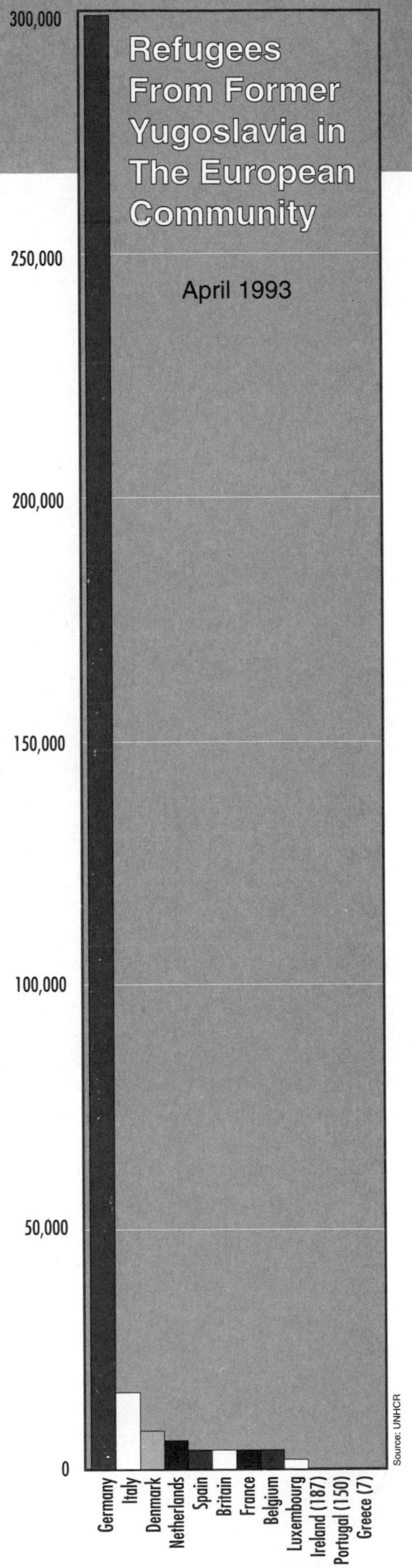

Refugees From Former Yugoslavia in The European Community

April 1993

Source: UNHCR

Germany, Italy, Denmark, Netherlands, Spain, Britain, France, Belgium, Luxembourg, Ireland (187), Portugal (150), Greece (7)

	Population (millions)		Population annual growth rate 1980-1991	Fertility (children per woman) 1991	Percent of population under 16 1991	Percent of population urbanized 1992	Life expectancy 1990-1995	Infant mortality per 1,000 live births 1990-1995	Under 5 mortality per 1,000 live births		Maternal mortality per 100,000 live births 1980-1990
	1992	2000							1960	1991	
Africa (sub-Saharan)	**561**	**713**	**3.0**	**6.5**	**54**	**29**	**51**	**102**	**262**	**180**	**600**
Angola	9.9	13.1	2.9	7.2	58	30	46	124	345	292	..
Benin	4.9	6.3	2.9	7.1	56	40	46	87	310	149	160x
Botswana	1.3	1.7	3.2	5.2	54	27	61	60	169	85	200
Burkina Faso	9.5	11.8	2.6	6.5	53	17	48	118	363	206	810
Burundi	5.8	7.2	2.9	6.8	54	6	48	106	260	181	..
Cameroon	12.2	15.3	2.9	5.8	51	42	56	63	270	126	430
Cape Verde	0.4	0.5	2.1*	4.4	..	30	68	40	164	61	..
Central African Republic	3.2	3.9	2.6	6.2	52	48	47	105	294	180	600
Chad	5.8	7.3	2.2	5.9	51	34	48	122	325	213	960
Comoros	0.6	0.8	3.1*	7.1	..	29	56	89	248	133	..
Congo	2.4	3.0	2.9	6.3	52	42	52	82	220	110	900
Côte d'Ivoire	12.9	17.1	3.8	7.4	60	42	52	91	300	127	..
Djibouti	0.5	0.6	..	6.6	..	82	49	112	..	161	..
Equatorial Guinea	0.4	0.5	2.5*	5.9	..	30	48	117	316	202	..
Ethiopia	53.0	67.2	2.6	7.0	55	13	47	122	294	212	..
Gabon	1.2	1.6	3.6	5.2	42	47	54	94	287	161	190
Gambia	0.9	1.1	3.0*	6.2	..	24	45	132	375	234	..
Ghana	16.0	20.2	3.3	6.1	54	35	56	81	224	137	1,000
Guinea	6.1	7.8	2.6	7.0	56	27	45	134	337	234	800
Guinea-Bissau	1.0	1.2	2.0	5.8	50	21	44	140	336	242	700x
Kenya	25.2	32.8	3.5	6.4	57	25	59	66	202	75	170x
Lesotho	1.8	2.2	2.7	4.8	44	21	61	79	210	137	..
Liberia	2.8	3.6	3.2	6.8	56	47	55	126	310	200	..
Madagascar	12.8	16.6	3.2	6.6	55	25	55	110	364	173	570
Malawi	10.4	12.6	4.3	7.6	58	12	44	142	365	228	170
Mali	9.8	12.6	3.0	7.1	57	25	46	159	400	225	2,000
Mauritania	2.1	2.7	2.7	6.5	52	49	48	117	321	209	..
Mauritius	1.1	1.2	1.1	2.0	27	41	70	21	104	28	99
Mozambique	14.9	19.4	1.7	6.5	53	30	47	147	331	292	300
Namibia	1.5	2.0	3.0	6.0	53	29	59	70	248	120	370x
Niger	8.3	10.6	3.3	7.1	58	21	47	124	321	218	700
Nigeria	115.7	147.7	3.3	6.6	56	37	53	96	212	188	800
Rwanda	7.5	9.8	3.1	8.5	59	6	46	110	255	189	210x
Senegal	7.7	9.6	2.8	6.2	52	41	49	80	299	182	600
Sierra Leone	4.4	5.4	2.4	6.5	51	34	43	143	385	253	450
Somalia	9.2	11.9	2.6	7.0	57	25	47	122	294	211	1,100
South Africa	39.8	47.9	2.5	4.2	43	50	63	53	126	72	83x
Sudan	26.7	33.2	3.0	6.2	52	23	52	99	292	169	550
Swaziland	0.8	1.0	2.7*	5.0	..	28	58	73	233	113	..
Tanzania	27.8	35.9	3.4	6.8	57	22	51	102	249	178	340x
Togo	3.8	4.8	3.0	6.6	56	29	55	85	305	144	420
Uganda	18.7	23.4	2.9	7.3	57	12	42	104	223	190	300
Zaire	39.9	51.0	3.3	6.7	57	28	52	93	300	180	800
Zambia	8.6	10.7	3.5	6.5	57	42	44	84	220	200	150
Zimbabwe	10.6	13.2	3.3	5.5	52	30	56	59	181	88	..
South Asia	**1,183**	**1,392**	**2.2**	**4.3**	**42**	**25**	**59**	**97**	**238**	**131**	**490**
Afghanistan	19.1	26.8	1.0	6.9	55	19	43	162	360	257	640
Bangladesh	119.3	144.3	2.5	4.8	47	18	53	108	247	133	600
Bhutan	1.6	1.9	2.2	5.9	44	6	48	129	324	205	1,310
India	879.5	1018.7	2.1	4.0	40	26	60	88	236	126	460
Nepal	20.6	24.9	2.7	5.6	50	12	54	99	298	147	830
Pakistan	124.8	154.8	3.2	6.3	51	33	59	98	221	134	500
Sri Lanka	17.7	19.4	1.5	2.5	34	22	72	24	130	21	80
East Asia and the Pacific	**1,725**	**1,930**	**1.7**	**2.5**	**33**	**31**	**69**	**35**	**198**	**42**	**160**
Burma (Myanmar)	43.7	51.6	2.1	4.3	43	25	58	81	237	117	460
Cambodia	8.8	10.6	2.5	4.5	48	12	51	116	217	188	500
China	1188.0	1309.7	1.5	2.3	31	28	71	27	205	27	95
Fiji	0.7	0.8	1.0*	3.0	..	40	71	23	97	30	..
Hong Kong	5.8	6.1	1.2	1.4	21	94	78	6	64	8	6
Indonesia	191.2	218.0	2.0	3.2	38	30	63	65	215	86	450
Korea, N.	22.6	25.9	1.8	2.4	33	60	71	24	120	34	41

Table 1 continued: Demographic Indicators

	Population (millions) 1992	2000	Population annual growth rate 1980-1991	Fertility (children per woman) 1991	Percent of population under 16 1991	Percent of population urbanized 1992	Life expectancy 1990-1995	Infant mortality per 1,000 live births 1990-1995	Under 5 mortality per 1,000 live births 1960	1991	Maternal mortality per 100,000 live births 1980-1990
Korea, S.	44.2	46.9	1.2	1.7	26	74	71	21	126	10	26
Laos	4.5	5.6	2.8	6.7	53	20	52	97	233	148	..
Malaysia	18.8	22.3	2.6	3.7	43	45	71	14	105	20	59
Mongolia	2.3	2.8	2.8	4.7	50	59	64	60	185	82	140
Papua New Guinea	4.1	4.9	2.3	5.0	45	17	56	54	248	79	900
Philippines	65.2	76.1	2.5	4.0	44	44	65	40	128	46	100
Singapore	2.8	3.0	1.1	1.7	26	100	74	8	50	10	10
Solomon Islands	0.3	0.4	3.3	5.5	..	16	70	27	..	..	..
Thailand	56.1	61.2	1.5	2.3	33	23	69	26	146	33	71
Vietnam	69.5	81.5	2.2	4.0	42	20	64	36	219	52	120
Latin America and the Caribbean	**458**	**520**	**2.1**	**3.2**	**39**	**73**	**68**	**47**	**161**	**57**	**180**
Argentina	33.1	36.2	1.3	2.8	32	87	71	29	70	24	140
Bolivia	7.5	9.0	2.5	4.7	47	52	61	85	282	126	600
Brazil	154.1	172.8	2.0	2.9	36	76	66	57	179	67	200
Chile	13.6	15.3	1.7	2.7	34	85	72	17	142	21	67
Colombia	33.4	37.8	1.9	2.7	37	71	69	37	130	21	200
Costa Rica	3.2	3.8	2.8	3.2	42	48	76	14	122	18	36
Cuba	10.8	11.5	0.9	1.9	25	74	76	14	91	14	39
Dominican Republic	7.5	8.6	2.3	3.5	41	62	68	57	200	76	..
Ecuador	11.1	13.1	2.6	3.8	43	58	67	57	184	82	170
El Salvador	5.4	6.4	1.4	4.2	47	45	66	46	210	67	..
Guatemala	9.7	12.2	2.9	5.5	53	40	65	49	220	92	200
Guyana	0.8	0.9	1.1	2.6	..	34	65	48	126	69	..
Haiti	6.8	8.0	1.9	4.9	45	30	57	86	270	137	340
Honduras	5.5	6.8	3.4	5.1	51	45	66	60	230	73	220
Jamaica	2.5	2.7	1.2	2.5	33	54	74	14	89	19	120
Mexico	88.2	102.6	2.3	3.3	41	74	70	35	138	37	110
Nicaragua	4.0	5.2	2.8	5.2	55	61	67	52	209	81	..
Panama	2.5	2.9	2.1	3.0	36	54	73	21	105	30	60
Paraguay	4.5	5.5	3.0	4.4	45	49	67	47	103	59	300
Peru	22.5	26.3	2.2	3.7	41	71	65	76	240	97	300
Suriname	0.4	0.5	..	2.8	..	49	70	28	96	37	..
Trinidad & Tobago	1.3	1.4	1.3	2.8	38	65	71	18	69	23	110
Uruguay	3.1	3.3	0.6	2.4	26	89	72	20	57	24	36
Venezuela	20.2	23.6	2.5	3.2	40	91	70	33	114	43	..
Middle East and North Africa	**317**	**384**	**3.0**	**4.9**	**48**	**57**	**65**	**55**	**242**	**83**	**181**
Algeria	26.3	32.7	2.9	5.0	49	53	66	61	243	61	140x
Bahrain	0.5	0.7	3.9*	3.8	..	83	71	12	208	18	..
Cyprus	0.7	0.8	0.7*	2.3	..	54	77	9	36	11	..
Egypt	54.8	64.8	2.5	4.2	44	44	62	57	260	85	320
Iran	61.6	77.9	3.9	6.1	54	58	67	40	233	62	120
Iraq	19.3	24.8	3.3	5.8	52	73	66	58	171	143	120x
Jordan	4.3	5.6	3.2	5.8	54	69	68	36	180	46	48x
Kuwait	2.0	1.7	3.6	3.8	33	93	75	14	128	17	6
Lebanon	2.8	3.3	0.4	3.2	39	86	69	34	91	46	..
Libya	4.9	6.4	4.0	6.5	55	84	63	68	269	108	80x
Morocco	26.3	31.7	2.6	4.5	45	47	63	68	265	91	300x
Oman	1.6	2.2	4.3	6.8	56	12	70	30	378	42	..
Qatar	0.5	0.5	..	4.5	..	90	70	26	239	35	..
Saudi Arabia	15.9	20.7	4.5	6.5	51	78	69	31	292	43	90
Syria	13.3	17.5	3.5	6.3	58	51	67	39	217	47	140
Tunisia	8.4	9.8	2.3	3.6	40	57	68	43	254	58	50
Turkey	58.4	68.2	2.3	3.6	39	64	67	56	216	89	150
United Arab Emirates	1.7	2.0	2.1*	4.6	31	82	71	22	239	29	..
Yemen	12.5	16.4	..	7.3	..	31	53	106	378	182	..
Industrial Countries	**1,230**	**1,290**	**0.6**	**1.9**	**23**	**73**	**75**	**12**	**45**	**17**	**15**
Albania	3.3	3.6	1.9	2.8	33	36	73	23	151	31	..
Australia	17.6	19.6	1.5	1.9	24	85	77	7	24	10	3
Austria	7.8	8.0	0.2	1.5	19	59	76	8	43	9	8
Belgium	10.0	10.1	0.1	1.6	19	96	76	8	35	10	3

Table 1 continued: Demographic Indicators

	Population (millions) 1992	Population (millions) 2000	Population annual growth rate 1980-1991	Fertility (children per woman) 1991	Percent of population under 16 1991	Percent of population urbanized 1992	Life expectancy 1990-1995	Infant mortality per 1,000 live births 1990-1995	Under 5 mortality per 1,000 live births 1960	Under 5 mortality per 1,000 live births 1991	Maternal mortality per 100,000 live births 1980-1990
Bulgaria	9.0	8.9	0.1	1.9	20	69	72	14	70	21	9
Canada	27.4	30.4	1.1	1.8	23	78	77	7	33	9	5
Czechoslovakia (former)	15.7	16.3	0.2	2.0	23	79	73	10	33	13	10
Denmark	5.2	5.2	0.1	1.7	18	85	76	7	25	9	3
Finland	5.0	5.1	0.4	1.8	20	60	76	6	28	7	11
France	57.2	58.8	0.5	1.8	21	73	77	7	34	9	9
Germany	80.3	82.6	0.2	1.5	19	86	76	7	40	9	5
Greece	10.2	10.3	0.5	1.5	19	63	78	8	64	11	5
Hungary	10.5	10.5	-0.1	1.8	20	66	70	14	57	17	15
Ireland	3.5	3.4	0.3	2.2	26	58	75	7	36	10	2
Israel	5.1	6.3	2.1	2.9	38	92	77	9	39	12	3
Italy	57.8	58.1	0.2	1.3	17	70	77	8	50	10	4
Japan	124.5	128.1	0.5	1.7	18	77	79	5	40	6	11
Netherlands	15.2	16.1	0.6	1.7	21	89	77	7	22	8	10
New Zealand	3.5	3.7	0.9	2.1	26	84	76	8	26	10	13
Norway	4.3	4.5	0.4	1.9	21	76	77	8	23	8	3
Poland	38.4	39.5	0.7	2.1	26	63	72	15	70	17	11
Portugal	9.9	9.9	0.1	1.5	20	35	75	12	112	12	10
Romania	23.3	24.0	0.4	2.2	24	55	70	23	82	34	150
Spain	39.1	39.6	0.4	1.4	19	79	78	7	57	9	5
Sweden	8.7	9.0	0.3	2.0	20	84	78	6	20	5	5
Switzerland	6.8	7.2	0.6	1.6	19	62	78	7	27	9	5
USA	255.2	275.3	0.9	2.0	24	76	76	8	30	11	8
USSR (former)	284.5	310.4	0.8	2.3	26	67	70	21	53	31	21
United Kingdom	57.7	58.8	0.2	1.9	21	89	76	7	27	9	8
Yugoslavia (former)	23.9	..	0.6	1.9	23	58	72	23	113	22	8
World	**5,479**	**6,220**	**1.8**	**3.4**	**36**	**44**	**65**	**62**	**178**	**82**	**266**

Table 2: Health, Nutrition, and Welfare

	Human development index (rank of 173 countries)	Mean years of schooling 1991 total	Mean years of schooling 1991 male	Mean years of schooling 1991 female	% infants with low birthweight 1990	% 1-year olds fully immunized 1989-91	Food production per capita (1979-81=100) 1988-90	Daily calorie supply (as % of requirements) 1988-90	Annual rate of deforestation 1981-85
Africa (sub-Saharan)	..	1.6	2.2	1.0	16	61	95	93	0.5
Angola	160	1.5	2.0	1.0	19	33	80	80	0.2
Benin	162	0.7	1.1	0.3	10	74	114	104	1.7
Botswana	104	2.4	2.5	2.4	8	85	63	97	0.1
Burkina Faso	170	0.1	0.1	0.1	21x	50	118	94	1.7
Burundi	154	0.3	0.5	0.2	..	86	88	84	2.7
Cameroon	133	1.6	2.5	0.8	13	61	79	95	0.4
Cape Verde	114	2.2	3.2	1.3	..	88	..	125	..
Central African Republic	156	1.1	1.6	0.5	15	86	93	82	0.2
Chad	165	0.2	0.3	0.1	..	33	97	73	0.6
Comoros	139	1.0	1.2	0.8	13	94	..	90	3.1
Congo	126	2.1	3.1	1.1	16	81	97	103	0.1
Côte d'Ivoire	136	1.9	2.9	0.9	14x	50	93	111	5.2
Djibouti	163	0.3	0.5	0.2	9	88	..	..	..
Equatorial Guinea	155	0.8	1.3	0.3	10	85	..	..	0.2
Ethiopia	151	1.1	1.5	0.7	16	46	87	73	0.3
Gabon	109	2.6	3.9	1.3	10	82	85	104	0.1
Gambia	167	0.6	0.9	0.2	10	89	..	..	2.4
Ghana	131	3.5	4.8	2.2	17	64	105	93	0.8
Guinea	173	0.8	1.3	0.3	21	26	88	97	0.8
Guinea-Bissau	164	0.3	0.5	0.1	20	52	104	97	2.7
Kenya	127	2.3	3.2	1.3	16	71	103	89	1.7
Lesotho	120	3.4	2.7	4.0	11	81	80	93	..
Liberia	144	2.0	3.2	0.8	..	43	63	98	2.3
Madagascar	128	2.2	2.6	1.7	10	48	83	95	1.2
Malawi	153	1.7	2.4	1.1	20	84	77	88	3.5
Mali	168	0.3	0.5	0.1	17	52	97	96	0.5
Mauritania	161	0.3	0.5	0.1	11	41	75	106	2.4

Table 2 continued: Health, Nutrition, and Welfare

	Human development index (rank of 173 countries)	Mean years of schooling 1991 total	male	female	% infants with low birthweight 1990	% 1-year olds fully immunized 1989-91	Food production per capita (1979-81=100) 1988-90	Daily calorie supply (as % of requirements) 1988-90	Annual rate of deforestation 1981-85
Mauritius	56	4.1	4.8	3.3	9	90	94	128	3.3
Mozambique	157	1.6	2.1	1.2	20	52	68	77	0.8
Namibia	135	1.7	1.7	1.7	12	58	92	..	0.2
Niger	169	0.1	0.2	0.1	15	24	73	95	2.6
Nigeria	142	1.2	1.8	0.5	16	66	124	93	2.7
Rwanda	149	1.1	1.6	0.5	17	86	86	82	2.2
Senegal	150	0.8	1.3	0.4	11	69	96	98	0.5
Sierra Leone	172	0.9	1.4	0.4	17	85	84	83	0.3
Somalia	166	0.2	0.3	0.1	16	24	81	81	0.1
South Africa	85	3.9	4.1	3.7	..	71	81	128	
Sudan	158	0.8	1.1	0.5	15	64	76	87	1.1
Swaziland	117	3.7	4.0	3.3	..	90	..	..	..
Tanzania	138	2.0	2.8	1.3	14	86	81	95	0.3
Togo	145	1.6	2.4	0.8	20	68	87	99	0.7
Uganda	146	1.1	1.6	0.6	..	82	97	93	0.8
Zaire	140	1.6	2.4	0.8	15	40	94	96	0.2
Zambia	130	2.7	3.7	1.7	13	83	98	87	0.2
Zimbabwe	121	2.9	4.2	1.7	14	71	76	94	0.4
South Asia	..	**2.3**	**3.4**	**1.2**	**34**	**86**	**113**	**99**	**0.5**
Afghanistan	171	0.8	1.4	0.2	20	25	73	72	..
Bangladesh	147	2.0	3.1	0.9	50	66	96	98	0.9
Bhutan	159	0.2	0.3	0.1	..	95	93	128	0.1
India	134	2.4	3.5	1.2	33	92	116	101	0.3
Nepal	152	2.1	3.2	1.0	26	80	124	100	4.0
Pakistan	132	1.9	3.0	0.7	25	82	102	99	0.4
Sri Lanka	86	6.9	7.7	6.1	25	88	89	101	3.5
East Asia and the Pacific	..	**4.8**	**5.9**	**3.7**	**11**	**94**	**127**	**112**	**0.8#**
Burma (Myanmar)	123	2.5	3.0	2.1	16	72	88	114	0.3
Cambodia	148	2.0	2.3	1.7	..	42	140	96	0.2
China	101	4.8	6.0	3.6	9	98	138	112	..
Fiji	71	5.1	5.6	4.6	18	94	..	108	0.2
Hong Kong	24	7.0	8.6	5.4	8	81	111	125	..
Indonesia	108	3.9	5.0	2.9	14	89	125	121	0.5
Korea, N.	91	6.0	7.4	4.6	..	99	109	121	..
Korea, S.	33	8.8	11.0	6.7	9	79	100	120	..
Laos	141	2.9	3.6	2.1	18	21	110	111	1.0
Malaysia	57	5.3	5.6	5.0	10	93	146	120	1.2
Mongolia	100	7.0	7.2	6.8	10	87	76	97	..
Papua New Guinea	129	0.9	1.2	0.6	23	74	98	114	0.1
Philippines	92	7.4	7.8	7.0	15	89	82	104	1.0
Singapore	43	3.9	4.7	3.1	7	89	70	136	..
Solomon Islands	118	1.0	1.2	0.8	20	77	..	84	<0.5
Thailand	74	3.8	4.3	3.3	13	91	109	103	2.5
Vietnam	115	4.6	5.8	3.4	17	88	131	103	0.6
Latin America and the Carribean	..	**5.2**	**5.3**	**5.1**	**11**	**79**	**105**	**114**	**1.5**
Argentina	46	8.7	8.5	8.9	8	92	95	131	..
Bolivia	122	4.0	5.0	3.0	12	48	125	84	0.2
Brazil	70	3.9	4.0	3.8	11	83	115	114	0.5
Chile	36	7.5	7.8	7.2	7	98	118	102	0.7
Colombia	61	7.1	6.9	7.3	10	89	104	106	1.7
Costa Rica	42	5.7	5.8	5.6	6	93	90	121	3.6
Cuba	75	7.6	7.5	7.7	8	95	96	135	0.1
Dominican Republic	97	4.3	4.6	4.0	16	81	81	102	0.6
Ecuador	89	5.6	5.8	5.3	11	71	99	105	2.3
El Salvador	110	4.1	4.1	4.1	11	72	103	102	3.2
Guatemala	113	4.1	4.4	3.8	14	68	95	103	2.0
Guyana	105	5.1	5.4	4.9	12	80	..	108	..
Haiti	137	1.7	2.0	1.3	15	46	83	89	3.7
Honduras	116	3.9	4.0	3.7	9	83	81	98	2.3
Jamaica	69	5.3	5.3	5.2	11	86	96	114	3.0

Table 2 continued: Health, Nutrition, and Welfare

	Human development index (rank of 173 countries)	Mean years of schooling 1991 total	male	female	% infants with low birthweight 1990	% 1-year olds fully immunized 1989-91	Food production per capita (1979-81=100) 1988-90	Daily calorie supply (as % of requirements) 1988-90	Annual rate of deforestation 1981-85
Mexico	53	4.7	4.8	4.6	12	78	97	131	1.3
Nicaragua	111	4.3	4.1	4.5	15	79	62	99	2.7
Panama	68	6.7	6.5	6.9	10	87	81	98	0.9
Paraguay	90	4.9	5.2	4.6	8	78	116	116	1.1
Peru	95	6.4	7.1	5.7	11	73	93	87	0.4
Suriname	65	4.2	4.3	4.0	13	76	..	..	<0.5
Trinidad & Tobago	31	8.0	8.0	8.1	10	80	87	114	0.4
Uruguay	30	7.8	7.4	8.2	8	89	108	101	..
Venezuela	50	6.3	6.4	6.2	9	65	99	99	0.7
Middle East and North Africa	..	3.3	4.4	2.2	10	87	110	126	..
Algeria	107	2.6	4.4	0.8	9	90	104	123	2.3
Bahrain	58	3.9	4.7	3.2	..	92	..	..	..
Cyprus	27	7.0	7.6	6.5	..	85	..	..	..
Egypt	124	2.8	3.9	1.6	10	90	106	132	..
Iran	103	3.9	4.6	3.1	9	91	114	125	0.5
Iraq	96	4.8	5.7	3.9	15	77	65	128	..
Jordan	99	5.0	6.0	4.0	7	90	82	110	..
Kuwait	52	5.4	6.0	4.7	7	95	..	..	..
Lebanon	102	4.4	5.3	3.5	10	68	132	127	..
Libya	87	3.4	5.5	1.3	..	82	74	140	..
Morocco	119	2.8	4.1	1.5	9	84	134	125	0.4
Oman	94	0.9	1.4	0.3	10	95	..	..	..
Qatar	55	5.6	5.8	5.4	6	85	..	..	..
Saudi Arabia	84	3.7	5.9	1.5	7	94	223	121	..
Syria	81	4.2	5.2	3.1	11	90	73	126	..
Tunisia	93	2.1	3.0	1.2	8	92	102	131	1.7
Turkey	73	3.5	4.7	2.3	8	82	99	127	..
United Arab Emirates	67	5.1	5.1	5.2	6	85	..	..	..
Yemen	143	0.8	1.3	0.2	19	88	79	..	..
Industrial Countries	..	10.0	10.4	9.6	6	80*	99	133	..
Albania	78	6.0	7.0	5.0	7	87*	62	107	
Australia	7	11.5	11.6	11.4	6	68*	92	124	
Austria	15	11.1	11.7	10.5	6	74*	103	133	
Belgium	16	10.7	10.7	10.7	6	75*	110	149	
Bulgaria	40	7.0	7.6	6.4	6	98*	88	148	
Canada	2	12.1	12.3	11.9	6	85*	117	122	
Czechoslovakia (former)	26	9.0	9.5	8.4	6	98*	118	145	
Denmark	13	10.4	10.5	10.3	6	84*	132	135	
Finland	14	10.6	10.7	10.5	4	95*	98	113	
France	8	11.6	11.5	11.7	5	69*	106	143	
Germany	12	11.1	11.7	10.6	..	59*	114	130	
Greece	25	6.9	7.3	6.5	6	76*	104	151	
Hungary	28	9.6	9.5	9.7	9	99*	114	137	
Ireland	21	8.7	8.6	8.8	4	78*	118	157	
Israel	19	10.0	10.9	9.0	7	88*	91	125	
Italy	22	7.3	7.4	7.3	5	43*	99	139	
Japan	1	10.7	10.8	10.6	6	73*	99	125	
Netherlands	9	10.6	10.4	10.8	..	94*	103	114	
New Zealand	17	10.4	10.2	10.6	6	90*	102	131	
Norway	3	11.6	11.7	11.5	4	87*	108	120	
Poland	48	8.0	8.3	7.7	..	96*	103	131	
Portugal	41	6.0	6.8	5.2	5	85*	117	136	
Romania	77	7.0	7.4	6.6	7	89*	70	116	
Spain	23	6.8	7.0	6.5	4	84*	111	141	
Sweden	5	11.1	11.1	11.1	5	84*	96	111	
Switzerland	4	11.1	11.5	10.7	5	94*	100	130	
USA	6	12.3	12.2	12.4	7	..	94	138	
USSR (former)	37R	9.0R	..	..	6	85*	96	132	
United Kingdom	10	11.5	11.4	11.6	7	89*	108	130	
Yugoslavia (former)	..	..	..	..	88	140*	..	..	

Table 3: Economic Indicators

	Per capita GNP 1991	Annual per cap. GNP growth (%) 1965-91	Military expenditure (as % of education & health expenditure) 1990	Total debt $ U.S. billions 1991	Debt servicing as % of exports 1991	Food as % of exports 1991	Food as % of imports 1991	Per capita energy consumption (kg of oil equiv.) 1991	Food as % of household consumption 1980-85
Africa (sub-Saharan)	**350**	**0.2**	**108**	**178.01**	**19.8**	**..**	**..**	**135**	**..**
Angola	b	..	..	8.78	5.8	..	21.2	..	..
Benin	380	-0.1	..	1.30	6.3	12.6	17.5	46	37
Botswana	2,530	8.2	16	.54	3.4	4.4	5.8	408	25
Burkina Faso	290	1.4	85	.96	..	7.6	12.5	17	..
Burundi	210	3.4	65	.96	31.6	..	9.7	24	..
Cameroon	850	2.8	51	6.28	..	18.7	19.5	147	24
Cape Verde	750	2.2G	..	.16	8.8	29.0	29.9	..	..
Central African Republic	390	-0.6	41	.88	8.2	23.2	22.9	29	..
Chad	210	-0.8	..	.61	4.4	19.1	5.3	17	..
Comoros	500	0.0	..	.18	4.9	66.8	45.5	..	..
Congo	1,120	3.0	50	4.74	23.4	1.7	15.9	214	37
Côte d'Ivoire	690	0.0	14	18.85	39.1	43.7	18.9	170	39
Djibouti	b	..	..	.20	..	7.5	25.7	..	..
Eqatorial Guinea	330	..	..	.25	7.4	7.7	15.8	..	..
Ethiopia	120	-0.3	239	3.48	25.4	8.3	36.0	20	49
Gabon	3,780	1.7	63	3.84	..	0.1	11.6	1,154	..
Gambia	360	2.7	..	.35	..	9.6	28.1	..	..
Ghana	400	-1.4	13	4.21	27.0	32.4	13.6	130	50x
Guinea	460	..	..	2.63	16.0	5.1	15.2	68	..
Guinea-Bissau	180	-1.1	..	.65	74.2	37.3	..	38	..
Kenya	340	1.8	31	7.01	..	12.3	7.0	104	38
Lesotho	580	4.1	..	.43	4.7	9.1	18.2	..	..
Liberia	450	-1.6	..	1.99	..	1.1	75.9	..	..
Madagascar	210	-2.0	34	3.72	34.3	33.6	11.8	39	59
Malawi	230	0.8	31	1.68	4.9	7.5	5.5	41	30
Mali	280	0.9	83	2.53	..	29.6	23.5	23	57
Mauritania	510	-0.6	..	2.30	16.8	8.1	57.3	111	..
Mauritius	2,410	4.7	5	.99	9.4	31.9	9.8	389	24
Mozambique	80	-1.1	..	4.70	12.2	14.7	18.7	59	..
Namibia	1460	-0.2	..	..	..	11.8	3.8	..	..
Niger	300	-2.5	21	1.65	47.3	17.4	17.2	41	..
Nigeria	340	0.3	65	34.50	25.2	1.3	6.9	154	48
Rwanda	270	0.9	35	.84	17.6	..	15.0	29	29
Senegal	720	-0.5	..	3.52	..	13.3	21.1	105	49
Sierra Leone	210	-0.2	11	1.29	..	12.5	54.1	75	56
Somalia	120	-0.1	500	2.44	..	41.5	19.9	..	..
South Africa	2,560	1.6	..	..	..	5.0	3.4	2,262	34
Sudan	400('90)	-0.5	..	15.91	3.9	37.2	21.5	54	60x
Swaziland	1,050	2.7	20	.26	3.5	42.8	6.2	..	..
Tanzania	100	-0.1	108	6.46	..	16.1	5.0	37	64
Togo	410	-0.1	46	1.36	7.5	6.5	14.2	47	..
Uganda	170	..	..	2.83	63.6	12.4	3.2	25	..
Zaire	220	-2.0	67	10.71	..	0.5	31.4	..	..
Zambia	460	-1.9	43	7.28	..	0.8	3.2	369	36
Zimbabwe	650	0.7	65	3.43	27.6	12.5	3.2	517	40
South Asia	**320**	**2.0**	**115**	**120.92**	**25.4**	**..**	**..**	**289**	**..**
Afghanistan	a	..	..	..	..	28.7	10.5	..	..
Bangladesh	220	0.7	57	13.05	19.9	0.9	15.9	57	59
Bhutan	180	3.1	..	.09	..	4.6	10.4	15	..
India	330	2.0	80	71.56	30.6	6.6	2.8	337	52
Nepal	180	0.7	61	1.77	13.6	19.9	9.4	22	57
Pakistan	400	2.8	239	22.97	..	7.8	11.2	243	37
Sri Lanka	500	2.9	62	6.55	14.1	5.8	15.1	177	43
East Asia and the Pacific	**715**	**5.2**	**..**	**268.71**	**13.3**	**..**	**..**	**571**	**..**
Burma (Myanmar)	a	1.8	..	4.85	..	31.3	11.4	..	..
Cambodia	200	..	..	..	..	..	4.6	..	..
China	370	5.9	97	60.80	12.0	..	..	602	61x,f
Fiji	1,930	2.5	9	.36	..	46.2	9.9	..	..
Hong Kong	13,430	5.9	..	..	..	1.4	3.9	1,438	12

Table 3 continued: Economic Indicators

	Per capita GNP 1991	Annual per cap. GNP growth (%) 1965-91	Military expenditure (as % of education & health expenditure) 1990	Total debt $ U.S. billions 1991	Debt servicing as % of exports 1991	Food as % of exports 1991	Food as % of imports 1991	Per capita energy consumption (kg of oil equiv.) 1991	Food as % of household consumption 1980-85
Indonesia	610	4.3	143	73.63	33.0	4.0	4.3	279	48
Korea, N.	b	..	..	..	..	0.2	8.4	..	..
Korea, S.	6,330	7.1	110	40.52	..	0.8	4.3	102	35
Laos	220	.6	..	1.12	..	18.4	6.3	42	..
Malaysia	2,520	4.0	65	21.45	8.4	8.5	4.9	1,066	23x
Mongolia	b	..	..	..	..	14.4	8.8	..	..
Papua New Guinea	830	0.1	..	2.76	29.6	6.7	13.7	231	..
Philippines	730	1.2	47	31.90	23.2	11.2	5.7	218	51
Solomon Islands	690	4.4	..	.13	11.3	19.0	13.3	..	..
Singapore	14,210	6.9	109	..	..	2.5	4.0	6,178	..
Thailand	1,570	4.5	74	35.83	13.1	12.8	1.3	438	30
Vietnam	a	..	..	..	..	19.7	3.1	..	..
Latin America and the Carribean	**2,410**	**1.6**	**64**	**439.7**	**29.5**	**..**	**..**	**1,051**	**..**
Argentina	2,790	-0.3	..	63.71	48.1	42.0	2.3	1,764	35
Bolivia	650	-0.7	144	4.08	34.0	12.1	6.8	251	33x
Brazil	2,940	3.1	22	116.5	30.8	11.1	9.7	908	35
Chile	2,160	0.4	..	17.90	33.9	15.7	4.0	892	29
Colombia	1,260	2.3	..	17.37	35.1	10.2	4.5	778	29
Costa Rica	1,850	1.1	4	4.04	18.4	39.1	7.1	570	33
Cuba	b	..	118	..	..	57.1	8.8	..	..
Dominican Republic	940	2.3	25	4.49	11.6	39.5	16.3	341	46
Ecuador	1,000	2.6	33	12.47	32.2	30.1	6.1	598	30
El Salvador	1,080	-0.4	121	2.17	17.3	10.0	10.2	230	33
Guatemala	930	0.7	87	2.70	17.1	31.1	8.3	155	36
Guyana	430	..	53	1.90	..	39.5	10.7	..	..
Haiti	370	0.1	45	.75	6.6	8.8	40.6	49	..
Honduras	580	0.5	102	3.18	28.1	47.8	9.8	181	39
Jamaica	1,160	-0.5	9	4.46	29.8	15.8	11.0	858	36
Mexico	3,030	2.7	8	101.74	30.9	7.0	9.1	1,383	35x,f
Nicaragua	460	-3.0	318	10.45	112.4	38.5	14.1	254	..
Panama	2,130	1.1	23	6.79	4.0	44.6	7.8	1,661	38
Paraguay	1,270	2.7	72	2.18	..	38.9	1.6	231	30
Peru	1,600	-0.5	70	20.71	27.4	3.5	14.7	451	35
Suriname	3,630	..	..	..	..	11.9	9.7	..	..
Trinidad & Tobago	3,670	-3.9G	33	2.33	..	3.9	13.2	4,907	19
Uruguay	2,840	0.6	51	4.19	38.2	35.1	4.2	816	31
Venezuela	2,730	-0.9	23	34.37	18.7	0.9	7.7	2,521	23
Middle East and North Africa	**1,910**	**1.1**	**275***	**200.18**	**26.9**	**..**	**..**	**..**	**..**
Algeria	1,980	1.9	18	28.64	68.4	0.2	23.6	1,956	..
Bahrain	7,130	-3.8G	134	..	..	<0.1	5.4	..	..
Cyprus	8,640	4.9G	25	3.21	..	18.3	7.2	..	..
Egypt	610	4.0	57	40.57	16.7	9.7	20.1	594	49
Iran	2,170	-0.4	..	11.51	4.6	2.4	8.7	1,078	37
Iraq	2,140	-3.5	511	..	..	1.9	30.3	..	..
Jordan	1,050	..	128	8.64	20.9	14.4	26.0	856	35
Kuwait	e	..	83	..	..	1.9	6.2	..	..
Lebanon	c	..	..	1.86	..	25.9	12.4	..	..
Libya	5,330	-3.0	56	..	..	0.0	15.0	..	..
Morocco	1,030	2.3	52	21.22	27.6	14.0	7.5	252	38
Oman	6,120	..	268	2.70	..	1.1	13.9	2,859	..
Qatar	15,870	..	..	..	..	0.2	16.8	..	..
Saudi Arabia	7,820	2.2	177	..	..	0.9	11.5	4,866	..
Syria	1,160	2.8	204	16.82	..	10.0	21.5	955	..
Tunisia	1,500	3.1	58	8.30	22.7	11.4	5.9	556	37
Turkey	1,780	2.6	118	50.25	30.5	21.0	3.5	809	40
United Arab Emirates	19,870('90)	..	174	..	..	1.7	11.4	..	..
Yemen	540	..	..	6.47	7.3	2.6	29.7	96	..
Industrial Countries	**21,530**	**2.4**	**..**	**..**	**..**	**..**	**..**	**5,106**	**..**

Table 3 continued: Economic Indicators

	Per capita GNP 1991	Annual per cap. GNP growth (%) 1965-91	Military expenditure (as % of education & health expenditure) 1990	Total debt $ U.S. billions 1991	Debt servicing as % of exports 1991	Food as % of exports 1991	Food as % of imports 1991	Per capita energy con-sumption (kg of oil equiv.) 1991	Food as % of household consumption 1980-85
Albania	b	..	..	..	..	21.1	16.6	..	..
Australia	17,050	1.8	15	..	..	15.4	2.7	5,211	13
Austria	20,140	3.2	8	..	..	2.3	3.6	3,500	16
Belgium	18,950	3.0	20	..	..	8.6	7.6	2,793	15
Bulgaria	1,820	1.7G	..	11.92	21.8	4.2	4.1	3,540	..
Canada	20,440	2.9	13	..	..	6.1	4.6	9,390	11
Czechoslovakia (former)	2,470	0.4G	..	9.79	11.5	5.1	4.7	4,681	..
Denmark	23,700	2.2	16	..	..	18.7	5.2	3,747	13
Finland	23,980	3.2	14	..	..	2.1	3.9	5,602	16
France	20,380	2.9	24	..	..	10.0	6.5	3,854	16
Germany	23,650	2.7	22	..	..	3.9	7.4	3,463	12
Greece	6,340	2.8	81	..	..	23.5	10.5	2,110	30
Hungary	2,720	1.7	..	22.66	32.5	19.1	2.0	2,830	25
Ireland	11,120	2.6	10	..	..	18.7	7.4	2,754	22
Israel	11,950	2.9	192	..	..	7.1	4.7	1,931	21
Italy	18,520	2.8	22	..	..	5.3	9.5	2,756	19
Japan	26,930	4.5	8	..	..	..	..	3,552	17
Netherlands	18,780	2.7	29	..	..	15.6	8.9	5,147	13
New Zealand	12,350	1.0	16	..	..	39.9	5.2	108	12
Norway	24,220	3.0	23	..	..	0.6	3.6	9,130	15
Poland	1,790	0.5G	24	52.48	5.4	8.7	5.0	3,165	29
Portugal	5,930	3.1	37	28.57	21.2	2.8	7.6	1,584	34
Romania	1,390	1.8	41	1.91	2.0	5.5	11.4	3,048	..
Spain	12,450	3.6	23	..	..	12.4	6.1	2,229	24
Sweden	25,110	1.9	15	..	..	1.5	4.3	5,901	13
Switzerland	33,610	1.5	12	..	..	2.0	4.1	3,943	17x
United Kingdom	16,550	2.2	36	..	..	3.6	7.5	3,688	12
USA	22,240	1.9	32	..	..	6.8	3.2	7,681	10
USSR (former)	3,220R	..	..	..	..	0.7	15.1	..	..
Yugoslavia (former)	2,940('90)	2.8	..	16.47	20.4	7.7	6.6	2,296	27

Table 4: Poverty and Hunger Statistics, Developing Countries

	% children under 5 suffering from				% without access to health facilities 1987-90	% without access to safe water 1988-90			Adult literacy rate 1990		
	underweight 1990	severe underweight 1980-91	wasting 1980-91	stunting 1980-91		total	urban	rural	total	male	female
Africa (sub-Saharan)	26.0	8	8	39	40	59	21	72	47	57	37
Angola	35.3	..	..	..	76	62	25	81	42	56	29
Benin	23.5	..	..	..	50	50	21	65	23	32	16
Botswana	26.8	..	6L	44	14	44	2	54	74	84	65
Burkina Faso	27.1	..	..	..	30	33	..	..	18	28	9
Burundi	29.1	10	6	48	20	62	0	66	50	61	40
Cameroon	16.7	..	2x	36x	85	66	53	73	54	66	43
Cape Verde	18.8x	..	3	26	18	26	13	35	67	..	..
Central African Republic	31.9	..	..	..	87	88	86	89	38	52	25
Chad	30.6	..	..	13L	74	..	..	..	30	42	18
Comoros	..	..	..	..	18	..	..	..	61	..	..
Congo	27.5	..	5	27	..	80	58	93	57	70	44
Côte d'Ivoire	12.3	2	9	17	40	17	0	25	54	67	40
Djibouti	..	..	11	22	..	..	50	79	19	..	..
Equatorial Guinea	..	..	..	..	..	..	..	..	50	..	..
Ethiopia	39.8	..	12	42	45	82	30	89	66	..	..
Gabon	15.1	5	..	18L	13	28	10	50	61	74	49
Gambia	17.1	..	7L	24L	10	23	8	27	27	..	..
Ghana	26.7	6	7	31	24	44	7	61	60	70	51
Guinea	24.0	..	..	..	68	67	44	75	24	35	13
Guinea-Bissau	23.4x	..	5L	22L	20	75	..	..	37	50	24
Kenya	17.4	3x	5	32	..	72	39	79	69	80	59
Lesotho	17.5	2	5	26	20	54	41	55	78	..	..

Table 4 continued: Poverty and Hunger Statistics, Developing Countries

	underweight 1990	% children under 5 suffering from severe underweight 1980-91	wasting 1980-91	stunting 1980-91	% without access to health facilities 1987-90	% without access to safe water 1988-90 total	urban	rural	Adult literacy rate 1990 total	male	female
Liberia	20.1	..	3x	37	66	50	7	78	40	50	29
Madagascar	38.1	8x	12	34	35	..	19	90	80	88	73
Malawi	23.5	..	2	56	20	47	18	50	47	..	..
Mali	21.6	9x	11	24	..	51	0	64	32	41	24
Mauritania	15.7	23	15	52	70	34	33	35	34	47	21
Mauritius	17.0	..	16	22	0	0	0	0	86	..	..
Mozambique	46.8	..	..	..	70	78	56	83	33	45	21
Namibia	29.0	6x	9	30	..	..	..	..	40		
Niger	44.0	9	23	38	70	41	0	48	28	40	17
Nigeria	35.4	12	9	43	33	54	0	80	51	62	40
Rwanda	31.7	4x	3	38	..	36	34	36	50	64	37
Senegal	19.6	6x	6	23	60	47	21	62	38	52	25
Sierra Leone	25.9	2x	5x	43	64	57	17	78	21	31	11
Somalia	38.8	..	..	..	80	44	42	45	24	36	14
South Africa	43.0	..	10[1]	53[1]	..	..	..	..	70	..	..
Sudan	33.7	..	14	32	30	..	..	..	27	43	12
Swaziland	8.8	..	1	30	45	70	0	93	72	..	..
Tanzania	24.2	6	5L	46L	7	48	25	54	65	93	88
Togo	18.4	6	5	30	..	29	0	39	43	56	31
Uganda	25.5	5	2L	45L	29	85	55	88	48	62	35
Zaire	33.2	..	3L	27L	41	34	41	83	72	84	61
Zambia	26.0	5x	4	54	25	41	24	57	73	81	65
Zimbabwe	14.1	2	1	29	29	64	..	86	67	74	60
South Asia	**62.0**	**25**	**12**	**63**	**22[2]**	**29**	**21**	**31**	**42**	**56**	**30**
Afghanistan	40.3	7	..	..	51	79	61	83	29	44	14
Bangladesh	65.8	27x	16	65	26	22	..	..	35	47	22
Bhutan	..	..	4	56	20	66	40	70	38	51	25
India	63.1	27x	21L	65	..	25	21	27	48	62	34
Nepal	50.5	..	14	69	..	63	34	66	26	38	13
Pakistan	41.6	14	9	50	15	50	16	65	35	47	21
Sri Lanka	42.0	2	18L	36L	10	40	20	45	88	93	84
East Asia and the Pacific	**26.0**	**.**	**5**	**34**	**..**	**33**	**16**	**38**	**77**	**86**	**67**
Burma (Myanmar)	33.0	9	11	50	52	67	57	71	81	89	72
Cambodia	37.7	3	..	..	..	..	..	..	35	48	22
China	21.0	3	4	32	..	29	13	32	73	84	62
Fiji	..	..	..	..	1	21	4	31	87	..	..
Hong Kong	..	..	..	..		0	0	0	90	..	..
Indonesia	38.0	..	..	..	57	58	35	68	73	84	62
Korea, N.	..	..	..	..	0	..	..	..	95	..	..
Korea, S.	..	..	2L	18L	0	22	9	51	96	99	94
Laos	34.0	..	11	40	33	72	53	75	54	..	..
Malaysia	17.6	4	..	..	12	22	4	34	78	87	70
Mongolia	..	..	..	..	0	34	22	50	93	..	..
Papua New Guinea	36.0	..	10L	47L	4	67	6	80	52	65	38
Philippines	33.5	5	6	37	..	19	7	28	90	90	90
Singapore	..	..	4x	11x	0	0	0	0	88	..	..
Solomon Islands	..	..	2L	34L	20	39	18	42	24	..	..
Thailand	13.0	4	6	22	41	28	..	..	93	96	90
Vietnam	41.9	14	12	49	3	50	30	67	88	92	84
Latin America and the Carribean	**12.0**	**3**	**3**	**21**	**14**	**19**	**9**	**44**	**85**	**87**	**83**
Argentina	1.2	4	..	..	..	..	..	..	95	96	95
Bolivia	11.4	3	9	38	..	54	23	85	78	85	71
Brazil	7.1	3	2	16	..	4	0	14	81	83	80
Chile	2.0	0x	1	10	5	14	0	79	93	94	93
Colombia	10.1	2	3	17	13	8	0	24	87	88	86
Costa Rica	8.1	..	2	8	3	6	0	16	93	93	93
Cuba	8.4	..	1	..	0	..	..	..	94	95	93
Dominican Republic	12.0	2x	1	19	..	38	..	..	83	85	82
Ecuador	13.0	0	2	34	20	42	25	63	86	88	84
El Salvador	19.4	..	5	30	..	59	24	90	73	76	70
Guatemala	25.0	8x	1	58	40	40	9	59	55	63	47
Guyana	18.0	..	9	21	4	19	6	26	96	..	..
Haiti	24.4	3x	9x	40x	55	58	44	64	53	59	47

Table 4 continued: Poverty and Hunger Statistics, Developing Countries

	underweight 1990	% children under 5 suffering from severe underweight 1980-91	wasting 1980-91	stunting 1980-91	% without access to health facilities 1987-90	% without access to safe water 1988-90 total	urban	rural	Adult literacy rate 1990 total	male	female
Honduras	19.8	4	2	34	38	48	44	51	73	76	71
Jamaica	7.2	1	3	9	..	28	5	54	98	98	99
Mexico	13.9	..	6	22	9	22	11	51	88	90	85
Nicaragua	18.7	1	1	22	0	47	22	81	81	..	..
Panama	11.0	..	6	22	18	17	0	34	88	88	88
Paraguay	4.2	1	<1	17	0	67	..	..	90	92	88
Peru	13.1	2x	1	37	0	42	27	78	85	92	79
Suriname	..	..	..	..	9	16	18	6	95	..	..
Trinidad & Tobago	9.0	0x	4	5	1	4	0	13	96	..	..
Uruguay	7.0	2x	..	16	0	16	5	73	96	97	96
Venezuela	5.9	..	2	6	0	11	11	11	88	87	90
Middle East and North Africa	**14.0**	..	**7**	**33**	**11**	**11**	**3**	**33**	**59**	**70**	**48**
Algeria	12.3	..	3	14	..	31	15	45	57	70	46
Bahrain	..	..	..	..	0	0	0	0	77	..	..
Cyprus	7.5	..	..	..	5	0	0	0	87	..	..
Egypt	10.0	3	4	30	1	14	4	18	48	63	34
Iran	39.0	..	13	50	27	11	0	25	54	65	43
Iraq	11.9	2	3	22	2	7	0	28	60	70	49
Jordan	12.7	1	3	19	10	1	0	2	80	89	70
Kuwait	5.0	..	3	12	0	0	0	0	73	77	67
Lebanon	8.9	..	..	..	5	2	..	..	80	88	73
Libya	4.0	..	..	..	0	3	0	20	64	75	50
Morocco	12.0	4x	4	26	38	27	0	50	50	61	38
Oman	..	..	..	..	11	43	13	53	35	..	..
Qatar	..	..	..	..	..	9	0	52	82	..	..
Saudi Arabia	12.6	..	..	..	2	5	0	26	62	73	48
Syria	12.5	..	..	..	1	21	9	32	65	78	51
Tunisia	8.9	2x	3	18	9	35	5	69	65	74	56
Turkey	10.5	..	..	..	..	8	..	..	81	90	71
United Arab Emirates	7.0	..	..	..	10	0	0	0	55	58	38
Yemen	19.1	..	8	34	..	..	..	..	39	53	26

Table 5: United States Poverty Trends

	1970	1980	1982	1984	1985	1986	1987	1988	1989	1990	1991
Population in millions	205.1	227.8	232.5	237	239.3	241.6	243.9	246.3	248.3	248.7	252.2
Total poverty rate (%)	12.6	13.0	15.0	14.4	14.0	13.6	13.4	13.1	12.8	13.5	14.2
White poverty rate (%)	9.9	10.2	12.0	11.5	11.4	11.0	10.4	10.1	10.0	10.7	11.3
Black poverty rate (%)	33.5	32.5	35.6	33.8	31.1	31.1	32.6	31.6	30.7	31.9	32.7
Hispanic poverty rate (%)	..	25.7	29.9	28.4	29.0	27.3	28.1	26.8	26.2	28.1	28.7
Elderly poverty rate (%)	24.6	15.7	14.6	12.4	12.6	12.4	12.5	12.0	11.4	12.2	12.4
Total child poverty rate (%)	15.1	18.3	21.9	21.5	20.7	20.5	20.5	19.7	19.6	20.6	21.1
White child poverty rate (%)	..	13.9	17.0	16.7	16.2	16.1	15.4	14.6	14.8	15.9	16.1
Black child poverty rate (%)	..	42.3	47.6	46.6	43.6	43.1	45.6	44.2	43.7	44.8	45.6
Hispanic child poverty rate (%)	..	33.2	39.5	39.2	40.3	37.7	39.6	37.9	36.2	38.4	39.8
Poverty rate of people in female-headed households (%)	38.1	36.7	40.6	38.4	37.6	38.3	38.3	37.2	32.2	33.4	39.7
Percent of federal budget spent on food assistance	0.5	2.4	2.1	2.1	2.0	1.9	1.9	1.9	1.9	1.9	2.0
Total infant mortality rate	20.0	12.6	11.5	10.8	10.6	10.4	10.1	10.0	9.7	9.1	8.9
White infant mortality rate	17.8	11.0	10.1	9.4	9.3	8.9	8.6	8.5	8.5	7.7	..
Black infant mortality rate	32.6	21.4	19.6	18.4	18.2	18.0	17.9	17.6	17.6	17.0	..
Unemployment rate (%)	4.9	7.1	9.7	7.5	7.2	7.0	6.2	5.5	5.3	5.5	6.7
Income distribution (per quintile in percentages)											
Lowest	..	5.0	4.5	4.4	4.4	4.3	4.3	4.4	3.8	3.9	3.8
Second	..	11.6	11.0	10.7	10.8	10.8	10.6	10.7	9.5	9.6	9.6
Middle	..	17.3	16.9	16.7	16.7	16.7	16.6	16.7	15.8	15.9	15.9
Fourth	..	24.5	24.2	24.1	24.1	24.2	24.1	24.2	24	24	24.2
Highest	..	41.5	43.5	44.2	44.1	44.2	44.4	44.1	46.8	46.6	46.5

Table 6: United States – State Poverty Conditions

	Population in millions July 1992	% Population in poverty 1991	Unemployment rate 1992	AFDC and food stamp benefits as % of poverty level – 4-person family 1992	Infant mortality rate 1992	% of children (under 12) hungry 1991	% of population (all ages) hungry 1991
Alabama	4.14	18.8	7.2	46.4	10.8	17.0	15.8
Alaska	.59	11.8	9.1	93.5	8.5	8.3	9.9
Arizona	3.83	14.8	7.4	65.3	8.5	12.1	12.4
Arkansas	2.40	17.3	7.2	53.2	9.8	18.4	14.5
California	30.87	15.7	9.1	87.6	6.9	13.1	13.2
Colorado	3.47	10.4	6.9	66.1	7.3	9.9	8.7
Connecticut	3.28	8.6	7.5	87.8	7.5*	7.8	7.2
Delaware	.69	7.5	5.3	64.6	9.7	10.6	6.3
District of Columbia	.59	18.6	8.4	70.2	20.0*	17.1	15.6
Florida	13.49	15.4	8.2	62.0	9.1	13.2	12.9
Georgia	6.75	17.2	6.9	59.9	10.4	13.1	14.4
Hawaii	1.16	7.7	4.5	99.3	6.6	10.8	6.4
Idaho	1.07	13.9	6.6	61.5	8.2	15.6	11.6
Illinois	11.63	13.5	7.5	65.5	10.0	13.9	11.3
Indiana	5.66	15.7	8.5	60.9	9.5	12.0	13.2
Iowa	2.81	9.6	4.6	69.9	7.8	14.7	8.0
Kansas	2.52	12.3	4.2	72.0	8.4	10.5	10.3
Kentucky	3.76	18.8	6.9	56.5	8.7	14.3	15.8
Louisiana	4.29	19.0	8.1	52.1	9.6	15.9	15.9
Maine	1.24	14.1	7.1	74.4	5.7	11.2	11.8
Maryland	4.91	9.1	6.5	69.2	8.1*	7.9	7.6
Massachusetts	6.00	11.0	8.5	77.9	6.8	9.3	9.2
Michigan	9.44	14.1	6.9	74.9	10.5	13.3	11.8
Minnesota	4.48	12.9	5.1	77.5	7.0	9.8	10.8
Mississippi	2.61	23.7	8.1	44.3	11.6	18.9	19.9
Missouri	5.19	14.8	5.7	60.7	9.0	12.7	12.4
Montana	.82	15.4	6.7	69.5	8.5	14.7	12.9
Nebraska	1.61	9.5	3.0	66.3	6.7	13.2	8.0
Nevada	1.33	11.4	6.6	64.6	6.6	12.9	9.6
New Hampshire	1.11	7.3	7.5	74.7	5.4	5.8	6.1
New Jersey	7.79	9.7	8.4	70.3	8.6	10.0	8.1
New Mexico	1.58	22.4	6.8	63.5	8.3	17.2	18.8
New York	18.12	15.3	8.5	87.4	8.5	14.6	12.8
North Carolina	6.84	14.5	5.9	57.5	10.2	12.4	12.2
North Dakota	.64	14.5	4.9	69.7	7.8	12.8	12.2
Ohio	11.02	13.4	7.2	65.4	8.7	11.7	11.2
Oklahoma	3.21	17.0	6.7	64.3	9.2	13.5	14.2
Oregon	2.98	13.5	7.5	77.2	7.4	11.3	11.3
Pennsylvania	12.01	11.0	7.6	71.0	8.6	12.3	9.2
Rhode Island	1.00	10.4	8.9	81.9	7.9	12.2	8.7
South Carolina	3.60	16.4	6.2	53.6	10.5	15.0	13.7
South Dakota	.71	14.0	3.1	67.2	10.0	13.4	11.7
Tennessee	5.02	15.5	6.4	51.4	9.5	14.7	13.0
Texas	17.66	17.5	7.5	50.9	7.7	13.6	14.7
Utah	1.81	12.9	4.9	68.4	6.2	11.3	10.8
Vermont	.57	12.6	6.6	84.6	6.8	10.0	10.6
Virginia	6.38	9.9	6.4	64.7	9.7*	9.7	8.3
Washington	5.14	9.5	7.5	80.3	7.4*	10.7	8.0
West Virginia	1.81	17.9	11.3	58.8	9.1	18.3	15.0
Wisconsin	5.01	9.9	5.1	77.2	7.1	11.4	8.3
Wyoming	.47	9.9	5.6	63.5	8.8	10.2	8.3

Notes

For categories in which a range of years is cited, data are generally from one year within range. Growth rates refer to entire range.

.. Data not available

Table 1: * Growth rates for 1960-91.
x Data pre-1980 or apply only to certain region within country.

Table 2: # Excluding China.
* % of children immunized for measles only.
R Russian federation only.

Table 3: a GNP per capita estimated less than $500.

b GNP per capita estimated in $500-$1,499 range.
c GNP per capita estimated in $1,500-3,499 range.
d GNP per capita estimated in $3,500-6,000 range.
* except Turkey and Iran.
x Years outside range specified.
 f Includes beverages and tobacco.
R Russian federation only.

G figures for GNP growth rate 1980-91

Table 4: ¹ Black population only.
² Excluding India.
x Pre-1980.
L Local or regional studies, may not reflect entire country.

Table 6: *1991.

Sources for Tables

SWP U.N. Fund for Population Activities, *The State of World Population 1993* (New York: UNFPA, 1993).

SWC UNICEF, *The State of the World's Children 1993* (Oxford: Oxford University Press, 1993).

HDR United Nations Development Program, *Human Development Report 1993* (Oxford: Oxford University Press, 1993).

Table 1
Population: SWP. Projections for 2000 from HDR.
1980-91 population growth rate: SWC.
Fertility: HDR.
Percent under 16: SWC.
Percent urbanized: SWP.
Life expectancy: SWP.
Infant, under five, and maternal mortality rates: SWC.

Table 2
Human Development Index: HDI components are life expectancy, knowledge (measured by literacy and years of schooling), and income. HDR.
Average years of schooling: HDR.
Low birthweight: SWC, HDR.
Percent of one-year-olds immunized: For developing countries, HDR. For developed countries (measles only), SWC.
Per capita food production and calorie supply: HDR.
Deforestation rate: World Resources

Institute, *World Resources 1992-93* (New York and Oxford: Oxford University Press, 1992).

Table 3
Per capita GNP and per capita GNP growth rate: The World Bank, *Social Indicators of Development 1993* (Baltimore: Johns Hopkins University Press, 1993), and *The World Bank Atlas* (Washington: The World Bank, 1992).
Military expenditure as percent of health and education expenditure: HDR.
Total debt and debt service as percent of exports (**debt service ratio**): The World Bank, *World Debt Tables 1992-93* (Washington: The World Bank, 1992).
Food as percent of imports and exports: Food and Agriculture Organization of the UN, Rome.
Per capita energy use and food as percent of household consumption: The World Bank, *World Development Report 1993* (Oxford: Oxford University Press, 1993).

Table 4
Percent of children underweight: U.N. Administrative Committee on Coordination/Subcommittee on Nutrition, *Second Report on the World Nutrition Situation*, Vol. 2. (Washington: International Food Policy Research Institute, 1993).
Severely underweight: SWC.
Stunting and wasting: UNICEF, *Child Malnutrition: Progress Toward the World Summit for Children Goal* (New

York: UNICEF, 1993); The World Bank, *Global Indicators of Nutritional Risk* (Washington: The World Bank, 1993).
Percent without access to health facilities and safe water, and adult literacy rate: HDR.

Table 5
Population and Poverty statistics are from U.S. Census Bureau, except as follows:
Food and nutrition assistance as percent of federal budget: *The Budget of the United States Government, FY 1992* (Washington: Office of Management and Budget, 1991).
Infant mortality rates: Center for the Study of Social Policy, *Kids Count Data Book 1993* (Washington: CSSP, 1993), and the National Center for Health Statistics.

Table 6
Unemployment rate: U.S. Bureau of Labor Statistics.
AFDC and food stamp benefits as percent of poverty level: *Kids Count Data Book 1993*.
Infant mortality rate: National Center for Health Statistics, *Monthly Vital Statistics Report*, Vol. 41, No. 12 (May 19, 1993).
Proportion of children hungry: Food Research and Action Center, Community Childhood Hunger Identification Project.
Percent of population hungry: Center on Hunger, Poverty, and Nutrition Policy, Tufts University.

Abbreviations

AID – U.S. Agency for International Development

BFW – Bread For The World

CCHIP – Community Childhood Hunger Identification Project

EC – European Community

ESF – Economic Support Fund

FAO – Food and Agriculture Organization of the United Nations

FRAC – Food Research and Action Center

GDP – Gross Domestic Product

GNP – Gross National Product

IMF – International Monetary Fund

NGO – Nongovernmental Organization

TEFAP – The Emergency Food Assistance Program

UN – United Nations

UNHCR – U.N. High Commissioner for Refugees

U.S. – United States

USDA – U.S. Department of Agriculture

WFP – U.N. World Food Program

WIC – Special Supplemental Food Program for Women, Infants, and Children

WHO – World Health Organization

Glossary

Absolute poverty – The income level below which a minimally nutritionally adequate diet plus essential non-food requirements are not affordable.

Anemia – A condition in which the hemoglobin concentration (the number of red blood cells) is lower than normal as a result of a deficiency of one or more essential nutrients, such as iron, or due to disease.

Daily calorie requirement – The average number of calories needed to sustain normal levels of activity and health, taking into account age, sex, body weight, and climate.

Famine – A situation of extreme scaricity of food, potentially leading to widespread starvation.

Food security – Assured access for every person, primarily by production or purchase, to enough nutritious food to sustain productive human life.

Foreign exchange – Currency acceptable for use in international trade, such as U.S. dollars. The value of one currency in terms of another is the **exchange rate**.

Gross domestic product (GDP) – The value of all goods and services produced within a nation during a specified period, usually a year.

Gross national product (GNP) – The value of all goods and services produced by a country's citizens, wherever they are located.

Hunger – A condition in which people lack the basic food intake to provide them with the energy and nutrients for fully productive, active, and healthy lives.

Infant mortality rate (IMR) – The annual number of deaths of infants under one year of age per one thousand live births.

Inflation – An increase in overall prices, which leads to a decrease in purchasing power.

International Monetary Fund (IMF) – An intergovernmental agency which makes loans to countries that have foreign exchange and monetary problems. These loans are conditioned upon the willingness of the borrowing country to adopt economic policies designed by IMF.

Low birthweight infants – Babies born weighing 2,500 grams (5 pounds, 8 ounces) or less who are especially vulnerable to illness and death during the first month of life.

Malnutrition – Failure to achieve nutrient requirements, which can impair physical and/or mental health. Malnutrition may result from consuming too little food or a shortage or imbalance of key nutrients, e.g. refined sugar and fat.

Poverty Line – An official measure of poverty defined by national governments. In the United States, for example, it is based on ability to afford USDA's Thrifty Food Plan.

Recession – A period in which a country's GDP declines in two or more consecutive three-month periods.

Structural adjustment – Economic policy changes, often imposed upon an indebted country by its lenders as a condition for future loans, intended to stimulate economic growth. These generally involve reducing the role of government in the economy and increasing exports.

Stunting – Failure to grow to normal height caused by chronic undernutrition during the formative years of childhood.

Sustainabilty – Society's capacity to shape its economic and social systems so as to maintain both natural resources and human life.

World Bank – An intergovernmental agency which makes long-term loans to the governments of developing nations.

Under five mortality rate – The annual number of deaths of children under five years of age per one thousand live births.

Underemployment – A situation where a large portion of the population is not fully employed year round.

Undernutrition – A form of mild, chronic, or acute malnutrition which is characterized by inadequate intake of food energy (measured by calories), usually due to eating too little. Stunting, wasting, and being underweight are common forms of undernutrition.

Underweight – A condition in which a person is seriously below normal weight for her/his age. The term can apply to any age group, but is most often used as a measurement of undernutrition in children under five years of age.

Vulnerability to hunger – Individuals, households, communities, or nations who have enough to eat most of the time, but whose poverty makes them especially susceptible to changes in the economy, climate, or political conditions.

Wasting – A condition in which a person is seriously below the normal weight for her/his height due to acute undernutrition.

Notes and Sources

Part I: Transforming the Politics of Hunger

1. Feeding People – Half of Overcoming Hunger (pp. 11-30)

A. The U.S. Feeding Movement – Fertile Ground for an Anti-Hunger Movement (pp. 11-19)

1. New York City Coalition Against Hunger, "No Soup at the Soup Kitchen: Hunger in NYC," (New York, 1992).

2. Based on organizations that file IRS Form 990, Independent Sector, *Nonprofit Almanac 1992-93* (Washington, 1992).

3. *The Chronicle of Philanthropy* 4.8 (Feb. 11, 1992):24.

4. Gibson Winter, *Community and Spiritual Transformation: Religion and Politics in a Communal Age* (New York: Crossroad, 1989), p. 99.

5. Robert Cameron Mitchell, "From Conservation to Environmental Movement: The Development of the Modern Environmental Lobbies," in Michael J. Lacey, ed., *Government and Environmental Politics: Essays on Historical Developments since World War II* (Washington: Wilson Center, 1988), p. 9.

6. Doug McAdam, John D. McCarthy and Mayer N. Zald, "Social Movements" in Neil J. Smelser, ed., *Handbook of Sociology*, (Beverly Hills: Sage Publications, 1988), p. 702.

7. Mark Wolfson, *The Consequences of a Social Movement: An Organizational Analysis of the Impact of the Citizens' Movement Against Drunk Driving*, Ph.D. dissertation, Catholic University, 1988.

B. From Relief Toward Development and Empowerment (pp. 20-30)

1. Letter from Paul Derstine, executive director, Interchurch Medical Assistance, Inc., to A. Cecilia Snyder, Dec. 14, 1992.

2. *InterAction Member Profiles 1993* (Washington: InterAction, 1993).

3. *Catholic Relief Services Annual Report 1991* (Baltimore. CRS, 1992).

4. *Development Cooperation, 1992 Report* (Paris: Organization for Economic Cooperation and Development, 1992), pp. a/72-73.

5. David C. Korten, "Third Generation NGO Strategies: A Key to People-Centered Development," *World Development* [Great Britain] 15: Supplement (1987):145-149. See also his *Getting to the 21st Century* (West Hartford, CT: Kumarian Press, 1990), especially Chapter 10.

6. *Ibid.*, p. 124.

7. For a discussion of public opinion data on these topics, see Gary Gunderson and Tom Peterson, "What We Think: American Views on Development and U.S.-Third World Relations," *Seeds*, June 1987, pp. 6-12.

8. Works such as Bob Smucker's *The Nonprofit Lobbying Guide* (San Francisco: Jossey-Bass, 1991) and the Council on Foundations' *Foundations and Lobbying: Safe Ways to Affect Public Policy* (Washington: Council on Foundations, n.d.) provide simple and useful guidance. The Advocacy Forum of the Alliance for Justice in Washington, D.C., offers *Being a Player: A Guide to the IRS Lobbying Regulations for Advocacy Charities* (Washington: Harmon, Curran, Gallagher, and Spielberg, 1991).

9. *Development Cooperation*, p. A-13; figures from U.S. Agency for International Development.

NGOs and Europolitics: An Overview (pp. 21-23)

A Churches Guide to European Institutions. Brussels: The Ecumenical Center, May 1992.

EURO-CIDSE News Bulletin. Brussels: International Cooperation for Development and Solidarity, May 1993.

Liaison Committee of Development NGOs to the European Communities. *Annual Report 1992-93* (Brussels: 1993).

Wilkinson, Mick. "Lobbying in Brussels: The NGDO Experience." Unpublished paper. University of Hull, U.K., 1992.

2. Religious Communities Respond to Hunger (pp. 31-46)

1. Independent Sector, *Giving and Volunteering 1992* (Washington: Independent Sector, 1992), p. 263.

2. Bedell, Kenneth B. and Alice M. Jones, eds., *Yearbook of American and Canadian Churches* (Nashville: Abingdon Press, 1992), p. 283.

3. *The Lutheran*, July, 1993, p. 53. Citing a study by Independent Sector sponsored by Lilly Endowment.

4. BFW Institute chose medium-sized cities in the northeast, northwest, and middle states where we could access a current and complete list of congregations. A telephone follow-up of congregations which did not return the questionnaire showed they were less likely than those which returned the questionnaire to have hunger-focused worship and education, but just as likely to be involved in a food distribution program.

5. Search Institute, *Effective Christian Education: A National Study of Protestant Congregations* (Minneapolis: Search Institute, 1990).

6. Robert Wuthnow, *The Restructuring of American Religion: Society and Faith Since World War II* (Princeton, NJ: Princeton University Press, 1988). Robert Wuthnow, *The Struggle for America's Soul: Evangelicals, Liberals, and Secularism* (Grand Rapids, MI: William B. Eerdmans, 1989).

7. Walter H. Capps, *The New Religious Right: Piety, Patriotism, and Politics* (Columbia, SC: University of South Carolina Press, 1989).

8. Thomas M. Guterbock, "What Do Christians Expect From Christian Relief and Development?," *Stewardship Journal* 2.3 & 4:17.

9. Kathryn Collmer, "From Hand to Mouth," *Soujourners*, 22:5 (June, 1993):18.

10. Edward H. McKinley, *Marching to Glory: The History of the Salvation Army in the United States of America 1880-1990* (San Fransisco: Harper & Row, 1989). The Salvation Army, *Handbook of Doctrine* (London: International Headquarters, 1969). Clark C. Spence, *The Salvation Army Farm Colonies* (Tucson: University of Arizona Press, 1985).

11. Dwight N. Hopkins, and George C.L. Cummings, eds., *Cut Loose Your Stammering Tongue: Black Theology in the Slave Narratives* (Maryknoll, NY: Orbis Books, 1991).

12. C. Eric Lincoln and Lawrence H. Mamiya, *The Black Church in the African American Experience* (Durham: Duke University Press, 1990), p. 397.

13. *Ibid.*, p. 225.

14. Independent Sector, *Nonprofit Almanac 1992-1993* (San Fransisco: Jossey-Bass, 1992), p. 229.

15. Lester M. Salamon and Alan J. Abramson, "The Federal Budget and the Nonprofit Sector: FY 1993," *Occasional Paper* No. 13 (Baltimore: The Johns Hopkins University Institute for Policy Studies, 1992):iii.

16. Largest Private Support from *The Chronicle of Philanthropy* 5.2, Nov. 3, 1992. Largest Income from *The Nonprofit Times* 6.11, Nov., 1992.

17. Search Institute, *Effective Christian Education: A Report for the United Church of Christ* (Minneapolis: Search Institute, 1990), p. 26.

18. *Ibid.*, p. 3.

19. Independent Sector, *Giving and Volunteering*, pp. 162-163.

MAZON: A Jewish Response to Hunger (pp. 41-43)

1. Albert Vorspan and David Saperstein, *Tough Choices: Jewish Perspectives on Social Justice* (New York: Union of American Hebrew Congregations Press, 1992), p. 178.

2. *MAZON Newsletter*, Spring 1993.

3. Speaking For Ourselves (pp. 47-66)

A. Organizing U.S. Low-Income People to End Hunger (pp. 47-55)

1. Personal interview, May 1, 1993.

2. One recent example is Kim Bobo, Jackie Kendall, and Steve Max, *ORGANIZE! Organizing for Social Change: A Manual for Activists in the 1990s* (Cabin John, MD: Seven Locks Press, 1991).

3. Personal interview, May 1, 1993.

4. Personal interview, May 1, 1993.

5. See, for example, *Poor People's Movements: Why They Succeed, How They Fail* (New York: Vintage Books, 1979).

Hunger and Poverty in the Hispanic Community (pp. 49-53)

1. Select Committee on Hunger, "Urban Grocery Gap," hearing held in Washington, D.C., Sept. 30, 1992 (Washington: U.S. Government Printing Office, 1992). Mark Bellinger, Public Voice for Food and Health Policy, Washington, D.C., communication to BFW Institute, July 26, 1993.

2. Committee on Ways and Means, *Overview of Entitlement Programs: 1992 Green Book* (Washington: U.S. Government Printing Office, 1992).

B. People's Movements: An Alternative Development Vision (pp. 56-66)

1. Daniel Siegel and Jenny Yancey, *The Rebirth of Civil Society: The Development of the Nonprofit Sector in East Central Europe and the Role of Western Assistance* (New York: The Rockefeller Brothers Fund, 1992), pp. 15-17, 21-27.

2. This discussion is drawn from David C. Korten, "The Role of Nongovernmental Organizations in Development: Changing Patterns and Perspectives," in Samuel Paul and Arturo Israel, eds., *Nongovernmental Organizations and the World Bank: Cooperation for Development* (Washington: The World Bank, 1991), pp. 20-43.

3. For further ideas and information on bridges between Northern and Southern grassroots movements, see *Global Exchanges*, the newsletter of Global Exchange.

4. David J. Suley, "The Impact of Third World Experience on American Christians," Doctor of Ministry Dissertation, Wesley Theological Seminary, Washington, D.C., May 1993.

4. Transforming Media Coverage of Hunger (pp. 67-82)

1. David Breskin, "Bob Geldof: The Rolling Stone Interview," *Rolling Stone* (Dec. 5, 1985):67.

2. Paul Harrison and Robin Palmer, *News Out of Africa*, (London: Hilary Shipman, 1986), p. 97.

3. William Boot, "Ethiopia: Feasting on Famine," *Columbia Journalism Review* 23 (March/April 1985):47.

4. Mohamed Amin, "A Vision of the Truth," *Refugees* 69 (Oct. 1989):24.

5. Shanto Iyengar, *Is Anyone Responsible? How Television Frames Political Issues* (Chicago: University of Chicago Press, 1991), p. 48.

6. Michael Moss, "The Media and Poverty: A Journalist's Approach," *Food Monitor* (Winter 1988): p. 53.

7. Ernest Hemingway, quoted in Hillier Kriegbaum, *Pressure on the Press* (New York: Apollo, 1973), p. 112.

8. Media General/Associated Press, Sept. 1989.

9. Joint Center for Political Studies poll, Sept. 1988.

10. Penn & Schoen Associates, 1991.

11. Floris W. Wood, ed., *An American Profile: Opinions and Behavior, 1972-1989* (New York: Gale Research, 1990).

12. Michael Parenti, *Make-Believe Media: The Politics of Entertainment* (New York: St. Martin's Press, 1992).

13. Amin, p. 22.

14. Steve Askin, "Hunger in Africa: A Story Still Untold," *Extra!* (Sept. 1992):5.

15. John Maxwell Hamilton, "`Juju' News from Abroad," *Gannet Center Journal* 3:4 (Fall 1989):144.

16. "Are You on the Nightline Guest List?" *Extra!* (Feb. 1989).

17. W. Russell Neuman, Marion R. Just, and Ann N. Crigler, *Common Knowledge: News and the Construction of Political*

Meaning (Chicago: University of Chicago Press, 1992).

18. Peter Carlson, "The Image Makers," *The Washington Post Magazine* (Feb. 11, 1990):15.

19. Shirley Biagi, *Media/Impact* (Belmont, CA: Wadsworth, 1990), p. 225.

20. William A. Henry, "News as Entertainment," in *What's News*, Elie Abel, ed. (San Francisco: Institute for Contemporary Studies, 1981).

21. Quoted in Stephen Vito, "Inside 60 Minutes," *American Film*, (Dec./Jan. 1972):55.

22. Fred Barnes, "Flix Mix in Politix," *The New Republic* (Oct. 1989):23.

23. Alan Atkisson, "Redefining Entertainment: An Interview with Norman Fleishman," *In Context* No. 23 (Fall 1989).

24. Marilyn Kern-Foxworth, "Martin Luther King, Jr.: Minister, Civil Rights Activist, and Public Opinion Leader," *Public Relations Review* 18:3 (Fall 1992):288.

25. Scott M. Cutlip, "Public Relations: The Manufacture of Opinion," *Gannet Center Journal* 3:1 (Winter 1989):114.

26. *Ibid.*, p. 105.

27. Carlson, p. 15.

28. Jeff & Marie Blyskal, *PR: How the Public Relations Industry Writes the News* (New York: William Morrow, 1985). Martin Lee and Norman Solomon, *Unreliable Sources: A Guide to Detecting Bias in News Media* (New York: Carol Publishing Group, 1990), p. 104.

29. Dorothy Levy, "The Emerging Wisdom from the Great PR Firms," *Public Relations Quarterly* (Fall 1990):33.

30. Robert Rutherford Smith, "Mythic Elements in Television News," *Journal of Communication* (Winter 1979):78-82.

31. Quoted in Biagi, p. 269.

32. Quoted in Philip Shabecoff, *A Fierce Green Fire: The American Environmental Movement* (New York: Hill & Wang, 1993), p. 144.

33. *Strategic Media* (Washington: Benton Foundation, 1991), p. 7.

34. Theodore White, *The Making of the President 1972* (New York: Bantam, 1973), p. 327.

35. Michael Moss, "The Poverty Story," *Columbia Journalism Review* (July/Aug. 1987):43.

5. Thirty Years of Anti-Hunger Advocacy (pp. 83-98)
1. Nick Kotz, *Let Them Eat Promises: The Politics of Hunger in America, 1967-1969* (Englewood Cliffs, NJ: Prentice-Hall, 1969).

2. *Bread for the World Newsletter*, May 1973.

3. *Bread for the World Newsletter*, Dec. 1973.

Barkan, Steven E., Cohn, Steven F., Whitaker, William H. "Professionalization in the Contemporary Anti-Hunger Movement," manuscript.

Birch, Bruce C. and Rasmussen, Larry L. *The Predicament of the Prosperous*. Philadelphia: Westminster Press, 1978.

Blaustein, Arthur I., ed. *The American Promise: Equal Justice and Economic Opportunity*, final report of the National Advisory Council on Economic Opportunity. New Brunswick, NJ: Transaction Books, 1982.

Borgstrom, Georg. *The Hungry Planet: The Modern World at the Edge of Famine*. New York: Macmillan Co., 1965.

Brown, Lester R., with Eckholm, Erik P. *By Bread Alone*. New York and Washington: Praeger Publishers for Overseas Development Council, 1974.

Caudill, Harry M. *Night Comes to the Cumberlands: A Biography of a Depressed Area*. Boston: Atlantic, Little, Brown, 1963.

Citizens' Board of Inquiry into Hunger and Malnutrition in the United States. *Hunger USA*. Boston: Beacon Press, by arrangement with New Community Press, Washington, 1968.

Coles, Robert. *Still Hungry in America*. New York: New American Library, 1969.

George, Susan. *How the Other Half Dies: The Real Reasons for World Hunger*. Montclair, NJ: Allenheld, Osmun, 1977.

Gremillion, Joseph, ed. *Food/Energy and the Major Faiths*, report of the Interreligious Peace Colloquium, Bellagio, Italy, May 1975. Maryknoll, NY: Orbis Books, 1978.

Gussow, Joan Dye. *The Feeding Web: Issues in Nutritional Ecology*. Palo Alto: Bull Publishing, 1978.

Harrington, Michael. *The Other America*. New York: Macmillan, 1962.

Hollings, Ernest F. *The Case Against Hunger: A Demand for a National Policy*. New York: Cowles Book Co., 1970.

Knowles, Louis L., ed. *To End Hunger: An Exploration of Alternative Strategies in the Struggle Against World Hunger*, report of the Church-University Conference on World Hunger (National Council of Churches of Christ in the U.S.A.), April 1981, Madison, WI. 1983.

Kotz, Nick. *Hunger in America: The Federal Response*. New York: The Field Foundation, 1979.

Kutzner, Patricia L. *World Hunger: A Reference Handbook*. Santa Barbara: ABC Clio, 1992.

Lappé, Frances Moore and Collins, Joseph. *Food First: Beyond the Myth of Scarcity*, revised. New York: Ballantine, 1978.

McLaughlin, Martin with Cooper, Mary. *Advocates for Justice: How different religious people learned to work together to advocate for justice in U.S. policies*. Washington: Interfaith Impact for Justice and Peace, Aug. 1991.

Minear, Larry. *New Hope for the Hungry? The Challenge of the World Food Crisis*. New York: Friendship Press, 1975.

Overseas Development Council. *Global Justice and Development: Report of the Interfaith Aspen Consultation on Global Justice, June 4-7, 1974*. Washington: Overseas Development Council, 1975.

Roundtree, Estelle and Halverstadt, Hugh. *Sometimes They Cry: A Study/Action Book*. New York: Friendship Press, 1970.

Sider, Ronald J. *Cry Justice: The Bible on Hunger and Poverty*. New York: Paulist Press for Bread for the World, 1980.

———— *Rich Christians in an Age of Hunger: A Biblical Study*. Downersgrove, IL:

InterVarsity Press, 1977.

Simon, Arthur. *Bread for the World* and *Bread for the World*, revised 1984. New York: Paulist Press and Grand Rapids, MI: Wm. B. Eerdmans, 1975.

Simon, Paul and Simon, Arthur. *The Politics of World Hunger.* New York: Harper's Magazine Press in association with Harper & Row, 1973.

Taylor, Richard K. *Economics and the Gospel: The First of Four Adult Primers on Shalom.* Edited by Charles McCullough. Cleveland: United Church Press, 1973.

Toton, Suzanne C. *World Hunger: The Responsibility of Christian Education.* Maryknoll, NY: Orbis Books, 1982.

Withers, Leslie and Peterson, Tom, eds. *Hunger Action Handbook: What You Can Do and How To Do It.* Decatur, GA: *Seeds Magazine,* 1987.

6. The Road Not Taken – The United States Government and Hunger (pp. 99-114)

1. Presidential Commission on World Hunger, *Overcoming World Hunger: The Challenge Ahead* (Washington: U.S. Government Printing Office, 1980), p. 185.

2. *Ibid.*

3. *Ibid.*, pp. 189-190.

4. Barbara E. Cohen and Martha R. Burt, "Eliminating Hunger: Food Security Policy for the 1990s," *Urban Institute Project Report* (Oct. 1989): 25-26.

5. Will Marshall and Elaine Ciulla Kamarck, "Replacing Welfare with Work," in Will Marshall and Martin Schram, eds., *Mandate for Change* (New York: Berkley Books, 1993), p. 223.

6. Cohen and Burt, pp. 14, 20, 22, 34-35, 38-39, 56.

7. Marshall and Kamarck, p. 223.

8. Patricia Ann James, "North America Hunger Update," in Marc J. Cohen, ed., *Hunger 1993: Uprooted People* (Washington: BFW Institute, 1992), p. 159.

9. B. Cohen and Burt, p. 30. Marshall and Kamarck, pp. 220-221, 228-229.

10. *Ibid.*, pp. 221, 235-236. *How the Poor Would Remedy Poverty* (Washington: Coalition on Human Needs, n.d.), p. iii.

11. Marshall and Kamarck, pp. 223-224, 226-227.

12. See *Hunger 1990: A Report on the State of World Hunger* (Washington: BFW Institute, 1990), pp. 92-98, 121. Marc J. Cohen, ed., *Hunger 1993: Uprooted People* (Washington: BFW Institute, 1992), p. 182, based on U.S. Census Bureau data.

13. *Hunger 1990*, pp. 94-96. Patricia Ann James, "Structural Economic Change and Hunger in the United States," in *Hunger 1993*, pp. 114-120.

14. Elaine Ciulla Kamarck and William Galston, "A Progressive Family Policy for the 1990s," in Will Marshall and Martin Schram, eds., *Mandate for Change* (New York: Berkley Books, 1993), pp. 156-160. Marshall and Kamarck, p. 218.

15. U.S. Department of Agriculture and U.S. Department of Health and Human Services, "International Conference on Nutrition Paper Submitted by the United States of America," April 1992, pp. I/8-I/9.

16. Letter from Dr. Larry Brown, director, Center on Hunger, Poverty, and Nutrition Policy, Tufts University, to U.S. Rep. Tony Hall, chairman, House Select Committee on Hunger (Sept. 8, 1992). Spencer Rich, "Ranks of Poverty Swell by 2 Million," *The Washington Post*, Sept. 4, 1992. M. Cohen, *Hunger 1993*, p. 182.

17. Total aid calculated by Larry Q. Nowels, "Foreign Aid: Budget, Policy, and Reform," *CRS Issue Brief*, Congressional Research Service, The Library of Congress, June 22, 1992, p. 2. *The World Food Day Report: The President's Report to the U.S. Congress*, Oct. 16, 1992. BFW Institute, "Foreign Aid: What Counts Toward Sustainable Development and Humanitarian Relief, A Discussion Paper" (hereafter cited as "What Counts?"), June 8, 1993. This last study was funded with a grant from the Ford Foundation. Much of the analysis of foreign aid which follows draws on the findings of "What Counts?" The paper rates programs as to whether they are *intended* to support sustainable development and humanitarian relief; it is not based on actual field assessments.

18. *International Conference on Nutrition: Nutrition and Development – A Global Assessment, 1992*, rev. ed. (Rome: FAO and WHO, 1992). *Human Development Report 1993* (New York: Oxford University Press for the United Nations Development Program, 1993), p. 141.

19. *International Food Policy Research Institute Annual Report, 1990* (Washington: IFPRI, 1991), pp. 37-39.

20. "Partnerships for Global Development: The Clearing Horizon, A Report of the Carnegie Commission on Science, Technology, and Government," (New York: Carnegie Commission, Dec. 1992), p. 83.

21. "Partnerships for Global Development," pp. 86, 88, 93-95. Frank C. Conahan, assistant comptroller general, National Security and International Affairs Division, U.S. General Accounting Office, "Foreign Assistance: Management Problems Persist at the Agency for International Development," testimony before the Committee on Appropriations, Subcommittee on Foreign Operations, United States Senate, May 1, 1992. Al Kamen and Thomas W. Lippman, "Task Force Favors Restructuring and Refocusing Troubled AID," *The Washington Post*, July 3, 1993.

22. United Nations Conference on Trade and Development, *Handbook of International Trade and Development Statistics, 1991* (New York: United Nations, 1992).

23. "Partnerships for Global Development," p. 83.

24. Dellia Leyva, "Season of Death in the Land of Sugar," *Hunger Notes* 18:1 (Summer 1992): 5,6. Joseph Collins, *The Philippines: Fire on the Rim* (San Francisco: Institute for Food and Development Policy, 1989).

25. *Defense Monitor* XXI:5 (1992).

26. "Partnerships for Global Development," pp. 36, 38.

27. Quoted in *Many Neighbors, One Earth: Transforming Foreign Aid, Bread for the World's 1993 Offering of Letters Kit* (Washington: Bread for the World, 1993), p. 4.

Part II: Regional Hunger Updates Africa (pp. 115-124)

ACCESS: A Security Information Service. "Somalia: A Country at War with Itself,"

Resource Brief 6, No. 5. Washington.: ACCESS, Nov. 1992.

Amnesty International. *Somalia: A Human Rights Disaster.* London: Amnesty International, Aug. 1992.

Africa Confidential Vol. 34, No. 12, June 11, 1993.

African Rights. *A Preliminary Assessment of Operation Restore Hope.* London: African Rights, May 1993.

Africa Watch. *Somalia Beyond the Warlords: The Need for a Verdict on Human Rights Abuses.* London: Africa Watch, March 1993.

Bonner, Ray. "Why We Went." *Mother Jones,* April 1993.

Brittain, Victoria. "When Democracy Is Not Enough: Denying Angola's Electoral Result." *Southern Africa Report,* Jan.-Feb. 1993.

Buchanon, Rob. "Twenty-Five Years of Civil War in Sudan." *The Nonviolent Activist,* April 1993.

Crocker, Chester A. *Nigh Noon in Southern Africa: Making Peace in a Rough Neighborhood.* New York. Norton & Co., 1992.

Davidson, Basil. *The Black Man's Burden: Africa and the Curse of the Nation-State.* New York: Times Books, 1992.

de Waal, Alex. "The Shadow Economy." *Africa Report,* Vol. 38, No. 2, March/April 1993.

European Parliamentarians for Southern Africa. *Mozambique Peace Process Bulletin,* Issue 3. Amsterdam: EPSA, May 1993.

Food and Agriculture Organization of the United Nations. *Food Outlook* No. 2. Rome: FAO, Feb. 1993.

Food and Agriculture Organization of the United Nations. *Foodcrops and Shortages* No. 3. Rome: FAO, March 1993.

Food and Agriculture Organization of the United Nations. *Eritrea Assessment,* Special Alert No. 230. Rome: FAO, Nov. 1992.

Gallagher, Dennis and Martin, Susan Forbes.

The Many Faces of the Somali Crisis. Washington: Refugee Policy Group, Dec. 1992.

Global Coalition for Africa. *1992 Annual Report.* Washington: GCA, 1992.

Hanlon, Joseph. *Mozambique: Who Calls the Shots?* London: James Currey, 1991.

Hansch, Steven. *Nutrition, Food Security and Health in Somalia: Assessment and Recommendations.* Washington: Food Aid Management, Feb. 1993.

Harsch, Ernest. "Somalia: Restoring Hope," *Africa Recovery Briefing Paper* No. 7. New York: United Nations, Jan. 1993.

Holcomb, Bonnie K. and Ibassa, Sisai. *The Invention of Ethiopia.* Trenton, NJ: Red Sea Press, 1992.

Life and Peace Institute. *Horn of Africa Bulletin.* Vol. 4, No. 4, July-Aug. 1992.

Johnson, Phyllis. *Mozambique is not Angola or Cambodia but the UN is Running Out of Excuses (And Time).* Harare: Southern African Research and Documentation Center (SARDC), March 1993.

Kadenge, Phineas, ed. *Zimbabwe's Structural Adjustment Program: The First Year Experience.* Harare: SAPES Books, 1992.

MacGarry, Brian. *Growth? Without Equity?* Harare: Mambo Press, 1992.

Marcum, John A. "Angola: War Again." *Current History,* May 1993.

Meldrum, Andrew. "Two Steps Back." *Africa Report* Vol. 38, No. 2, March/April 1993.

Nduru, Moyiga. "Eritrean Referendum." *African Business,* April 1993.

New Internationalist. "Horror and Hope: The Horn of Africa." No. 238, Dec. 1992.

Noble, Kenneth. "Angolan Rebels Rebound, Within Reach of a Victory." *New York Times,* April 13, 1993.

Physicians for Human Rights. *Hidden Enemies: Land Mines in Northern Somalia.* Boston: Physicians for Human Rights, Nov. 1992.

Prendergast, John. Trip Report to the Horn. Washington: Center of Concern, Feb. 1993.

SADC Regional Early Warning Unit. *Food Security Quarterly Bulletin.* Harare: Jan. 31 and March 31, 1993.

Sogge, David. *Sustainable Peace: Angola's Recovery.* Harare: SARDC, 1992.

Tafirenyika, Masimba. "Lessons of Angola." *New African,* March 1993.

Taylor, Paul. "The Meltdown of Angola's Peace Accord." *The Washington Post,* March 29, 1993.

Thompson, Carol. *Drought Management Strategies in Southern Africa.* Nairobi: UNICEF, 1993.

United Nations. *Africa Recovery Briefing Paper,* Vol. 6, No. 4, Dec. 1992-Feb. 1993.

United Nations Operation in Somalia. *U.N. Relief and Rehabilitation Programme for Somalia.* New York: UN, March 1993.

World Bank. *Zimbabwe: A Policy Agenda for Private Sector Development.* Washington: The World Bank, 1992.

World Food Program. *Emergency Report No. 10.* Rome: WFP, March 12, 1993.

Asia-Pacific (pp. 125-132)

1. *Far Eastern Economic Review* (hereafter *FEER*), Jan. 14, 1993 and Feb. 18, 1993. University of London scholar Anne Booth cautions that while the decline in poverty in Indonesia is real, measures of poverty for that country understate the problem; see "Review Article: The World Bank and Indonesian Poverty," *Journal of International Development* 4:6 (1992):633-642. Also, the official Indonesian poverty population of 30 million is larger than the total population of over 75 percent of the world's nations; see "A Survey of Indonesia," *The Economist,* April 17, 1993.

2. U.S. Dept. of Agriculture, Economic Research Service, *Global Food Assessment: Situation and Outlook Report,* GFA-3, Nov. 1992, p. 61 (hereafter *GFA*).

3. International Conference on Nutrition, *Nutrition and Development – A Global Assessment, 1992* rev. ed. (Rome:FAO and WHO, 1992), p. 6.

4. See United Nations Administrative Committee on Coordination/Subcommittee on Nutrition (ACC/SCN), *Second Report on the World Nutrition Situation, Vol. I: Global and Regional Results,* Oct.

1992. Communication from Dr. Howarth Bouis, International Food Policy Research Institute.

5. ACC/SCN, pp. 10, 39-40, 43. *Nutrition and Development*, pp. 9, 14-15, 48. Siddharth Dube, "Hunger in India: Malnutrition Paradox Persists," *First Call for Children*, Jan.-March 1993, p. 7, notes inadequate adult nutrition levels.

6. ACC/SCN, p. 24.

7. *Ibid.*, p. 24, 26-27, 51. Dube, p. 7. John Ward Anderson and Molly Moore, "The Burden of Womanhood," *The Washington Post National Weekly Edition*, March 22-28, 1993, pp. 6-7.

8. *Ibid.*, p. 6.

9. This section summarizes newly collected data on malnutrition among women aged 15-49. See ACC/SCN, pp. 24, 26, 30, 40-57.

10. Shah M. Tarzi, "Afghanistan in 1992: A Hobbesian State of Nature," *Asian Survey* XXXIII:2 (Feb. 1993):165-174. Hiram Ruiz, "Left Out in the Cold: The Perilous Homecoming of Afghan Refugees," *U.S. Committee for Refugees Issue Paper*, Dec. 1992, p. 11. Food and Agriculture Organization of the United Nations, *Foodcrops and Shortages* No. 12 (Rome: FAO, Dec. 1992):3, 21-22. *FEER*, March 18, 1993.

11. *Far Eastern Economic Review Asia 1993 Yearbook* (Hong Kong: Review Publishing, 1992, hereafter *Asia 1993*), p. 93. *FEER* May 7, 1992. *B.U.R.M.A.* 2:4 (April 1992):3. *World Refugee Survey 1993* (Washington: U.S. Committee for Refugees, 1993), p. 79.

12. Lisa Morris Grobar and Shiranthi Gnanaselvam, "The Economic Effects of the Sri Lankan Civil War," *Economic Development and Cultural Change* 41:2 (Jan. 1993):395-405. *Global Food Assessment*, p. 66. ACC/SCN, p. 26. "Financial Survey: Sri Lanka," *Financial Times*, Oct. 27, 1992.

13. *Asia 1993*, p. 192. "National Ecumenical Conference on the Philippines – 1993 Sustainable Peace Campaign,'" *Philippine Witness* No. 42 (Oct./Dec. 1992):1, 10. Alan Vaughan, "Ramos' First 100 Days," *in ibid.*, pp. 3-4. *Asia 1993*, p. 193. Measuring poverty in the Philippines involves the opposite of the problem

with Indonesia's measures: the official poverty line income is higher than that used by other countries in the region, and so the poverty rate is overstated.

14. This section is taken from *World Refugee Survey 1993*.

15. Le Dang Doanh, "Vietnam's Economic Reform and Some Social Aspects," paper presented at the International Development Conference, Washington, Jan. 11-13, 1993. *FEER*, April 23, 1992; June 4, 1992; May 27, 1993. Carol Levin, "Vietnam's Recent Policy Reforms and Their Effect on Agriculture and Trade," *Asia and Pacific Rim Agriculture and Trade Notes*, U.S. Dept. of Agriculture (Dec. 15, 1992):19-23. Carol Levin and Mark Giordano, "New Directions for Vietnam's Economy," *Agricultural Outlook* (March 1993):28-32. Judith Ladinsky, "Changes in the Health Care System of Vietnam in Response to the Emerging Market Economy," (American Public Health Association: Nov. 1992):3-4. Personal interview with Dr. Carol Levin, U.S. Dept. of Agriculture, Economic Research Service, April 21, 1993.

16. *Asia 1993*, p. 49. "China's Economic Reforms," *Overseas Development Institute Briefing Paper* (Feb. 1993). James L. Tyson and Ann Scott Tyson, "Chinese Reforms Widen Gap Between Coast and Hinterland," *The Christian Science Monitor*, July 22, 1992.

17. *Foodcrops and Shortages* No. 1/2 (Feb. 1993):26; No. 4 (April 1993):25. *Asia 1993*, pp. 168, 170. Personal interview with Ruth Elleson, USDA/ERS, April 21, 1993.

18. John Merrill, "North Korea in 1992: Steering Away from the Shoals," *Asian Survey* XXXIII:1 (Jan. 1993):47. *Asia 1993*, pp. 143, 145. Personal interview with John Dyck, USDA/ERS, April 21, 1993. Data on this country must be regarded with some skepticism.

19. *GFA*, pp. 67-68. "A Survey of Indonesia." *Asia 1993*, p. 132.

20. *FEER*, Aug. 20, 1992 and Feb. 18, 1993.

21. *FEER*, June 25, 1992; Sept. 17, 1992; March 11, 1993. *Asia 1993*, p. 128. ACC/SCN, p. 26.

22. *FEER*, Oct. 1, 1992. *Foodcrops and Shortages* No. 12 (Dec. 1992):26. Personal

interview with Dr. Anwarul Hoque, USDA/ERS, April 21, 1993.

23. *Foodcrops and Shortages* No. 1/2 (Feb. 1992):26-27. *Asia 1993*, p. 173. Girish Chendra Regmi, "Nepal in 1992: Exercising Parliamentary Politics," *Asian Survey* XXXIII:2 (Feb. 1993):148-149.

24. "Monsoon Floods Kill 983 in Asia," *The Washington Post*, July 22, 1993.

25. *Foodcrops and Shortages* No. 1/2 (Feb. 1993):45. *Foodcrops and Shortages* No. 5/6 (May/June 1993):46.

26. *ADB Quarterly Review* (Jan. 1993):14.

27. ACC/SCN, pp. 27-28, 68.

Seed the Killing Fields (pp. 129-132)

1. Benedict, Kiernan. *How Pol Pot Came to Power* (New York: Routledge Chapman Hall, 1985).

2. "Most Cambodians See Nothing of Aid," *The New York Times*, Feb. 21, 1993. Letter to BFW Institute from Craig Etcheson, executive director, Campaign to Oppose the Return of the Khmer Rouge, May 3, 1993.

Former Soviet Union, Central and Eastern Europe (pp. 133-138)

1. *Radio Free Europe/Radio Liberty News Briefs* (Feb. 1-5 1993), p. 2.

2. Alan Backema, Mark Drabenstoff, and Karl Skold, "Agriculture in the Soviet Union: The Long Road Ahead," *Federal Reserve Bank of Kansas City Economic Review*, Fourth Quarter 1992, p. 80.

3. *RFE/RL Research Report* 2 (Feb. 5, 1993):34.

4. *RFE/RL News Briefs* 2, No. 8 (1993):7. *RFE/RL Research Report* 1, No. 32 (Aug. 14, 1992):62.

5. Murray Feshbach and Alfred Friendly, Jr., *Ecocide in the U.S.S.R.: Health and Nature Under Siege.* (New York: Basic Books, 1992).

6. Simon Johnson and Oleg Ustenko, "Ukraine on the Brink of Hyperinflation," *RFE/RL Research Report* 1, No. 50 (Dec. 18, 1992):58.

7. Food and Agriculture Organization of the United Nations. *Foodcrops and Shortages* No.11 (Rome: FAO, Nov. 1992):38.

8. *Armenpress*, March 2, 1993. As reported in *Foreign Broadcasting Information Service* SOV-93-040, p. 68.

9. As reported in *Foreign Broadcasting Information Service*, SOV-93-043 (March 8, 1993):85.

10. Timothy W. Ash, "Agricultural Food Supply in the Former Soviet Union," *RFE/RL Research Report* 1, No. 45 (Nov. 13, 1992):14.

11. *Ibid.*, p. 44.

12. *Foodcrops and Shortages*, No. 12 (Dec. 1992): 39.

13. Patrick Moore, "War Returns to Croatia," *RFE/RL Research Report* 2, No. 9 (Feb. 26, 1993):42.

14. *Foodcrops and Shortages* No. 11 (Nov. 1992): 42.

15. Sonja Kiridzhievska, "Pessimism – A Part of Everyday Life," *Nova Makedonija*, Jan. 23, 1993, p. 15. As reported in *Joint Publications Research Service* EER-93-015-5 (March 2, 1993):25.

16. "Montenegro: The Status of Poverty," *Ekonomska Politika*, Feb. 8, 1993, p. 33. As reported in *Foreign Broadcasting Information Service*, EEU-93-044 (March 9, 1993):69.

17. As reported in *Foreign Broadcasting Information Service*, EEU-92-234 (Dec. 4, 1992):2.

18. *RFE/RL Research Reports* 1, No. 3 (July 31, 1992):55.

19. *RFE/RL Research Report* 1, No. 35 (Sept. 4, 1992):37.

20. Dan Ionescu, "Romania's Winter of Shortages," *RFE/RL Research Report* 2, No. 6 (Feb. 5, 1993):47.

21. *PlanEcon Report* VIII, No. 47-49 (Dec. 28, 1992):21.

22. *Foodcrops and Shortages* No. 12 (Dec. 1992):39.

23. Mrs. Sandor Jellen, Ministry of Agriculture, in *Magyar Nemzet*, Feb. 1993, p. 1. As cited in *Joint Publications Research Service*, EER-93-017-8 (March 4, 1993):20-22.

24. *Budapest MTI* in English, 0811 GMT, March 24, 1993. As reported in *Foreign Broadcasting Information Service*, EEU-93-055 (March 24, 1993):25.

25. *CTK*, March 12, 1993. As reported in *Foreign Broadcasting Information Service*, EEU-93-048 (March 15, 1993):8.

26. *Joint Publications Research Service*, EER-93-017-5 (March 4, 1993):43.

Latin America (pp. 139-144)

1. FAO data on food needs; "Brazil – Hungry," *The Economist*, July 10, 1993, pp. 35, 38.

2. *Foodcrops and Shortages* No. 5/6 (May/June 1993):30. Communication to BFW Institue from Jo Marie Griesgraber, Latin America Research Associate, Center of Concern, July 6, 1993.

3. Information on Haiti and Peru from *Global Food Assessment: Situation and Outlook Report*, U.S. Department of Agriculture, Economic Research Service, GFA-3, November 1992, pp.72-77. *Foodcrops and Shortages* No. 3 (March 1993): 29-30, 32.

Middle East (pp. 145-150)

Development Foundation of Turkey. "Alternative Approaches to Rural and Agricultural Development," Position Paper. Ankara, Turkey: DFT, 1992.

Food and Agriculture Organization of the United Nations. *Foodcrops and Shortages No. 12*. Rome: FAO, Dec. 1992; and *Foodcrops and Shortages No.4*. Rome: FAO, April 1993.

FAO. *Food Outlook*. Rome: FAO, Dec. 1992, Feb. 1993, March 1993.

Kawar, Ramzi N. "The Case of Jordan," presented at Middle East Council of Churches Children of War Seminar, Amman, Jordan, Sept. 1992.

Lowman, Shep. "Our Duty to Help Kurds," *The Washington Post*, Dec. 29, 1992.

"Radical Movements," *Middle East Report* 181, March/April 1993.

Miller, Judith. "Iraq Accused: A Case of Genocide," *New York Times Magazine*, Jan. 3, 1993.

Muir, Jim. "Weary of War, Turkish Kurds Try Talking," *The Christian Science Monitor*, April 12, 1993.

Natali, Denise. "Kurds in Northern Iraq Badly Needed Help," *The Christian Science Monitor*, March 12, 1993.

Nelan, Bruce. "Saddam Still," *Time*, March 29, 1993.

Randal, Jonathan C. "Kurds' Winter of Discontent," *The Washington Post*, Jan. 25, 1993.

————"Obstacles Keeping Food and Fuel from Iraqi Kurds," *The Washington Post*, Jan. 22, 1993.

Safir, Nadji. "Migratory Currents in the Middle East," *Development: Journal of the Society for International Development* 1993:1.

El Sarraj, Dr. Eyad. "Palestinian Children Under Siege: Psychological Effects of Extended Curfews," presented at International Conference on the Mental Health and Psychological Wellbeing of Refugees and Displaced Persons, Stockholm, Sweden, Oct. 1991.

Sfeir, Jacqueline. "Selected Studies of Childhood Anemia," paper presented at the Middle East Council of Churches Children of War Conference, Amman, Jordan, Sept. 1992.

Shahin, Miriam M. "Children in Iraq," paper presented at the Middle East Council of Churches Children of War Conference, Amman, Jordan, Sept. 1992.

UNICEF. *The State of the World's Children 1992*. New York: Oxford University Press, 1992.

United Nations Relief and Works Agency, "Palestine Refugees Today," *UNRWA Newsletter* No. 133, Jan. 1993.

Waldman, Peter. "A Disgruntled Army and Mounting Unrest Face Egyptian Regime," *The Wall Street Journal*, June 14, 1993.

North America (pp. 151-156)

1. House Select Committee on Hunger, "Hunger & Poverty in America," Sept. 1992.

2. "Mayors Find Hunger Aid Falls Short," *The Washington Post*, Dec. 12 1992.

3. Jonathan Yenkin, "30 Million Americans Go Hungry, Report Says," *The Boston Globe*, Sept. 10, 1992. Larry Brown, communication to BFW Institute, March 23, 1993.

4. For example, using 1989 data, the Food Research and Action Center found that 5.5 million children under age 12 were hungry and another 6 million were vulnerable to hunger; see *Community Childhood Hunger Identification Project: A Survey of Childhood Hunger in the United States* (Washington: FRAC, 1991).

5. Sonia Nozario, "Hunger, High Food Costs Founder in Inner-City Area," *The Los Angeles Times*, June 11, 1993.

6. Sheldon Danziger, and Peter Gottschalk, "A 20-Year Glitch in America," *The Washington Post*, Jan. 5, 1993.

7. Larry Brown and John T. Cook, *Two Americas*, Tufts University Center on Hunger, Poverty, and Nutrition Policy, January 1993, p. 16.

8. *Ibid.*, p. 13.

9. *The State of America's Children 1992* (Washington: Children's Defense Fund, 1992), pp. 28-29. Frank Swoboda, "Workers Generally Worse Off Than a Decade Ago, Study Finds," *The Washington Post*, Sept. 7, 1992.

10. *Ibid.*

11. *Ibid.*

12. *Ibid.* Communications from Teresa Amott, July 30, and John T. Cook, June 10, 1993.

13. Swoboda.

14. Hobart Rowan, "A Recovery Without Jobs," *The Washington Post*, April 8, 1993.

15. John Berry, "Productivity Growth at 20-Year High in '92," *The Washington Post*, Feb. 5, 1993. Hobart Rowan, "Economy Lacks Engine to Spark Jobs Growth," *The Washington Post*, May 16, 1993. Communication from Cook (see note 12).

16. "State Jobless Claims," *The Washington Post*, Digest, April 2, 1993.

17. *Nutrition Week* XXIII:21 (June 4, 1993): 1. Steven Pearlstein, "A Wave of Change Sweeps U.S. Firms," *The Washington Post*, January 27, 1993. Steven Pearlstein, "Jobs Report Shakes Faith in Recovery," *The Washington Post*, April 3, 1993.

18. Rowan, "Economy Lacks Engine."

19. Hobart Rowan, "Besieged Clinton Needs Fed Help With Economy," *The Washington Post*, May 23, 1993.

20. Jane Gross, "On the Edge of Poverty in California: A Welfare Mother Fears Deeper Cuts," *The New York Times*, August 11, 1992, cited in Teresa Amott, *Caught in the Crisis: Women and the U.S. Economy Today* (New York: Cornerstone Books, 1993), pp. 123-124.

21. Brown and Cook, p. 21.

22. Unless otherwise noted, this section is based on "Child Poverty in Canada," Report Card 1992, Campaign 2000 and "Statistics Canada." *Canadian Social Trends,* Spring 1992.

23. Timothy M. Smeeding, "Why the U.S. Anti-Poverty System Doesn't Work Very Well," *Challenge,* Jan.-Feb. 1992, pp. 32-33.

Western Europe (pp. 157-160)

1. "Europeans Fear Unemployment Will Only Rise," *The New York Times*, June 13, 1993.

2. Bérnard Dandrel, Secrétaire Général, Fédération Européene des Banques Alimentaires. Communication to the author, Dec. 14, 1992.

3. "Down and Out in Europe," *Newsweek,* June 29, 1992, p. 32.

4. Commission of the European Communities, "Employment in Europe – 1992" (Luxembourg: Office for the Official Publications of the European Communities, 1992), pp. 3, 7-9, 157.

5. Commission of the European Communities, "The Community's Battle Against Social Exclusion" (Luxembourg: Office for the Official Publications of the European Communities, 1992), p. 3.

6. "Homeless in Europe." *Parade Magazine*, August 15, 1993.

7. "The Community's Battle Against Social Exclusion," p. 5.

8. "For Richer, For Poorer," *The Economist*, Jan. 30, 1993, p. 50.

9. "Europe's 'Rio Grande' Floods With Refugees," *The Washington Post*, June 11, 1993.

10. U.S. Committee for Refugees, *World Refugee Survey 1993* (Washington: U.S. Committee for Refugees, 1993), pp. 122-123.

11. *Ibid.*, p.5.

Food Banks in Europe (p. 159)

1. Brochure, Fédération Belge des Banques Alimentaires (Brussels: 1992).

2. "The Clearinghouse," Foodbanking, Inc. (Phoenix, AZ: 1992).

3. Fédération Européene des Banques Alimentaires (Arceuil, France: 1990).

Sponsors and Cosponsors Of *Hunger 1994*

Sponsors

Bread for the World Institute seeks to inform, educate, nurture, and motivate concerned citizens for action on policies which affect hungry people. Based on policy analysis and consultation with poor people, it develops educational resources and activities including its annual report on the state of world hunger, occasional papers, policy briefs, and study guides, together with workshops, seminars, and briefings. Contributions to the Institute are tax-deductible. It works closely with Bread for the World, a Christian citizens' movement of 44,000 members, who advocate specific policy changes to help overcome hunger in the United States and overseas.
*1100 Wayne Ave., Suite 1000
Silver Spring, MD 20910
Ph. (301) 608-2400
Fx. (301) 608-2401*

BROT für die Welt is an association of German Protestant churches which seeks to overcome poverty and hunger in developing countries, as an expression of their Christian faith and convictions, by funding programs of relief and development. Founded in 1959, BROT has funded more than 15,000 programs in over 100 nations in Africa, Latin America, and Asia. For nearly 35 years the emphases of the programs which BROT funds has shifted from relief to development and empowerment. BROT's programs of education in Germany are intended to

lead to changes – in understanding and lifestyle at the personal level, and to policy changes at the national, European Community, and international levels.
Stafflenbergstrasse 76; Postfach 10 11 42; D-7000 Stuttgart 10, Germany; Ph. 07 11-2159-0 Fx. 07 11-2159-368.

Robert Cahill

Ambassador and Mrs. William H. Crook

Christian Children's Fund is the largest independent child-care agency in the world, providing assistance to more than half a million children and their families in 40 countries and the United States. An international, not-for-profit, nonsectarian agency, free of political associations, Christian Children's Fund provides education, medical care, food, clothing, and shelter to children around the world. Services are provided based on need and without regard to sex, race, creed, or religion. Christian Children's Fund recently began new programs in Central and Eastern Europe and the Middle East.
2821 Emerywood Parkway, PO Box 26227, Richmond, VA 23261-6227 Ph. (804) 756-2700; Fx. (804) 756-2718.

LCMS World Relief (Lutheran Church – Missouri Synod) provides relief and development funding for domestic and international projects. Based under the Synod's Department of Human Care Ministries, LCMS World Relief pro-

vides domestic grants for Lutheran congregations and social ministry organizations as well as other groups with Lutheran involvement which are engaged in ministries of human care. Domestic support is also provided to Inter-Lutheran Disaster Response and Lutheran Immigration and Refugee Service. International relief and development assistance is channeled through the Synod's mission stations and partner churches as well as Lutheran World Relief.
*1333 So. Kirkwood Road, St. Louis, MO 63122-7295
Ph. (314) 965-9000
Fx. (314) 822-8307*

United Methodist Committee on Relief (UMCOR) was formed in 1940 in response to the suffering of people during World War II. It was a "voice of conscience" expressing the concern of the church for the disrupted and devastated lives churned out by the war. UMCOR has expanded its ministry into more than 80 countries to minister with compassion to "persons in need, through programs of relief, rehabilitation, and service: to refugees, to those suffering from root causes of hunger and their consequences, and to those caught in other distress situations." The ministry of UMCOR, a program department of the General Board of Global Ministries of The United Methodist Church, is carried out through a worldwide network of national and international church agencies which cooperate in the task of alleviating human suffering.

Sponsors and Cosponsors

475 Riverside Drive, Room 1374
New York, NY 10115
Ph. (212) 870-3816
(800) 841-1235
Fx. (212) 870-3624

Malcolm and Anita Street

The **United Nations Children's Fund** (UNICEF) for more than 40 years has supported countries to improve and expand their services for children, to help establish priorities, and to reach the neediest children. UNICEF promotes the well-being of children throughout their formative years in 127 countries and territories. Almost all UNICEF resources are invested in the poorest developing countries, with the greatest share supporting children up to age five. UNICEF support is provided for emergencies and for longer-term programs in such areas as health, water supply and sanitation, nutrition, and education. UNICEF is an integral, yet semi-autonomous part of the UN system. It is also unique among U.N. organizations in that it relies entirely on voluntary public and government contributions.
3 United Nations Plaza
New York, NY 10017-4414
Ph. (212) 326-7035
Fx. (212) 888-7465

World Vision, founded in 1950, is a Christian humanitarian aid organization carrying out relief and development activities in 94 countries, including the United States. The U.S. national support office is headquartered in Los Angeles, and national support offices in 16 other countries raise funds for transform-

ing the lives of the poor in Africa, Asia, Latin America, and Eastern Europe. Meeting the health care, educational, vocational, and nutritional needs of children and their families is the focal point of programs leading to the long-term sustainable development of communities. Through 6,243 projects, worldwide, World Vision affirms the right of every child to education, good nutrition, health care, and spiritual nurture. More than 1 million children are sponsored through World Vision donors from industrialized nations.
919 West Huntington Drive
Monrovia, CA 91016
Ph. (818) 357-7979
Fx. (818) 303-7651

Cosponsors

Adventist Development and Relief Agency International (ADRA) is the worldwide agency of the Seventh-day Adventist church set up to alleviate poverty in developing countries and respond to disasters. ADRA works on behalf of the poor in more than seventy developing countries spanning Africa, Asia, the Middle East, and Central and South America, without regard to ethnic, political, or religious association. ADRA's projects include working to improve the health of mothers and children, developing clean water resources, teaching agricultural techniques, building and supplying clinics, hospitals, and schools, training people in vocational skills, and feeding people in countries where hunger is a long-term problem. When disasters strike, ADRA

sends emergency supplies and stays in the disaster area to help rebuild.
12501 Old Columbia Pike
Silver Spring, MD 20904
Ph. (301) 680-6380
Fx. (301) 680-6370

CARE is the world's largest relief and development organization not affiliated with a government or religion. Each year, CARE reaches more than 25 million people in over 40 nations in Africa, Asia, and Latin America. The organization's work began in 1946, when its famous CARE packages helped Europe recover from World War II. Today, CARE improves health care and the environment, helps subsistence farmers and small business owners produce more goods, addresses population concerns, and reaches disaster victims with emergency assistance. The scope of CARE's work is broad, but its vision focuses on a single concept – helping people help themselves.
151 Ellis Street Atlanta, GA 30303
Ph. (404) 681-2552
Fx. (404) 577-6271

Catholic Relief Services (CRS) is the official overseas relief and development agency of the United States Catholic Conference. Established in 1943 to help displaced people in war-torn Europe, CRS now works in 74 countries in Africa, Asia, Latin America, Europe, the Caribbean, and the Middle East. CRS exists to serve the poor and disadvantaged throughout the developing world to achieve social justice and economic self-sufficiency. Working in partnership with the Catholic church in each country, CRS provides disaster relief and development assistance throughout the world strictly on the basis of need.

209 West Fayette Street
Baltimore, MD 21201-3443
Ph. (410) 625-2220
Fx. (410) 685-1635

Christian Reformed World Relief Committee (CRWRC) is the relief and development agency of the Christian Reformed Church in North America, with offices in Grand Rapids, Michigan, and Burlington, Ontario, Canada. CRWRC was begun in 1962 to respond to the needs of Korean war victims, Cuban refugees, and victims of natural disasters in North America. Today, it focuses on helping the poorest of the poor meet their own needs through community development in more than 30 countries around the world. Through cooperative efforts with national Christian churches and organizations, CRWRC staff enables more than 75,000 families to free themselves from material and spiritual poverty. CRWRC also helps strengthen churches and community organizations.

2850 Kalamazoo Ave., S.E.
Grand Rapids, MI 49560-0600
Ph. (616) 247-5875
Fx. (616) 246-0806

Church World Service (CWS) is a global relief, development, and refugee assistance ministry of the 32 Protestant and Orthodox communities that work together through the National Council of Churches. Founded in 1946, CWS works in partnership with local church organizations in more than 70 countries worldwide, supporting sustainable self-help development of people which respects the environment, meets emergency needs, and addresses root causes of poverty and powerlessness. Within the United States, CWS resettles refugees, assists communities in responding to disasters, advocates for justice in U.S. policies which relate to global issues, provides educational resources, and offers opportunities for communities to join a people-to-people network of global and local caring through participation in a CROP walk.

475 Riverside Drive, Suite 678
New York, NY 10115-0050
Ph. (212) 870-2257
Fx. (212) 870-2055

CODEL (Coordination in Development) is a membership association of Catholic, Protestant, and Orthodox organizations that respond globally to our Lord's invitation, "whatever you do to the least of mine, you do unto me," through environmentally sustainable socioeconomic development. CODEL seeks to inform and awaken the consciousness of the people of the U.S. to human needs. The purpose of CODEL throughout the developing world is to support training and other development activities identified by people of all faiths who have limited opportunities to participate in economic, social, environmental, and political decisions that affect their lives.

CODEL supports these activities wherever that support fosters ecumenical collaboration and Christian unity.

475 Riverside Dr., Suite 1842
New York, NY 10115-0050
Ph. (212) 870-3000
Fx. (212) 870-3545

EuronAid is a European association of nongovernmental organizations which facilitates dialogue with the Commission of the European Community (CEC). EuronAid cooperates with the CEC in programming and procuring food aid for the NGOs, then arranges and accounts for delivery to Third World NGOs for distribution. In recent years, triangular operations (purchases within Third World nations) have accounted for half of EuronAid's food aid, which meets both emergency and development purposes. EuronAid assimilates the experiences of NGOs involved in food aid and employs this knowledge in its dialogue with CEC and the European Parliament to achieve improved management of food aid. EuronAid was created in 1980 by major European NGOs in cooperation with the Commission of the European Community. The association has at present 24 member agencies, and services an additional 50 European NGOs on a regular basis.

Rhijngeesterstraatweg 40; PO Box 79; 2340 AB Oegstgeest, The Netherlands; Ph. 71-169 261
Fx. 71-155 201

Sponsors and Cosponsors

Food for the Hungry International (FHI) is an organization of Christian motivation committed to working with poor people to overcome hunger and poverty through development and, where needed, appropriate relief. Founded in 1971, FHI is incorporated in Switzerland and works in 17 countries of Asia, Africa, and Latin America. As its name implies, FHI focuses on poverty needs that relate to food and nutrition. Its primary emphasis is on long-term development among the extremely poor, recognizing their dignity, creativity, and ability to solve their own problems. The international staff numbers more than 680 persons. Autonomous Food for the Hungry partner entities in several different countries, such as Food For the Hungry (USA) contribute resources.
7807 East Greenway Road, Suite 3
Scottsdale, AZ 85260
Ph. (602) 951-5090
Fx. (602)951-9035

Freedom from Hunger, founded in 1946 as Meals for Millions, launches innovative programs to eliminate chronic hunger – providing resources and information that empower the poorest families and communities to help themselves. Our *Credit with Education* program in developing countries on four continents supports self-help groups of poor people, particularly women, by providing cash credit and nonformal adult education. *Credit* enables participants to increase their income-earning and savings opportunities so they can buy or grow more and better food. *Education* enhances their money management and offers knowledge and motivation to improve their health, nutrition, and family planning practices. In the United States, Freedom From Hunger helps existing health and human service programs use their financial and technical resources more effectively to improve family health and nutrition.
1644 DaVinci Court
Davis, CA 95617
Ph. (916) 758-6200
Fx. (916) 758-6241

The Hunger Project is a global, not-for-profit organization focused exclusively on the human component of ending world hunger. It is neither a relief nor a development organization, but rather a *strategic* organization, seeking to identify "what's missing" in the global effort to end hunger, and to either provide it or ensure that it is provided. Headquartered in New York, The Hunger Project has offices in 12 countries and volunteer activities in 20 additional countries. Its current programs include "strategic planning-in-action" (a participatory, multi-sectoral methodology pioneered in India), the Africa Prize for Leadership, *African Farmer* magazine, the global "Youth Ending Hunger" movement, and initiatives to encourage international agencies to work together as a "common front for the end of hunger."
One Madison Avenue
New York, NY 10010
Ph. (212) 532-4255
Fx. (212) 532-9785

Lutheran World Relief, founded in 1945, acts in behalf of Lutheran Churches in the U.S.A. to "support the poor and oppressed of less-developed countries in their effort to meet basic human needs and to participate with dignity and equity in the life of their communities; and to alleviate human suffering resulting from natural disaster, war, social conflict, or poverty." The agency, headquartered in New York City, is geared to respond quickly to requests for emergency assistance and supports more than 200 long-range development projects in countries throughout Africa, Asia, the Middle East, and Latin America.
390 Park Avenue South, New York,
NY 10016; Ph. (212) 532-6350
Fx. (212) 213-6081

Mennonite Central Committee (MCC), founded in 1920, is an agency of the Mennonite and Brethren in Christ churches in North America, and seeks to demonstrate God's love through committed women and men who work among people suffering from poverty, conflict, oppression, and natural disaster. MCC serves as a channel for interchange between churches and community groups where it works around the world and North American churches. MCC strives for peace, justice, and dignity of all people by sharing experiences, resources, and faith. MCC's priorities include disaster relief and refugee assistance, rural and agricultural development, job creation (SELF-HELP Crafts), health; and education.
21 South 12th Street
Akron, PA 17501-0500
Ph. (717) 859-1151
Fx (717) 859-2171

Oxfam America works to fight hunger in partnership with people around the world. To feed themselves, poor people need access to basic resources like land, water, seeds, tools, and training. Since 1970, Oxfam America has helped get those resources. Oxfam America, a private, nonprofit, international agency, funds self-help development and relief in Africa, Asia, the Americas, and the Caribbean. It also produces and distributes educational materials for people in the United States on issues of hunger and development, conducts educational campaigns, and speaks out about public policies that affect the work of grassroots partners. Oxfam America is one of seven autonomous Oxfams around the world.
115 Broadway, Boston, MA 02116
Ph. (617) 482-1211
Fx. (617) 556-8925

Oxfam UK and Ireland (UKI) supports poor people in their struggle against hunger, exploitation, and poverty in 70 countries in Africa, Asia, Latin America, the Caribbean, Middle East, and Eastern Europe through development, emergency relief, and advocacy. Through its extensive network of overseas programme staff and offices, Oxfam UKI works closely with local counterparts in supporting the efforts of poor people to gain sustainable livelihoods and basic rights. In this development work, it prioritizes gender considerations and the need to strengthen institutions at all levels which empower and address the needs of poor people. Oxfam UKI

is involved in extensive emergency relief and in public education, lobbying, and campaigning. The organization is independent of government and depends largely on voluntary work and donations from the public.
274 Banbury Road Oxford, OX2 7DZ; England; Ph. 0865 311 311 Fx. 0865 312 600

Save the Children (SC) helps make lasting, positive differences in the lives of disadvantaged children in the United States and 35 countries overseas. Programs are guided by a set of principles known as CBIRD – community-based integrated rural development. This approach includes community participation in identifying goals and implementing projects. The CBIRD approach relies on non-formal educational techniques – transferring skills and encouraging self-help and the maximum use of available resources. In SC's international programs, the four key development sectors are: primary health; environmentally sound sustainable agriculture; productivity, especially through small-scale enterprises; and education. Save the Children also supports refugee assistance programs in Africa, Asia, and the Middle East, and provides disaster relief.
54 Wilton Road, Westport, CT 06880; Ph. (203) 221-4000 Fx. (203) 221-4123

Save the Children-UK (SCF-UK) works to achieve lasting benefits for children within the communities in which they live, by influencing policy and practice based on

its experience and study in different parts of the world. In all of its work, Save the Children endeavors to make a reality of children's rights. SCF-UK works in more than 50 countries in Africa, Asia, Latin America, and the Caribbean, and has a large programme of development activities within the United Kingdom itself. Areas of particular expertise include food security, relief and refugee assistance, health-systems development, and child welfare and development. In all of its work, SCF-UK endeavors to link programme activities with research, information, and advocacy at the national and international levels.
17 Grove Lane; London, SE5 8RD, England; Ph. 071-703-5400 Fx. 71 703 2278

Second Harvest is a network of 185 affiliated food banks in the United States which provide food to the hungry through nearly 50,000 social service agencies. As the largest charitable source of food in the United States, the Second Harvest network annually distributes more than 500 million pounds of donated food and grocery products. The Second Harvest Mission is to:

• Feed the hungry by soliciting and judiciously distributing marketable but surplus food and grocery products to a nationwide network of food banks;

• Develop, certify, and support Second Harvest food banks that channel food and grocery products to local nonprofit charities that provide services to the needy;

• Serve as a liaison between food

banks and donors; and
• Educate the public about the nature of, and solutions to, the problems of hunger.
116 South Michigan Avenue, Suite 4, Chicago, IL 60603-6001
Ph. (312) 263-2303
Fx. (312) 263-5626

Share Our Strength is a nationwide network of creative professionals who use their skills and resources to help alleviate the causes and consequences of hunger in the United States, Canada, and in developing countries. One of the nation's largest private, nonprofit sources of funds for hunger relief, SOS promotes self-sufficiency among those in need through funding, public education, and community outreach. Founded in 1984 to organize the food industry on behalf of hunger relief groups, SOS now includes more than 5,000 chefs, restauranteurs, writers, artists, photographers, and creative professionals from a variety of fields. Since its inception, SOS has raised almost

$11 million for distribution to more than 300 hunger relief and community development organizations. Some of Share Our Strength's programs include: Share Our Strength's Taste of the Nation, presented by American Express; Writers Harvest: The National Reading; Share our Strength's Book Projects; SOS Market Booths; and Quarters for Kids.
1511 K Street, N.W., Suite 940 Washington, DC 20005
Ph. (202) 393-2925
Fx. (202) 347-5868

Shield-Ayers Foundation

The Trull Foundation (and predecessor B.W. Trull Foundation) has been interested in educational, religious, cultural, and social programs since 1948. Current priorities include concern for:
1. The needs of the Palacios, Texas area where the Foundation has its roots;
2. Pre-adolescents, and opportunities to direct lives away from child abuse, neglect, and hunger,

towards an adolescence of good mental and physical growth; and
3. Mexican-Americans in South Texas, to help them "catch up," hurdle a language barrier, a poverty barrier, and system which has consistently kept them poor, uneducated, and unrepresented.
404 Fourth St., Palacios, TX 77465
Ph. (512) 972-5241

World Relief is the relief and development arm of the National Association of Evangelicals in the United States. Since 1944, World Relief has provided both immediate and long-term assistance to people who suffer from poverty, disease, hunger and war. Working with groups in Asia, Latin America, Africa, the Middle East, and the United States, World Relief supports programs focused on disaster relief, refugee assistance, income generation, and health.
PO Box WRC, Wheaton, IL 60189
Ph. (708) 665-0235
Fx. (708) 653-8023